STRIKE INJUNCTIONS
IN THE NEW SOUTH

SEE THE LAST PAGES OF THIS BOOK FOR A COMPLETE LIST OF
THE UNIVERSITY OF NORTH CAROLINA SOCIAL STUDY SERIES

*The University of North Carolina Press, Chapel Hill, N. C.;
The Baker and Taylor Co., New York; Oxford University
Press, London; Maruzen-Kabushiki-Kaisha, Tokyo; Edward
Evans & Sons, Ltd., Shanghai.*

STRIKE INJUNCTIONS
IN THE NEW SOUTH

BY

DUANE McCRACKEN, Ph.D.

Professor of Economics, Guilford College
Formerly Instructor in Economics, University of Minnesota

WITH A FOREWORD BY

MAURICE T. VAN HECKE, Ph.B., J.D.

Professor of Law and Dean of the Law School,
University of North Carolina

CHAPEL HILL
THE UNIVERSITY OF NORTH CAROLINA PRESS
1931

COPYRIGHT, 1931, BY
THE UNIVERSITY OF NORTH CAROLINA PRESS

TO MY WIFE

FOREWORD

As the industrial revolution in the South heads into the unionization of labor, one of the legal weapons at hand will be the labor injunction. Whether to use it or not, how to use it, and with what probable costs and results, are questions that will face the manufacturer and his lawyer. Professor McCracken's book will help to answer those questions.

It is not a compendious digest of the accumulated decisions and statutes. Nor is it the epic of the evolution of the labor injunction as a legal institution. Rather, these case-histories of the actual effects of the injunctions at Raleigh, Asheville, Marion, Elizabethton, and Danville, show the labor injunction in action amid southern industrial conditions. True, the injunctions in question were neither extreme nor complicated. And only at Elizabethton did they precipitate contempt proceedings. The manufacturer's lawyer will thus find less in these chapters for use in his preparation of injunction litigation than he will as a basis for advice to the board of directors. But in that connection, as raw material for a decision by the company executives as to what may be gained by resort to the injunction, the studies are invaluable.

The effort Professor McCracken has made to be strictly impartial, to be critical of both sides, and to refrain from polemics, as well as his realization that the root of the trouble lies far deeper than any legal instrumentality may plow, will disappoint the extremists in both camps. His findings of fact, however, and his provocative evaluation of the conventional arguments pro and con in the light of those findings, will delight the seeker for truth as to what the injunction's use in industrial controversies has accomplished.

As source-material, the pleadings and other legal documents in the appendices, especially the Danville answer and the Danville letter-poster are excellent. Only the Asheville case is otherwise adequately available.

M. T. VAN HECKE

Chapel Hill
May, 1931

PREFACE

This book represents an attempt to do a thing which students of the subject have considered vitally necessary for many years. There have been many reviews and digests of the law on the subject. Comment and criticism, dealing with various phases, have been voluminous. Information as to the actual effects of injunctions growing out of industrial disputes is, on the other hand, quite fragmentary.

The special function of this work is expressed clearly in a personal letter from Professor Felix Frankfurter, of the Harvard Law School, from which we quote the following:

"We need light very badly—and social economists are the ones who ought to give it to us—upon the economic effects of the labor injunction in specific situations in which injunctions are issued. . . . I suggest an intensive study of the instances in which the injunction was employed in industrial controversies in North Carolina, and particularly the influences which such legal intervention exerted in the industrial conflicts in which the law intervened."

Because the experience with this legal remedy in the state of North Carolina was found to be very narrowly limited, the recent cases in Elizabethton, Tennessee, and Danville, Virginia have been included in the study. Chapters I and II are largely introductory. Chapters III and IV are designed to give a theoretical background for the more concrete material. Chapter V may be regarded as the distinctly original contribution to the subject.

The writer wishes it were possible to give full credit to all the persons who have assisted in this study. Special mention should be made of Professor Alvin H. Hansen, of the University of Minnesota, whose wise counsel at all stages of the study has been invaluable. Hardly second in importance are the advice and suggestions of Professor M. T. Van Hecke, of the University of North Carolina Law School, and Professor Henry Rottschaefer, of the University of Minnesota Law School. To Dean R. A. Stevenson, Professor F. B. Garver, and Professor Morris B. Lambie of the University of Minnesota, the writer is indebted for helpful suggestions during the preparation of the original manuscript. Dean Charles T. McCormick,[1] of the University of North Carolina Law School, Professor Harry D. Wolf, of the Department of Economics, University of North Carolina, and Miss Harriet L. Herring, Research Assistant of the Institute for Research in Social Science, have made helpful suggestions for the revision of the manuscript. Mr. Murray T. Quigg, editor of *Law and Labor*, has generously responded to requests for material. The unselfish service of Dr. E. E. Witte, of the Wisconsin Legislative Reference Library, in placing a portion of his large fund of material at the writer's disposal is worthy of strong commendation. The assistance of Professor Felix Frankfurter in isolating the problem has been mentioned above. The writer feels indebted to Professor John R. Commons for first arousing his interest in the subject. Of fundamental importance is the assistance given by employers, labor leaders, union members, lawyers on both sides of the controversy, public offi-

---

[1] Resigned, June 1931.

cers, and the many others who have supplied the concrete materials used here.

It should be made clear that those who have given their advice and assistance are not responsible for the conclusions reached. Full responsibility is assumed by the author.

DUANE McCRACKEN

Guilford College, N. C.
May, 1931

CONTENTS

FOREWORD BY PROFESSOR MAURICE T. VAN HECKE   vii
PREFACE   ix
I. THE INJUNCTION PROBLEM   3
II. THE INJUNCTION AS A LEGAL REMEDY   7
III. THE CASE FOR INJUNCTIONS IN INDUSTRIAL DISPUTES   22
IV. THE CASE AGAINST INJUNCTIONS IN INDUSTRIAL DISPUTES   32
V. THE EFFECTS OF INJUNCTIONS IN THE NEW SOUTH   47

    Case I. McGinnis v. Raleigh Typographical Union, and Others   49
    Case II. Citizen Company v. Asheville Typographical Union, and Others   62
    Case III. Marion Manufacturing Company v. United Textile Workers, and Others   79
    Case IV. American Glanzstoff Corporation and American Bemberg Corporation v. George Miller, United Textile Workers, and Others   94
    Case V. Riverside and Dan River Cotton Mills, Incorporated, v. Francis J. Gorman, and Others..   144

VI. GENERAL SUMMARY AND CONCLUSIONS   131

APPENDICES

    I. The Shipstead Bill, Limiting the Jurisdiction of Equity Courts   145
    Senate Substitute for Shipstead Bill...........   146
    II. Complaint and Affidavit, Case I.............   156
    III. Restraining Order, Case I..................   163

CONTENTS

IV. Judgment, Case I 166
V. Argument of Counsel for Plaintiffs, Case I.... 169
VI. Interview with Dr. Charles Lee Smith, Case I.. 173
VII. Excerpts from Brief of Defendants,
  Appellants, Case I........................ 175
VIII. Interview with L. E. Nichols, Assistant Commissioner of Labor and Printing, State of North Carolina (1921), Case I 181
IX. Summary of Interviews with Defendants, Case I 183
X. Complaint and Affidavit, Case II............. 187
XI. Summons for Relief, Case II................. 192
XII. Restraining Order, Case II.................. 194
XIII. Interview with Charles A. Webb, Case II...... 197
XIV. Excerpts from the Opinion of the Supreme Court, Case II 203
XV. Summary of Interviews with Defendants, Case II 205
XVI. Judgment, Case II 212
XVII. Complaint and Affidavit, Case III........... 215
XVIII. Restraining Order, Case III.................. 223
XIX. Modified Order, Case III.................... 225
XX. Letter from N. A. Townsend, Executive Counsellor to the Governor of North Carolina, Case III 228
XXI. Summary of Interviews with Defendants, Case III 230
XXII. Certified Copies of Writs of Injunction and Order to Sheriffs, Case IV 234
XXIII. Summary of Interviews with Defendants, Case IV 238
XXIV. Bill for Injunction, Case V 248
XXV. Restraining Order, Case V 254
XXVI. Answer, Case V 257
XXVII. Letter Poster Number 192, Issued Feb. 12, 1931 by H. R. Fitzgerald, Case V.......... 265
XXVIII. Wisconsin Statute (1931) 269

SELECTED BIBLIOGRAPHY 281
INDEX.. 285

STRIKE INJUNCTIONS IN THE NEW SOUTH

CHAPTER I

THE INJUNCTION PROBLEM

THE injunction problem has grown out of a conflict of interests. We have, on the one hand, the employing group composed of men who are seeking maximum protection for property rights. We have, on the other hand, the trade unionists, who are interested in promoting collective bargaining and are seeking the maximum freedom in the use of those means which will make collective bargaining effective. The equity process of injunction is regarded as sacred by the employing group because it is intended to give property rights more complete protection. The trade union group bitterly oppose the injunction process because they believe it takes away part of their liberty to engage in collective bargaining. This conflict of interests would not constitute a social problem, in the sense implied here, if there were not a widespread belief that the equity process works badly in this class of cases. This belief is held, not only by trade unionists but also by disinterested scholars and citizens. Evidence of this is found in the long agitation in Congress and in a number of state legislatures for the curtailment of the equity powers of our courts.[1] Further evidence is found in the Reports of Proceedings of the American Federation of Labor, in the writings of members of the legal profession, including judges, practising attorneys, and

---

[1] See Frankfurter and Greene, *The Labor Injunction* (1930), chap. IV. This book is a thorough, critical discussion of the legal theory and practice involved in labor injunction cases. See also Edward Berman, *Labor and the Sherman Act* (1930).

teachers of law, in the writings of prominent men in the fields of economics, sociology, and political science, and also in the platforms of political parties. Critics have pointed to the fact that the national platform of every political party entering the contest in 1928 contained a section advocating the removal of abuses in this branch of our judicial system.

In an abstract sense, the laborer has the same right of access to our courts as the employer. However, the writ of injunction was originally intended, and has mainly been used, to protect property. Since the laborer supplies only his labor, which is not property, in the employment relation, he has in the past had little or no occasion to seek the protection of an equity court in this connection. There are, of course, rights growing out of contracts which can be protected by injunction in appropriate cases. With the advent of the trade agreement, the opportunity which laborers have for obtaining relief by injunction has increased. However, it is still true that a vast majority of injunctions, growing out of industrial disputes, are obtained by the employer.[2] Everyone is aware of the fact that there has been much criticism of the writ in this class of cases. The conservative answer to this criticism is that the same rules of equity are applied in this class of cases as in others. It is contended that there is, therefore, no

---

[2] Dr. E. E. Witte gives the number obtained by employers as eighteen hundred as against thirty-three obtained by organized labor. Of these, twenty-four were against employers and nine were against public officers. 39 *Yale Law Journal*, 374-75 (January, 1930). Two recent notable cases of injunctive relief for labor as against employers are the following: Texas & New Orleans R. R. Co. v. Brotherhood of Ry. Clerks, 50 Sup. Ct. 427, 281 U. S. 548, 74 L. ed. 1034 (1930); and David Adler & Sons Co. v. Moglio, 228 N. W. 123 (Wis., Dec. 3, 1929).

just cause for criticism. This leads to the heart of the controversy. Are there peculiar facts and circumstances connected with employer-employee relations which make the law of injunctions, as now practised in our equity courts, an exceptionally serious interference with liberty?

A complete answer to this question is not attempted in the present study, which is, essentially, an inquiry into the effects of the injunction in five specific cases. No apology is made for the fact that the method used is qualitative rather than quantitative. In the present state of our knowledge of the subject, the case method promises more satisfactory results than the mathematical method. In preparing the material on these cases, the writer made a first-hand investigation at each of the places where the events had occurred. Throughout the study, he has endeavored to be fair and to deal with the subject as objectively as possible. As anyone learned in the law will easily discover, the writer is not a lawyer. However, a real effort has been made to present the legal material accurately.

It will help to clarify the atmosphere if we distinguish sharply three fundamentally different attitudes toward the problem of industrial relations. At one extreme we have certain powerful, well-organized groups who regard trade unions as a sinister force in American life, which should be destroyed root and branch. At the other extreme are those who believe that capitalism is a vampire system which serves no good end and which must be discarded. According to this view, there is no danger of invasion of legitimate rights to private property, since they do not exist. There are doubtless many sincere people in both groups. For the purposes of this study, however, a third group is vastly more significant. The members of this third, or intermediate, group believe that private ownership of capital has a legitimate functional basis. They believe that, within reasonable limits, property rights should be protected. They believe, on the other hand, that trade unions, when properly conducted, perform a useful social function. The right to collective bargaining, on which trade unions are based, should therefore be protected.

It may be well to warn the reader, at this point, that no claim of universality is made for the conclusions reached in the closing chapter. While one might reasonably infer that similar results would be found in similar cases elsewhere, no such assertion is made here.

CHAPTER II

THE INJUNCTION AS A LEGAL REMEDY

Definition.—"*A writ of injunction* may be defined as a judicial process, operating *in personam* (i.e., against the person), and requiring the person to whom it is directed to do or refrain from doing a particular thing."[1]

The injunction has been called "extraordinary relief." In a very real sense this is true. The temporary restraining order, which is one form of injunction, orders the person or persons restrained to do or not to do something without a previous notice and without an opportunity for a hearing. This is obviously a harsh method. Because of its drastic nature, there must be very compelling circumstances to justify a court in granting this type of relief. The primary purpose of the writ of injunction is not to punish for acts already committed or to make restitution for damage done but to prevent threatened wrongs.

Types of Injunctions.—There are two distinct types of injunctions: *temporary*, or *interlocutory*, and *perpetual*.[2] There is a great deal of variation in terminology and procedure among our various states but this general classification is applicable to all. In the Federal Courts and in several of the state courts we have the *temporary restraining order* which is an interlocutory injunction issued without notice or hearing for the defendants, usually upon affidavits filed by the complainant. The purpose of this writ is to hold the subject of litigation in *statu quo*

---
[1] High, *A Treatise on the Law of Injunctions*, I, 2.
[2] *Ibid.*, pp. 4-5.

until the merits of the case can be determined. "The *status quo* is the last actual peaceable uncontested *status* which preceded the pending controversy. . . ."[3]

The *final*, or *perpetual, injunction* is a final decree of the court issued after a full hearing of the case on its merits and a determination by the court of the rights of the parties involved.[4] At the final hearing the court may make the temporary order perpetual, modify the order, or dissolve it entirely. A few of the variations may be indicated. In the Federal Courts we have a *temporary injunction* which is issued only after a preliminary hearing of the defendants. In other respects it is similar to the temporary restraining order. Where the temporary restraining order is used, it is common to give the defendants a preliminary hearing within a few days, at which time the court decides whether the order shall be dissolved, modified, or continued until the final hearing.

In the absence of a statute on the subject, the interlocutory injunction continues until the final hearing, unless dissolved or modified by the court.[4a] A time limit for the pendency of a temporary restraining order has been fixed by statute in several jurisdictions.

Writs of injunction are issued by courts of equity or chancery courts. These courts were separate and distinct from the law courts in England and are today in some of our states—e.g., New Jersey and Tennessee. In our federal government and in most of the states, the functions of both are combined in one set of courts.

---
[3] *Bouvier's Law Dictionary*, Rawle's third revision, p. 1570.
[4] *Ibid.*
[4a] It has been held, however, that parties may, by agreement, render the injunction inoperative. See Chapter V, Case IV below.

Bases of Injunctive Relief.—The primary purpose of the writ of injunction is to afford protection especially to property or a property right where there is no adequate remedy at law. If strict rules of equity are observed, the party making the complaint must furnish very strong evidence that an important property right is about to be invaded, that the loss will be irreparable, and that the remedy at law is inadequate. Perhaps the simplest illustration is an order which restrains the cutting of timber on land where ownership is in dispute. It would be impossible to replace the full-grown trees after the question of ownership has been settled. If the subject of litigation can be held in *statu quo* until the rights of the parties have been determined, the desired result has been obtained.

But even in cases where the damage could be repaired by a payment of money, an injunction may issue on the ground that the defendant does not have property which could be reached in a damage suit. Another special reason for injunctive relief is that otherwise a plaintiff would have to bring or defend a "multiplicity of suits."

"It may be laid down, as a general rule that whenever the rights of a party aggrieved cannot be protected or enforced in the ordinary course of proceedings at law, except by numerous and expensive suits, a court of equity may properly interpose and afford relief by injunction."[5]

The last two special grounds for relief, i.e., financial irresponsibility and multiplicity of suits, have special applicability in cases growing out of disputes between employers and employees. In the typical case, the laborer has little or no property which could be attached to satisfy

[5] High, *op. cit.*, p. 12.

a judgment for damages. Furthermore, in a strike involving hundreds of men, it would be expensive to sue each of them separately. If the damage can be prevented, these difficulties are avoided. This is just what the injunction is supposed to do. High says it is "to be regarded as a preventive rather than as a remedial process."[6]

Contempt of Court.—The regular method of enforcing an injunction is by proceedings in contempt. Parties enjoined may be cited for contempt if they violate the order. They are required to appear before the court and answer the charge of violating the injunction. If the court is convinced, after hearing, that the defendant is guilty of contempt, he can be fined or sentenced to jail at the discretion of the court. Maximum penalties are provided by statute in some states. In the absence of a statute on the subject, the person charged with contempt is not entitled to jury trial. A federal statute requiring jury trial where the contempt is also a crime has been sustained.[7]

Frequently a large police force is required to carry out the order of the court. This may be provided by swearing in more deputy sheriffs, asking the governor to send militia, calling upon the state constabulary (in states where it exists), or, in the case of federal injunctions, swearing in a sufficient number of United States marshals.

The Scope of Injunctions in Industrial Disputes.[7a]—Some idea of the scope of injunctions may be obtained by reviewing the list of acts which may be enjoined. When applied against employers or groups of employers, there

---

[6] *Ibid.*, p. 3.
[7] Michaelson v. U. S., 45 Sup. Ct. 18, 266 U. S. 42, 69 L. ed. 162 (1924).
[7a] See Frankfurter and Greene, *op. cit.*, chap. III.

is a limited range of acts which labor organizations have endeavored to use as a basis for injunctive relief. Dr. E. E. Witte has found that most of the successful cases come under three heads; namely, violation of trade agreements, eviction from company houses, and interference with pickets or with strike meetings.[8] Injunctions against black-listing have been sought but generally denied.[9] The total of successful cases in Dr. Witte's list, which is probably the most complete of any in existence, is thirty-three. When compared with the eighteen hundred[10] injunctions which have been obtained against labor organizations, this number seems very small.

The prohibitions contained in injunctions against labor organizations show a wide range and considerable complexity. In this brief review, illustrative cases only are cited. On several points, hundreds of cases could be cited. An excellent list is found in Oakes, *The Law of Organized Labor and Industrial Conflicts*, Sections 586-606.

Violence, Threats of Violence, and Intimidation.—In a very large number of cases, these acts are enjoined.[11] Assaulting employees is also enjoinable.[12] While all these offenses are frequently mentioned together, intimidation

---

[8] "Labor's Resort to Injunctions," 39 *Yale Law Journal* (January, 1930), 374-87.
[9] *Ibid.* [10] *Ibid.*
[11] Recent illustrations are New York Trust Company, Trustee for New Orleans Public Service Company, v. Amalgamated Association of Street and Electric Railway Employees, U. S. D. C. E. D. of Louisiana (July 9, 1929); Citizens Company v. Asheville Typographical Union, 187 N. C. 42, 121 S. E. 31 (1924). For additional cases, see Oakes, *The Law of Organized Labor and Industrial Conflicts*, pp. 936-38.
[12] Marion Manufacturing Company v. United Textile Workers. See Case III in Chapter V below.

is sometimes mentioned separately.[13] Messrs. Brissenden and Swayzee have found these acts to be enjoined almost universally in the New York Needle Trades.[14] It may be laid down as a general rule that violence, threats of violence, and intimidation may be enjoined in cases where they are seriously threatened. Destruction of property is also enjoinable.[15]

Trespassing.—Striking employees or former employees may be enjoined against trespassing upon the property of their former employer.[16]

Picketing.—A wide range of activities connected with industrial disputes is included in the term "picketing" and the acts incidental thereto. In several cases, picketing as such has been enjoined without qualification.[17] The justification for this is made on the ground that it really amounts to intimidation. In other cases, picketing is enjoined but the defendants are allowed a specified number of representatives at each point of access to the premises.[18]

[13] American Glanzstoff Corporation *et al.* v. Miller. See Case IV, Chapter V below; McGinnis v. Raleigh Typographical Union. See Case I, Chapter V below.

[14] "Use of the Labor Injunction in the New York Needle Trades," 44 *Political Science Quarterly* (December, 1929), 458.

[15] Gasaway v. Borderland Coal Corporation, 278 Federal 56 (1921); New York Trust Company v. Amalgamated Association of Street and Railway Employees, U. S. D. C. E. D. of Louisiana (July 9, 1929).

[16] Great Northern Railway Company v. Brosseau, 286 Federal 414 (1923); Citizens Company v. Asheville Typographical Union, 187 N. C. 42, 121 S. E. 31 (1924); Marion Manufacturing Company v. United Textile Workers (Case III below); American Glanzstoff Corporation v. Miller (Case IV below).

[17] Atchison, T. & S. F. R. Company v. Gee, 139 Federal 582 (1905); Pierce v. Stablemen's Union, 156 Cal. 70, 103 Pac. 324 (1909); Barnes v. Chicago Typographical Union, 232 Ill. 424, 83 N. E. 940 (1908); U. S. v. Railway Employees Department, 283 Federal 479 (1922).

[18] American Steel Foundries v. Tri-City Central Trades Council, 42 Sup. Ct. 72, 257 U. S. 184, 66 L. ed. 189 (1921); Great Northern Railway Company v. Brosseau, 286 Federal 414 (1923); New York Trust Company v. Street Railway Employees, U. S. D. C. E. D. Louisiana (July 9, 1929).

A single representative has been specified as in the Tri-City case referred to in footnote 18, while two or three have been allowed in several cases. The more widely accepted view seems to be that there are two general classes of picketing; namely, peaceful picketing, which is lawful, and threatening or coercive picketing, which is unlawful.[19] The law on this subject shows such wide variation that it is difficult to generalize. A detailed study of precedents in the particular jurisdiction is necessary in all cases.

Abusive Epithets.—The use of abusive epithets occurs most frequently in connection with picketing. However, it is frequently enjoined specifically.[20] The use of such terms as "rats," "scabs," "runts," and "bowery bums" has been enjoined.[21]

Boycotts.—The extent to which engaging in a boycott may be enjoined cannot be stated clearly without distinguishing between a *primary* boycott and a *secondary* boycott. By the former is meant action directly against the offending party. The latter refers to a combination to harm one person by coercing others to harm him.[22] Primary boycotts have generally been held to be legal while secondary boycotts have been enjoined.[23]

---

[19] Citizens Company v. Asheville Typographical Union, 187 N. C. 42, 121 S. E. 31 (1924). For detailed list see Oakes, *op. cit.*, pp. 459-60.

[20] Iron Molders' Union v. Allis Chalmers Company, 166 Federal 45 (1908); Gasaway v. Borderland Coal Corporation, 278 Federal 56 (1921); Michaels v. Hillman, 111 Miscellaneous 284, 181 N. Y. Supp. 165 (1920).

[21] McGinnis v. Raleigh Typographical Union (Case I, Chapter V below). Dissolved on appeal; Michaels v. Hillman (cited above).

[22] L. D. Clark, *The Law of the Employment of Labor*, pp. 289-90.

[23] Duplex Printing Press Company v. Deering, 41 Sup. Ct. 172, 254 U. S. 443, 65 L. ed. 349 (1921); Booth v. Burgess, 72 N. J. Eq. 181, 65 Atl. 226

Inducing Breach of Contract.—Acts by which it is sought to induce others to break their contracts can be enjoined.[24] This applies to efforts to induce laborers to join a trade union when they have signed individual contracts (called "yellow dog" contracts) with the employer whereby they agree that so long as they stay in his employ they will not belong to a labor union.[25] Cases on this point are especially significant for the reason that union organizers for the United Mine Workers were enjoined from entering the non-union coal fields and endeavoring to persuade the miners to join the union. The last two cases cited in footnote 25 were used as a basis for defeating the nomination of the Honorable John J. Parker for the United States Supreme Court.[26]

Calling a Strike.—Union officers may be enjoined against calling a strike if the court considers the strike unlawful.[27] The same is true if the strike call would be in violation of union rules.[28] Calling a strike in violation of a contract may be enjoined.[29] Officers may also be en-

---

(1906); Thomson Machine Company v. Brown, 89 N. J. Eq. 326, 104 Atl. 129 (1918); Bedford Cut Stone Company v. Journeymen Stone Cutters Association, 47 Sup. Ct. 522, 274 U. S. 37, 71 L. ed. 916 (1927). See Martin, *Modern Law of Labor Unions*, p. 109.

[24] Keeney v. Borderland Coal Corporation, 282 Federal 269 (1922); McMichael v. Atlanta Envelope Company, 151 Ga. 776, 108 S. E. 226 (1921).

[25] Hitchman Coal and Coke Company v. Mitchell, 38 Sup. Ct. 65, 245 U. S. 229, 62 L. ed. 245 (1917); United Mine Workers v. Red Jacket Consolidated Coal and Coke Company, 18 Federal (2nd) 839 (1927); Bittner v. West Virginia-Pittsburgh Coal Company, 15 Federal (2nd) 652 (1926).

[26] See Hearings before subcommittee of the Judiciary (April 5, 1930), p. 41.

[27] Toledo A. A. and N. M. R. Company v. Pennsylvania Company, 54 Federal 730 (1893).

[28] Burgess v. Georgia F. O. A. R. Company, 148 Ga. 415, 96 S. E. 864 (1918).

[29] Barnes v. Berry, 156 Federal 72 (1907).

joined against directing a strike or issuing any strike orders.[30]

The Use of Money to Carry on a Strike.—The use of money may be enjoined if the court is convinced that it invades the employer's rights.[31] The payment of strike benefits has been enjoined.[32] The collection of money for strike purposes has also been enjoined.[33] Aiding and abetting striking employees in resisting eviction from company houses has been enjoined.[34]

Residual Clauses.—In addition to the specific prohibitions, injunctions usually contain clauses which are very general in meaning and wide in scope. Dr. Witte has called these "catch-all clauses." The defendants are restrained from "interfering with complainants *in any way.*"[35] Messrs. Brissenden and Swayzee have found the following clause to be generally included in the injunctions growing out of industrial disputes in the New York Needle Trades: The defendants are restrained from "combining, conspiring, or agreeing to obstruct plaintiff's business in any way."[36] In the Debs case, the defendants are enjoined "from in any way or manner interfering with,

[30] U. S. v. Railway Employees Department, 283 Federal 479 (1922).
[31] Tunstall v. Stearns Coal Company, 192 Federal 808 (1911); Everett-Waddey v. Richmond Typographical Union, 105 Va. 188, 53 S. E. 273 (1906).
[32] Reynolds v. Davis, 198 Mass. 294, 84 N. E. 457 (1908); Barnes v. Berry, 156 Federal 72 (1907).
[33] Borderland Coal Corporation v. United Mine Workers, 275 Federal 871 (1921). Reversed on appeal, 278 Federal 56 (1921).
[34] Pittsburgh Terminal Coal Corporation v. United Mine Workers, 22 Federal (2nd) 565 (1927); United Mine Workers v. Red Jacket Company, 18 Federal (2nd) 839 (1927).
[35] Glanzstoff Corporation v. Miller (Case IV in Chapter V below).
[36] 45 *Political Science Quarterly*, 107-9.

hindering, obstructing or stopping any of the business" of the complainants.[37]

The prohibitions contained in some of the recent orders will illustrate recent tendencies. In the case of *Clarkson Coal Company v. United Mine Workers* (D. C. of U. S., S. D. of Ohio, E. D., September 10, 1927), the temporary restraining order enjoined the defendants as follows:[37a]

1. From interfering with, obstructing or preventing in any way or attempting to do so, the carrying on of the business of the plaintiffs;

2. From destroying or damaging physical property of the complainant;

3. From exploding dynamite or other explosives in the neighborhood;

4. From trespassing upon the property of the plaintiff;

5. From doing any acts of violence or making threats of violence;

6. From displaying signs or banners, containing words designed to intimidate or insult present or prospective employees, within ten miles of the mines. This applies to signs on property owned or leased by the defendants as well as elsewhere;

7. From interfering in any way with the carrying out of any contract of employment (persuasion in the presence of three or more persons is prohibited);

8. From blockading any of the public highways leading to the mines;

---
[37] United States v. Debs, 64 Federal 724 (1894).
[37a] 9 *Law and Labor* (October, 1927), 290.

9. From gathering or loitering in groups near the mines (peaceful assemblies not on mining company's property permitted);

10. From picketing except as herein specifically permitted: Picket posts allowed provided they are not within 100 feet of complainant's property and not closer together than 700 yards. Not more than three pickets allowed at each post. Picket posts must not be more than 100 feet long. The president of the district union must furnish the United States Marshal a plot of picket posts and a complete list of pickets. Each picket must be a citizen of the United States and able to speak the English language. Relief pickets must not stay in the vicinity of picket posts when not on duty. Pickets may peacefully observe, communicate with, and endeavor to persuade peacefully prospective employees not to enter employment or may endeavor to persuade peacefully present employees to cease work at the expiration of an existing contract. But this permission *"does not include peacefully persuading one to break an existing employment contract."*[37b] The erection or maintenance of tents within 100 yards of plaintiff's property or within 100 yards of any picketed highway is restrained.

11. From doing any acts in the furtherance of any combination or conspiracy.

12. The United States Marshal is ordered to have this order published in a newspaper of general circulation in each of the counties involved and to have a certified copy of the order printed in the English, Italian, and

---

[37b] Italics mine.

Polish languages, posted in twenty-five conspicuous places in each of the counties involved.

13. The Marshal is ordered to enforce this injunction by arresting violators and by calling to his assistance such Deputy Marshals as he may deem necessary.

An injunction, growing out of the same strike, and similar in many respects, is that allowed in the case of *Pittsburgh Terminal Coal Corporation v. United Mine Workers* (22 Federal—2nd—559), 1927. The novel feature of this order relates to resisting eviction from company houses. The defendants are restrained:

"From hereafter detaining or occupying any mining house or houses of plaintiff by causing the same to be occupied against the plaintiff's will.

"From disbursing any funds for any further appeal-bonds, attorney services, court costs, or otherwise for the purpose of enabling, aiding, encouraging, or procuring any person to occupy against the plaintiff's will any such mining houses of plaintiff, from signing any further appeal bond or depositing, providing, or furnishing security for such appeal bond to prolong or aid in litigation respecting the possession of said houses; . . ."[38]

The widening scope of injunctions in industrial disputes was emphasized in an address made by the Honorable George Wharton Pepper at the meeting of the American Bar Association in 1924.[39] After a careful examination of practically all the orders, issued by Federal courts, in recent years, and especially the three hundred growing out of the railway shopmen's strike of 1922, he finds "an

---

[38] Order printed in full in 9 *Law and Labor* (November, 1927), 311.
[39] 49 *A. B. A. Proceedings* (1924), 174-80.

evolution mildly comparable to the corporate mortgage. The injunction orders have become more and more comprehensive and far-reaching in their provisions until they culminate in the Shopmen's Injunction Order already referred to."[40]

A digest of the injunction obtained by the Attorney-General in this case will give some idea of its comprehensiveness.[41] This injunction enjoined the defendants and their "attorneys, servants, agents, associates, members, employees, and all persons acting in aid of or in conjunction with them" from the following:

1. Hindering, interfering with, or obstructing interstate commerce and the mails;

2. Picketing;

3. Inducing or attempting to induce by the use of threats, etc., entreaties, argument, persuasion, rewards, or otherwise, any person or persons to abandon the employment of the railway companies, or any of them, or to refrain from entering such employment;

4. Inducing or attempting to induce by the use of threats, etc., entreaties, argument, persuasion, rewards, or otherwise, any person or persons to abandon the employment of said railway companies, or any of them or to refrain from entering such employment;

5. In any manner by letters, printed or other circulars, telegrams, word of mouth, oral persuasion, or suggestion or through interviews to be published in newspapers or otherwise in any manner whatsoever, encourage, direct, or

---

[40] *Ibid.*, pp. 176-77. The reference is to the injunction secured by the government in U. S. v. Railway Employees Department, 283 Federal 479 (1924).

[41] This digest was made by Senator Pepper in an unpublished memorandum entitled: *The Use by the Federal Courts of the Injunction in Labor Disputes.*

command any person whether a member of any or either of said labor organizations or associations defendant therein, or otherwise, to abandon the employment of said railway companies, or any of them, or to refrain from entering the service of said railway companies or either of them.

6. The said defendants (by name) as officers, are enjoined from

(a) Issuing any instructions, requests, public statements, or suggestions in any way to any defendant herein, or to any official or member of any said labor organization constituting the said Federated Shop Crafts, or to any official or member of any system federation thereof with reference to their conduct or the acts they shall perform subsequent to the abandonment of the employment of said railway companies by the members of the said Federated Shop Crafts, or for the purpose of or to induce any such officials or members or any other persons whomsoever, to do or say anything for the purpose or intended or calculated to cause any employee of said railway companies or any of them, to abandon the employment thereof, or to cause any persons to refrain from entering the employment thereof, to perform duties in aid of the movement and transportation of passengers and property in interstate commerce and the carriage of the mails.

(b) Using, causing, or consenting to the use of any funds or monies of said labor organizations in aid of or to promote or encourage the doing of any of the matters or things hereinbefore complained of.

The opinion of the Court is based on its finding that

the strike is illegal, as an unlawful conspiracy to obstruct the mails and as an unlawful conspiracy in restraint of interstate commerce under the Sherman Act. The object of the strike being illegal, all acts directed toward its promotion are illegal and properly enjoinable.

This order seems to have gone farther in its prohibitions than any other order on record at the present time. However, the injunction against Debs and his associates was similar in many respects.[42]

[42] For a comparison of these two orders in parallel columns, see Frankfurter and Greene, *The Labor Injunction*, pp. 253-63.

CHAPTER III

THE CASE FOR INJUNCTIONS IN INDUSTRIAL DISPUTES

IN THE long and heated discussion of the writ of injunction in industrial disputes, there have been a number of eloquent defenders. Most of these have been members of the legal profession or representatives of organized employers. In the argument of the case, various points have been emphasized but we shall review only a few of them. These arguments are presented objectively without any attempt to test their validity in this chapter.

1. *The Injunction Prevents Unlawful Acts.*—As indicated in Chapter II, the chief purpose of the injunctive remedy has been to protect property. It has been strongly contended that prevention of unlawful acts which would result in the destruction of property, is vastly superior to a remedy which cannot be applied until after the damage has been done. As a general proposition, this doctrine has been widely accepted. The thoughtful student will naturally wish to know *how* the writ of injunction prevents lawlessness. Several answers to this have been given. Its virtue lies partly in the fact that *it places the defendants on notice*.[1] They may be vaguely aware of the criminal law, but the notice served at the time the unlawful acts are about to be committed reinforces the criminal law and applies it to the particular situation.

Closely related to this is the idea of *definite advice*.[2]

---

[1] Interview with Thomas A. Jones, Sr., attorney for complainants in the case of Citizen Co. v. Asheville Typo. Union, 187 N. C. 42, 121 S. E. 31 (1924).

[2] Walter Gordon Merritt, *Hearings on S. 1482* (December 18, 1928), p. 740.

The injunction tells the defendant specifically what acts he is restrained from doing. Instead of calling the militia or ordering out the entire police force to preserve order, the court of equity warns the defendant as to the rights which it appears he is about to infringe, thus avoiding the use of unnecessary force. This has been strongly relied upon as an argument for the peacefulness of the injunctive remedy. An excellent illustration of this argument is found in the opinion of the Supreme Court in the Debs case.[3] Mr. Justice Brewer, in delivering the opinion of the court, says:

> ... the right to use force does not exclude the right of appeal to the courts for a judicial determination and for the exercise of all their powers of prevention. Indeed, it is more to the praise than to the blame of the government that, instead of determining for itself questions of right and wrong on the part of these petitioners and their associates and enforcing that determination by the club of the policeman and the bayonet of the soldier, *it submitted all these questions to the peaceful determination of judicial tribunals*,[4] and invoked their consideration and judgment as to the measure of its rights and powers and the correlative obligations of those against whom it made complaint.

In support of the preventive nature of injunctions, it has also been pointed out that the dignity of the court commands respect and gives the order a wholesome restraining influence.[5]

2. *It Reinforces the Criminal Law.*—Taking note of the argument of critics that the injunction amounts to the assumption of criminal jurisdiction, the defenders have

---
[3] *In Re Debs*, 15 Sup. Ct. 1039, 158 U. S. 564, 39 L. ed. 1092 (1895).
[4] Italics mine.
[5] Interview with Gallatin Roberts, mayor of Asheville, N. C., Dec., 1929.

emphasized the function of an equity court in reinforcing the criminal law. Instances of statutory authorization for such intervention are frequently cited.[6] Perhaps the most notable of recent illustrations is a provision of this kind in the Volstead Act providing for enforcement of the Eighteenth Amendment. An unusually clear explanation of this point has been given by Mr. Murray T. Quigg, editor of *Law and Labor*:[7]

> Where, during an industrial dispute, acts are occurring which are of a criminal nature, the evidence may or may not associate the acts beyond a reasonable doubt with particular individuals, even though a preponderance of the evidence establishes that the acts are caused by parties to the industrial dispute. Punishment for crime . . . rarely, if ever, apprehends and punishes persons other than the criminal actually committing the damaging act, whereas he may have been instigated and even compelled to commit the act by other persons. . . .
>
> . . . the process of the injunction acts promptly. It reaches everybody who may be involved, and it particularly reaches those persons who stand behind the scenes and direct the activities which result in the criminal acts. It reaches not only the malefactors but it reaches the persons who may be morally responsible for the malefaction but who could not be reached by the criminal law.

The special applicability of this argument to industrial disputes is obvious. The complainants might seek protection against the "labor agitators" even though there is not sufficient proof of overt acts of a criminal nature to secure a conviction in a criminal court.

It may be noted that the argument quoted above re-

---
[6] See Testimony of James A. Emery, *Hearings on S. 1482* (1928), pp. 873-74.
[7] Personal letter dated January 17, 1930.

fers especially to what the courts have called "conspiracies." Stating the argument formally: *Injunctions are especially helpful in reaching conspiracies.* The same idea is emphasized by Mr. James A. Emery.[8] He strongly objects to the proposed legislation on the ground that it "repeals the fundamental distinction between the acts of an individual and the acts of a combination." Our Federal courts, especially, have considered a showing of conspiracy an exceptionally strong reason for granting relief by injunction. Evidence of this is found in two of the most important of recent cases before the Supreme Court.[9]

The injunction reinforces the criminal law in a special way if the local police authorities are unable or unwilling to act against the parties who are threatening the injury. Mr. Quigg considers this an important factor in "the hysterical situation in the small southern mill towns during the past year."[10] Federal authority for relief on this ground goes back at least as far as the Debs case.[11]

3. *Equity Procedure Is More Expeditious.*—This argument is in line with the fundamental bases of relief by injunction. The conduct threatened may be punishable by fine or imprisonment and the party who is about to sustain the loss may be entitled to an action for damages in case the loss is sustained, but punishment of the criminal offense does not restore his property and the offending party may not be answerable in damage. If

[8] *Hearings on S. 1482* (1928), p. 857.
[9] Duplex Printing Press Company v. Deering, 41 Sup. Ct. 172, 254 U. S. 443, 65 L. ed. 349 (1921); and Bedford Cut Stone Company v. Journeymen Stone Cutters, 47 Sup. Ct. 522, 274 U. S. 37, 71 L. ed. 916 (1927).
[10] Personal letter, January 17, 1930.
[11] *In Re Debs*, 15 Sup. Ct. 1039, 158 U. S. 564, 39 L. ed. 1092 (1895).

quick action by a court of equity can preserve his property, the desired result is achieved. The rights of the parties enjoined must be considered, but it is impossible to observe all the rules of procedure which law courts have worked out for the protection of parties accused, without leaving the complaining party remediless.[12] This argument is especially strong in view of the factors mentioned above, namely: the fact that defendants may not have property which could be attached in an action for damages and the inconvenience and expense involved in a multiplicity of suits.

4. *Injunctions Restrain Only Unlawful Acts.*—Even if the injury complained of is not seriously threatened, as a full hearing may later show, the injunction does no harm since it restrains only *unlawful acts*.[13] The parties enjoined are still free to engage in lawful acts. They are acting at their peril if they violate the injunction, but the injunction forbids nothing which the defendants have a lawful right to do. In a sense, it is even a protection to them. In the absence of an injunction, they may be uncertain as to just what acts are unlawful. But the injunction gives definite advice and thus indicates the bounds which must not be overstepped.

5. *Labor Organizations Cannot Lawfully Be Singled Out for Exemption.*—The injunction is an established remedy under our system of government. It is used in all classes of cases where irreparable injury to property rights is about to be sustained as a result of unlawful acts. It is

---

[13] See opinion of Chief Justice Taft in Truax v. Corrigan, 42 Sup. Ct. 124, 257 U. S. 312, 66 L. ed. 254 (1921).

[13] See *Hearings on S. 1482* (1928), p. 308.

contended that it would be unconstitutional and unjust to enjoin a group of capitalists from interfering with a property right and allow labor organizations to perform the same acts with impunity.[14]

6. *Trade Unions Have a Power for Evil Against Which the Public Should Be Safeguarded.*—This argument includes many diverse elements but it is a focal point for a large volume of testimony before investigating committees and for the argument of cases in court. It is charged that labor organizations have used the strike, picket, and boycott for extortion of graft, overthrow of arbitration awards, coercing men to join trade unions, forcing the discharge of men who will not be admitted to trade unions, suppression of products and materials which save labor, and the suppression of products and materials made by non-union men.[15]

Strikes, which may be justifiable under some circumstances, are frequently used to bring about industrial injustice against which the injunction is a safeguard. Various illustrations of this have been given.[16] The railway employees threaten a strike against any railroad which hauls non-union coal. By law the railroad is prohibited from discriminating against shippers in this manner. The injunction simply orders the officers of the union not to force the carrier into committing a crime.

Strikes have been called against contractors because the contractors do not maintain prices unlawfully set by

[14] Based upon the testimony of Walter Gordon Merritt, *Hearings on S. 1482* (1928), p. 764.
[15] Personal letter from Murray T. Quigg, January 17, 1930.
[16] Argument of Walter Gordon Merritt, *Information Service* (March 8, 1930), Federal Council of Churches, pp. 15-16.

collusion between a contractors' association and the trade union.[17] Strikes have been called against the employment of married women and Negroes to whom union membership is denied.[18]

Organized labor in the building trades in New York City decreed that no manufactured stone should be erected within twenty-five miles of New York City Hall which had not been made by union labor within that area.

The Decorative Stone Company, employers of union labor in New Haven, Connecticut, bid for the manufactured stone work on the Roosevelt High School at Yonkers, $18,814.00. The lowest bid from a local union concern for the same job was $52,000.00. . . . Similarly, the bid of the Decorative Stone Company on the Junior High School at New Rochelle was $33,000.00 under that of any other bidder. The stone was delivered but, through the coercive effort of the Union to prevent its erection, the completion of the building was delayed for more than two years. . . . Finally, an injunction out of a Federal Court . . . permitted the work to be completed.[19]

The investigations of the New York Legislative Committee on Housing (1922-23) disclosed a wide variety of oppressive practices of trade unions. The committee found that fines of from $500 to $2,000 had been imposed upon members for trifling infractions of union rules. They practically amounted to expulsion from the union and depriving the aggrieved parties of an opportunity for earning a livelihood since the closed union shop prevailed in the trade.[20] It was found that a jurisdictional dispute between plumbers and steamfitters, for which contractors were not to blame in any way, had tied up a large volume

[17] *Ibid.*   [18] *Ibid.*, p. 16.   [19] *Ibid.*
[20] Legislative Document (1923), No. 48 State of New York. Final Report of the Joint Leg. Committee on Housing, p. 53.

of business.[21] The committee found various instances in which competent workmen were kept out of the union by purely arbitrary action on the part of the trade unions. It is contended that these oppressive practices should be enjoined.

7. *Strikes Are Not Peaceful.*—Those who favor the continued use of injunctions in industrial disputes call attention to the fact that strikes and their incidents, especially picketing, are not as peaceful as they are claimed to be.

> The proofs of this are to be seen in the papers almost daily. We read of wanton attacks made upon men whose only offense was that they had taken the places of strikers, of dynamite placed under the houses in which they boarded, of shots fired through their windows, of poison placed in their food. . . . *Assault, riot, arson, murder, treason—this is a pretty list of offenses to compare with the impudent claim, made at every strike, that the strikers are acting only on their legal rights.*[22]

After showing the relation of these acts to the irreparable injury doctrine, this writer concludes: "This state of facts affords good ground for the interference of equity."[23]

At the hearings on the Clayton bill, H. R. 1567 (63rd Congress) 1914, Mr. O. P. Briggs, retiring president of the National Founders' Association, filed an exhibit entitled, "A Policy of Lawlessness—Partial Record of Riot, Assaults, Murder, Coercion and Intimidation Occurring in Strikes of the Iron Molders' Union during 1904, 1905, 1906 and 1907." This record contains forty-three pages

---
[21] *Ibid.*, p. 55.
[22] Ardemus Stewart, 33 *American Law Register & Review* (1894), 615.
[23] *Ibid.*, p. 617.

of affidavits and statements reciting various forms of violence, intimidation and coercion. The total number of affidavits and statements on this point is four hundred.[24] It was strongly urged that the situation depicted in this exhibit called for the continuance of equity power in this class of cases.

8. *Jury Trial Is Inappropriate.*—It has been contended that promptness is a necessity in cases of threatened irreparable injury. Jury trial would impose delay and seriously detract from the efficiency of the remedy.[25] It has also been suggested that the union movement is so widespread that it is almost impossible to secure a jury without union sympathies. For this reason, the remedy at criminal law is held to be inadequate.[26]

9. *Labor Organizations Can Use Injunctions.*—In recent years there has been strong advocacy of the use of injunctions by labor organizations. As a matter of fact, trade unions are applying for relief at the hands of equity courts in an increasing number of cases. As noted above, several of these have been granted. *Law and Labor*, the official organ of the League for Industrial Rights, strongly urges the desirability of this course of action. Trade unionists have the same right to approach the courts as other citizens. They may seek and obtain relief when the facts justify it. It is contended that there is thus equality before the law and no radical change is needed.

Summary.—In the course of this chapter we have sketched briefly the more important arguments advanced

---

[24] Hearings on H. R. 1567, Subcommittee of the Judiciary United States Senate (1914), pp. 709-52.
[25] William H. Taft, 34 *American Law Register* (1895), 608.
[26] Ardemus Stewart, 33 *American Law Register* (1894), 616.

in support of injunctions in industrial disputes. If the argument of its friends is true, the injunction has a fundamental basis in the necessity for protecting property against irreparable injury by unlawful acts. It prevents unlawful acts by placing the offending party on notice and giving him definite advice. It reinforces the criminal law by reaching those who counsel and induce lawlessness as well as those who actually commit the overt acts. It is exceptionally useful in reaching conspiracies. Equity is to be preferred to the remedy at law because it is more expeditious. Even if the court errs in granting the injunction, it does no harm since it enjoins only unlawful acts. The defendants are still free to engage in lawful acts. It would be unjust to exempt trade unions from injunctions without making the rule generally applicable. A special reason for retaining this remedy is the lawlessness and abuse of power which prevails in the labor movement. Jury trial would impose delay and often result in a miscarriage of justice. If the trade unionists would avail themselves of their opportunity to use injunctions, equality before the law would be obvious and no radical change would be needed.

Lengthy discussion of the points presented here has been omitted. In a later chapter, we shall have the opportunity to test the validity of the most important arguments involved.

CHAPTER IV

THE CASE AGAINST INJUNCTIONS IN INDUSTRIAL DISPUTES

THE intervention of courts of equity in industrial disputes has been a subject of criticism for many years. The first great outburst came at the time of the Debs injunction[1] in 1894. During the next half decade, a number of attacks upon the system were made in legal journals as well as in the popular press. The sweeping character of the injunction against Debs and his associates and the comparative novelty of the proceeding seem to have made a strong impression on the writers and public speakers of the time. In this early period, the attack was led by prominent men in the legal profession. In more recent years, the brunt of the attack seems to have shifted to the trade union leaders. While there is considerable overlapping, the argument may be classified as legal on the one hand and economic or social on the other. The arguments in both classes will be outlined briefly. No estimate of validity is made in this chapter.

LEGAL OBJECTIONS[1a]

1. *Evasion of Safeguards of Liberty.*—In the attack upon the use of injunctions, especially as applied in industrial disputes, attention has been called to certain safeguards which have been adopted to protect the rights of individuals and especially those accused of crime. Prominent among these is the right to a hearing before execu-

---
[1] *In Re Debs*, 15 Sup. Ct. 1039, 158 U. S. 564, 39 L. ed. 1092 (1895).
[1a] See Frankfurter and Greene, *op. cit.*, chap. II.

tion of the judgment of the court. It is charged that the granting of temporary restraining orders on the *ex parte* application of the complainant seriously infringes upon this safeguard.

"No trace of the proofs taken may be left on which a defendant is incarcerated as it may be all unwritten testimony, taken *ex parte* without the accused seeing the witnesses or having an opportunity to ask them a single question; or the proofs may be by affidavit."[2]

This is regarded as objectionable for special reasons in the case of an industrial dispute. A prominent labor attorney, Mr. Morris Hillquit, has expressed the opinion that "in most cases, the preliminary injunction, the *ex parte* injunction, without notice or hearing, has decided the fate of the strike."[3] This charge occurs frequently in the literature of the subject.

In this connection, the trustworthiness of affidavits submitted in applying for an injunction should be noted. Federal Judge Amidon has expressed a very definite opinion on this point:

> The experience both upon the hearings as to whether a preliminary injunction should issue, and upon the contempt proceedings, have convinced me that affidavits are an untrustworthy guide for judicial action. That is the case in all legal proceedings, but it is peculiarly true of litigation growing out of a strike, where feelings on both sides are necessarily wrought up, and the desire for victory is likely to obscure nice moral questions and poison the minds of men by prejudice. Many of the affidavits submitted on behalf of plaintiffs have been made by private detectives or

---

[2] Charles Noble Gregory, 11 *Harvard Law Review* (1898), 502-3. Also, see 31 *American Law Reg.* (n. s.), 2.

[3] 13 *Academy of Political Science* (June, 1928), 87. Also, see J. H. Benton, *What Is Government by Injunction?*, p. 63.

guards. As a class, they are overzealous through their desire to prove to the detective bureaus that they are efficient, and to the railway company (the plaintiff in this case) that they are indispensable. Speaking generally, such detectives are mostly drawn from a class of people in large cities which would cause little credence to be given to their statements in ordinary litigation. . . .

Experience . . . has caused me to be so incredulous of affidavits that I have required in all important matters the presence of the chief witnesses upon each side at the hearing. These witnesses have been subjected to oral examination. The court has had a chance to observe their demeanor. A comparison of the picture produced by their testimony with that produced by their affidavits has proven *the utter untrustworthiness of affidavits. Such documents are packed with falsehoods,*[4] or with half-truths which in such a matter are more deceptive than deliberate falsehoods.

The most serious complaint that can be made against injunctions, which have become so prominent a part of the law dealing with strikes in the United States, is the fact that courts have become accustomed to decide the most important questions of fact, often involving the citizen's liberty, upon this wholly untrustworthy class of proof.[5]

Similar in tone is the following preface to an opinion on a labor injunction case:

Hardly anything of greater private or public gravity is ever presented to the court, and yet these matters are constantly receiving adjudication without a single witness brought before the judge. It is a bad practice. I confess my inability to determine with any satisfaction from an inspection of inanimate manuscript questions of veracity. In disposing of the present rule, I am compelled to find, as best I may from perusing two hundred thirty-five lifeless, typewritten pages, of conflicting evidence, the facts which must determine respondent's guilt or innocence on the quasi-criminal charge of contempt.[6]

[4] Italics mine.
[5] Great Northern Railway Company v. Brosseau, 286 Federal 416 (1923).
[6] Long v. Bricklayers' Union, 17 Pa. Dist. R. 984.

The evasion of other constitutional safeguards for persons accused of crime is frequently charged by the critics of the system.[7] Included in this list are formal indictment, presumption of innocence, requirement of proof beyond a reasonable doubt, right to be confronted by witnesses, and, probably most important of all, JURY TRIAL. It has even been urged that the sole reason for preferring the injunction, enforced by contempt proceedings, to criminal prosecution is that in the latter case "those safeguards which have been thought essential to liberty interpose some delay or uncertainty."[8]

The United States Commission on Industrial Relations (1912-1916) inquired thoroughly into this subject. The testimony printed in the record covers four hundred sixty pages. One of the prominent witnesses before the Commission, Mr. S. S. Gregory, former President of the American Bar Association, was almost vehement in his criticism of the evasion of jury trial and other constitutional safeguards. He contends that "the obvious wisdom of permitting twelve men drawn from the body of the people to pass on questions of fact . . . has so far commended itself to the wisdom of our legislators and jurists to such a degree that it has become a permanent feature of our jurisprudence. . . ."[9]

This witness is also convinced that trial for contempt without a jury *"has been an injustice that has rankled in*

---

[7] See dissenting opinion of Justice Brandeis in Truax v. Corrigan, 42 Sup. Ct. 124, 257 U. S. 312, 66 L. ed. 254 (1921).
[8] Charles Noble Gregory, 11 *Harvard Law Review* (1898), 502. Also, see W. H. Dunbar, 13 *Law Quarterly Review* (1897), 347-67.
[9] *Report of United States Commission on Industrial Relations*, XI, 10, 539.

the minds of everybody that has been a victim of it and justly so."[10]

The literature of the subject is replete with criticism of this type.[11] The emphasis on this point in current labor literature and in the hearings before legislative committees indicates clearly that trade unionists, as well as members of the legal profession, are impressed by it. Critics on the labor side frequently combine with this the charge that the judges are reactionary and in sympathy with the other side.

The section of the Clayton Act providing jury trial for criminal contempt has been upheld as applied to acts which are crimes in the ordinary sense; i.e., acts which would be in violation of the criminal law, even if no injunction were involved.[12] In most of the states, however, there is no right to jury trial in contempt proceedings.

2. *Assumption of Executive Power.*—It has been charged that courts of equity, in granting injunctions and enforcing their orders, have gone beyond their constitutional powers and entered a sphere of activity which properly belongs to the executive branch of the government. In order to assure compliance with the order of the court, it is often necessary to direct the regular police officers, or United States Marshals in the case of Federal courts, to swear in a large number of deputies. In some cases, this has amounted to placing an army of men at the disposal

---

[10] *Ibid.* Italics mine.

[11] For recent attacks by prominent lawyers, see Newton D. Baker, 8 *A. B. A. Journal*, 734; George W. Pepper, 49 *A. B. A. Proceedings* (1924), 174-80; H. W. Ballantine, 98 *Central Law Journal*, 5-9.

[12] Michaelson v. United States, 45 Sup. Ct. 18, 266 U. S. 42, 66 L. ed. 162 (1924).

of the court. Familiar illustrations are the Debs case, the shopmen's strike of 1922, and the coal miners' strike of 1928. Less spectacular, but illustrative of the same point, is the recent Federal injunction issued against the street car strike in New Orleans. The United States Marshal was ordered to swear in two hundred fifty deputy marshals who should enforce the injunction.[13] In the case of *American Glanzstoff Corporation v. Miller*, which is discussed in detail in Chapter V below, a large force of militia was called to carry out the order of the court. The critics contend that it is no longer true that the judiciary holds "neither the purse nor the sword."

3. *Assumption of Legislative Power.*—Perhaps the most frequent criticism of equity courts, in connection with industrial disputes, is the charge that in exercising this jurisdiction they have assumed legislative power. It is claimed that they have done this by directing orders against "all other persons" and "all other persons whomsoever," by enjoining acts which have not been declared to be unlawful by the legislature or any other authority, and by substituting their judgment for the judgment of the legislators on matters of social policy. This argument, combined with those mentioned above, has been made the basis for the protest against "government by injunction."[14] The following quotation from the Boston *Herald*, October 2, 1897, gives the argument concisely:

> The criticism that can be made upon recent judicial action of the kind referred to (sweeping injunctions in industrial disputes and punishment for violation by contempt proceedings) is that, in

[13] E. E. Witte, *American Labor Legislation Review*, (Sept., 1929), p. 312.
[14] For a list of articles on this subject, see Sayre, *Cases in Labor Law*, p. 759.

the opinion of a large number of our people, it has gone beyond proper limitations, and, as a result, restraints have been imposed upon individual action which neither the national congress nor the legislatures of the various states would ever have imposed if the facts in the case had been brought to their attention.[15]

One finds frequent reference to this in current literature, especially in the writings of trade union leaders. A prominent labor leader[16] contends that equity courts have gone further in legislating than our legislative bodies could go.

If a citizen believes a law—an act of Congress or the Legislature—to be unconstitutional, he may challenge that law by disregarding or violating it and, if he can prove the law to be erroneous, no penalty attaches to his disobedience. . . . But our courts do not recognize any such liberty in relation to the judicial edicts or court orders known as injunctions. Even though the order of the judge be erroneous, and the citizen proves to the satisfaction of the higher courts that it was an improper order, nevertheless he is punished for having disobeyed it. [Under the American injunction system] a single judge may issue an order against any citizen which would be unconstitutional if enacted as a law by Congress.[17]

4. *Indefinite Language of Orders.*—It has been objected that the use of terms such as "conspiring against the plaintiff" or "interfering with the business of the plaintiff in any way" or other terms, which the laborers cannot understand, places the defendants at a great disadvantage.[18]

---

[15] Quoted by J. H. Benton in *What Is Government by Injunction?*, pp. 10-11.
[16] Victor A. Olander, Secretary-Treasurer, Illinois State Federation of Labor, Labor Day Address, 1928: *The Inequity of Injunctions*, pp. 5-6.
[17] *Ibid.*
[18] *Ibid.*, pp. 6-8.

Economic and Social Objections

1. *Property Rights Placed above Personal Rights.*—This argument rests upon the legal principle that the primary purpose of an injunction is to protect property. It has, of course, never been contended that all interference with property rights could be enjoined. It is only interference without proper justification which the courts condemn. However, the critics have charged that, as the writ has been used in labor cases, the courts have been very illiberal in recognizing personal rights which would constitute a justification. One frequently meets the accusation that the courts seem inclined to protect property rights against all forms of interference, thus disregarding personal rights instead of properly balancing the two.[19] This has been regarded as especially serious since jury trial, which might give more adequate consideration to personal rights, is denied in the contempt proceedings. The argument on this point has been tersely expressed by the late Samuel Gompers in his introduction to Mr. Frey's book on the subject:

"A careful study of this book will convince all who are open to conviction that the injunction, as used in industrial disputes, is a preposterous weapon of oppression, used without authority of the law or the constitution, and an instrument forged by cunning and usurpation *for the benefit of the possessors of property to the detriment of humanity.*"[20]

2. *Perversion of Status Quo Doctrine.*—It has been

---

[19] See Henry R. Seager, *Principles of Economics* (1923), pp. 593-94; Thomas Reed Powell, 13 *Academy of Political Science*, 65.

[20] John P. Frey, *The Labor Injunction*, p. 4. Italics mine.

seriously contended that the injunction, as now used, ties the hands of one party to the industrial dispute while arming the other for industrial conflict. The purpose of the temporary restraining order is to maintain the *status quo* but "an order which prohibits the union men from picketing, persuading prospective customers or employees to stay away, or using the other means necessary to make the strike effective, while the employer is left free to import strike-breakers, hire private guards, and otherwise break the strike, is not maintaining the *status quo*."[21]

3. *Inadequate Consideration of Economic Facts.*—It has been charged that our judges, in granting injunctions, have frequently not adequately considered economic facts which are necessarily involved in the cases. The employer comes to the court with a complaint of conspiracy to interfere with his business and cause irreparable injury. The threatened injury may be real and apparent but the critics contend that the courts have been less liberal in recognizing justification for interference in these cases than in other cases. Business competition may drive a man out of business but courts will not enjoin it. But both the competitors and the trade unionists are pursuing self interest. This view has been emphasized by Mr. Justice Holmes.[22] In a case involving only peaceful picketing and persuasion, he holds that the self interest of the laborers in the "free struggle for life" is a sufficient justification even though it results in injury. It is justified on the

---

[21] Hoxie, *Trade Unionism in the United States*, p. 233; also, see 13 *Academy of Political Science* (June, 1928), 84.
[22] Dissenting Opinion in Vegelahn v. Guntner, 167 Mass. 92, 44 N. E. 1077 (1896).

same basis as injury by business competition. Competition is worth more than its costs.

The conspiracy angle of these cases has come in for special criticism.

There is a notion which latterly has been insisted on a good deal, that a *combination* of persons to do what one of them lawfully might do by himself will make the otherwise lawful conduct unlawful. ... In the general form in which it [this proposition] has been presented and accepted by many courts, I think it is plainly untrue, both on authority and in principle. ...

If it be true that workingmen may combine with a view among other things, to getting as much as they can for their labor, just as capital may combine with a view to getting the greatest possible return, it must be true that when combined they have the same liberty that combined capital has to support their interests by argument, persuasion, and the bestowal or refusal of those advantages which they otherwise lawfully control.[23]

The same idea has been expressed by Commons and Andrews. In the view of these writers, the development of the modern industrial corporation has made the conspiracy doctrine an absurdity. One of these corporations, though a single person in the eyes of the law, has greater power to inflict injury than a trade union.[24] The use of this power for what is called a "secondary boycott" was demonstrated in the report of the Lockwood Investigating Committee of the New York Legislature in 1922.[25] Testimony showed that large steel companies would not sell steel to a contractor who employed union labor. President Grace of the Bethlehem Steel Company testified as follows:

[23] *Ibid.* See Sayre's *Cases in Labor Law*, pp. 205-6.
[24] *Principles of Labor Legislation* (1927), p. 107.
[25] Legislative Document Number 60, pp. 128-30.

"Our company refused to sell fabricated steel to any builder or contractor in the New York District who will not erect it on what we call the open shop principle.

"I do not know of any builder who can get any fabricated steel for construction in the City of New York without subscribing to that resolution (to operate with non-union labor). I do not know of any place where he can get it."[26]

The critics contend that if economic facts were adequately considered, the courts would either enjoin the secondary boycott against both the large corporation and the trade union or refuse this relief in both cases.

Injunctive relief in another class of cases has recently brought forth a great deal of criticism. These are the cases in which courts have enjoined efforts to organize employees who have signed individual "contracts" of employment, whereby they agree that so long as they remain in their present employ they will not be or become members of a trade union or other labor organization.[27] These decisions have been criticised on the ground that such agreements are not really contracts. The employer reserves the right to discharge the employee at any time for any reason. There is no guarantee of any particular wage. It has been maintained that such "contracts" are without consideration and therefore void.[28]

On the economic side, the argument involves certain

[26] *Ibid.*, p. 129.
[27] Hitchman Coal and Coke Company v. Mitchell, 38 Sup. Ct. 65, 245 U. S. 229, 62 L. ed. 260 (1917); United Mine Workers v. Red Jacket Consolidated Coal and Coke Company, 18 Federal (2nd) 839 (1927).
[28] Senator Borah, *Hearings on the Confirmation of Judge John J. Parker* (April 5, 1930), p. 29.

facts about the coal mining industry. The "central competitive field" of Illinois, Indiana, Ohio, and Pennsylvania, was organized. The mines in West Virginia were not. In order to hold the ground they had gained in the central competitive field, it was necessary for the United Mine Workers to prevent the undercutting by the West Virginia operators who employed lower paid non-union labor. It has been contended by spokesmen for the union that organization of the West Virginia field was the only way to prevent the undermining of their whole system of collective bargaining. The market for the coal was national, and collective bargaining, in order to be effective, must be national.[29] The trade unionists regard injunctions which prevent organization of these non-union fields as an unreasonable and unwarranted interference with the right to collective bargaining.[30]

4. *Injunctions as Now Used Increase Industrial Unrest.*—It is frequently asserted that injunctions cause industrial unrest. Ex-Senator Pepper has expressed the opinion that, because of the abuse of equity power, there is a growing bitterness of organized labor toward the courts, especially our Federal courts. He thinks the feeling on this subject, if unchecked, may easily develop into a revolutionary sentiment.[31] Another authority has expressed the opinion that "much of the bitterness manifested by workingmen in labor disputes arises from this cause. . . . As a source of friction and as a cause of com-

---

[29] Both legal and economic aspects of this class of cases are discussed fully by Francis B. Sayre, 36 *Harvard Law Review* (1923), 663.
[30] See testimony of William Greene, *Hearings on the Confirmation of Judge John J. Parker* (April 5, 1930), pp. 25, 31.
[31] 49 *A. B. A. Proceedings* (1924), 176.

plaint they [injunctions] rank among the most serious of present-day problems in industrial relations."[32]

5. *Injunctions Have Caused a Decrease in Respect for Our Courts.*—It is admitted by both sides of the controversy that respect for the courts is one of the requirements for a successful use of injunctions. In reading the criticism, one finds frequently the charge that the use and abuse of the writ in industrial disputes is causing a decrease in respect for the courts. One critic admits that injunctions, enforced by contempt proceedings, frequently accomplish the object for which they are issued but that this is accomplished "at a cost of a part of that respect for the court which . . . is the very force which makes these injunctions a success at the present time."[33]

Similar in tone is a more recent pronouncement by Newton D. Baker. He finds that the result of the courts' enlarging their equity jurisdiction in this direction has been a "loss of prestige in the courts and a widespread distrust of law and the courts. . . ."[34] Illustration of this is found in Mr. Gompers' testimony before the Lockwood Investigation Committee. Mr. Untermyer called his attention to a wide variety of oppressive practices of trade unions and asked if the courts should not be allowed to redress the wrong. Mr. Gompers answered "No" one hundred and fifty times and at one point exclaimed, "God save labor from the courts."[35]

---

[32] Commons and Andrews, *Principles of Labor Legislation*, p. 103. Also, see John A. Fitch, *Causes of Industrial Unrest*, chap. XV, "Trade Unions and the Injunction."

[33] William Draper Lewis, 46 *American Law Register* (1898), 10.

[34] 8 *A. B. A. Journal*, 734.

[35] *Ibid.*

A southern labor leader has expressed the opinion that injunctions, as he has recently seen them used, amount to persecution and result in a "deterioration of the respect for the courts of our country."[36]

Similar in tone is a statement made by Miss Jane Addams in 1908: "I should say perhaps that the one symptom among workingmen which most definitely indicates a class feeling is a growing distrust of the integrity of the courts, the belief that the present judge has been a corporation attorney, that his sympathies and experience and his whole view of life is on the corporation side. Either this distrust is growing rapidly or the statement of it is being more distinctly made every day."[37]

Summary.—The preceding paragraphs give a cursory review of some of the more important criticisms of equity practice in industrial disputes. Some of them are clear-cut, while others are nebulous. In the following chapter, the applicability of these criticisms to concrete cases may be estimated. An excerpt from a dissenting opinion of Mr. Justice Brandeis, in an injunction case of far-reaching importance, is presented below. It summarizes in a remarkable way the contents of this chapter:

It was asserted (by critics of "government by injunction") that in these proceedings an alleged danger to property, always incidental and at times insignificant, was often laid hold of to enable the penalties of the criminal law to be enforced expeditiously without that protection to the liberty of the individual which the Bill of Rights was designed to afford; that through such proceedings a single judge often usurped the functions not only of the

---

[36] Personal letter from Paul Aymon, President, Tennessee State Federation of Labor, December 13, 1929.
[37] 13 *American Journal of Sociology* (1908), 772.

jury but of the police department; that, in prescribing the conditions under which strikes were permissible and how they might be carried out, he usurped also the powers of the legislature; and that incidentally he abridged the constitutional rights of individuals to free speech, to a free press and to peaceful assembly.

It was urged that the real motive in seeking the injunction was not ordinarily to prevent property from being injured nor to protect the owner in its use, but to endow property with active, militant power which would make it dominant over men. In other words, that, under the guise of protecting property rights, the employer was seeking sovereign power. And many disinterested men, solicitous only for the public welfare, believed that the law of property was not appropriate for dealing with the forces beneath social unrest; that in this vast struggle it was unwise to throw the power of the State on one side or the other, according to principles deduced from that law; that the problem of the control and conduct of industry demanded a solution of its own; and that, pending the ascertainment of new principles to govern industry, it was wiser for the State not to interfere in industrial struggles by the issuance of an injunction.[38]

[38] Truax v. Corrigan, 42 Sup. Ct. 124, 142-143, 257 U. S. 312, 367-368, 66 L. ed. 254, 279-280 (1921). The majority opinion in this case held the Arizona statute, restricting the use of injunctions, to be unconstitutional.

CHAPTER V

THE EFFECTS OF INJUNCTIONS IN THE NEW SOUTH

As INDICATED in the introductory chapter, the material presented on the following cases is based upon a first-hand study of the actual operation and effects of injunctions in five cases. If we count each of the cases at Asheville and Danville separately, the total number is seven. Strangely enough, there are only two reported cases of this kind in the state courts of North Carolina. One unreported North Carolina case has been added. There may be other unreported cases, but a fairly thorough search has failed to reveal them. The writer has been informed that a temporary restraining order against the union of street railway employees of Asheville was issued at the time of a strike in 1913. However, the order was not served.[1]

The other two cases were added because they occurred in the same geographical area and because of their unusual significance. Each of them may be regarded as a crisis in the movement to organize the textile workers of the South. The Tennessee case especially gives an opportunity to note important differences in judicial procedure. In all cases, a diligent effort was made to get the viewpoint of both sides and to make the study as nearly objective as possible. Contemporaneous newspaper reports have been examined. It is a source of considerable gratification that, in most cases, the parties whose coöperation

---

[1] Interview with W. B. Plemmons, president of the union, Asheville, North Carolina.

was sought were extremely cordial. In practically all the interviews, there was an atmosphere of frankness and freedom which was very pleasing.

In collecting material on struggles which were as bitter as these, prejudice of one's informants is inevitable. For this reason, statements obtained are likely to be colored according to the point of view. Perhaps the most disconcerting aspect of the investigation is the flat contradiction in statements of fact which one obtains by listening to the two sides. However, this has an advantage as well as a disadvantage. It enables the student to appreciate more fully the problem of the judge who is called upon to decide these cases.

To facilitate comparison, a uniform outline is followed throughout. Beginning with the background of economic facts, we shall follow through the more detailed legal facts, the form of the injunction, the procedure, and the effects.

CASE I

McGINNIS V. RALEIGH TYPOGRAPHICAL UNION AND OTHERS

Supreme Court of North Carolina,
October 26, 1921

181 North Carolina 770; 108 Southeastern 728

In view of the long history of injunctions in industrial disputes, the date of this first case in the State of North Carolina is surprising. The newness of the whole proceeding is indicated by the following quotation from the Brief of Defendants in this case:[1]

"So far as we can learn, this court in passing upon this question is in new ground. Never before in the history of the State has an employer resorted to an injunction to fight a strike of his employees; . . ."

This case grew out of what is known as the Forty-four Hour Strike. The forty-four hour week in the printing trades was a nation-wide movement. About two years prior to this strike, the "Agreement of 1919" was reached by representatives of the International Unions in the printing trades, on the one hand, and the International Association of Employing Printers, on the other.[2] By the terms of this agreement, the hours of labor per week were to be forty-four instead of forty-eight beginning May 1, 1921.[3] The defendants contend that the plaintiffs in this case were aware of this agreement and were either members of the Association or in close sympathy with it.[4]

---
[1] Court record, p. 3.
[2] Affidavit of E. J. Wicker in the printed record, p. 28.
[3] *Ibid.*   *Ibid.*

The defendants also made affidavit that they had given sixty days' formal notice of their intention to abide by the national agreement.[5] An affidavit signed by officers of the respective firms states that they are not, and never have been, members of the International Association of Employing Printers. The affidavit further states that there are three divisions of the United Typothetae of America; namely, the General Division, the Closed Shop Division, and the Open Shop Division. Three of the firms, according to the affidavit, had belonged to the General Division but had never belonged to the Closed Shop Division, which was the only Division signing the forty-four hour agreement.[6] The plaintiffs admit notice of the proposed forty-four week in the fall of 1920 but flatly deny giving any indication that they would adopt it. On the contrary, they make affidavit that they told the union representatives that they would not consent to it.[7]

The struggle over this case was long and bitter, as well as expensive. Both sides were represented by able counsel. The diligence with which the cases were prepared is illustrated by the volume of affidavits. Affidavits filed by the plaintiffs cover sixty-nine printed pages, while those filed by the defendants cover one hundred eleven printed pages.[8]

The unions justified the strike on two grounds: first, that the nature of the work and the materials handled constituted a health hazard if the hours of labor were long, and second, that membership in the international unions,

---

[5] Ibid.
[6] Affidavit of Charles Lee Smith, J. W. Weaver, V. C. Moore, and M. E. Carroll, printed record, pp. 166-69.
[7] Ibid.
[8] See court record.

which had adopted the forty-four hour week, made their action in this case obligatory. The unions at first asked an increase in wages but later agreed to retain the existing rate per hour with time and a half for all time over forty-four hours per week.

The employing printers, on the other hand, stated that it was simply impossible for them to stay in business under the proposed new agreement.[9] They were in competition with the open shops in other cities and, since much of their business came through competitive bids, they would have to keep costs down. Otherwise, they contended, they could get no business.

The significant charges made in the bill of complaint are as follows:

1. Conspiracy to drive the non-union employees out of employment.

2. Making war on the printing houses and their employees.

3. Engaging in "a systematic course of espionage, annoyance, intimidation, threats, abuse, and insults, which are intended to make, are calculated to make, and are making, the lives of these complainants and all other employees of the several printing houses above mentioned miserable, intolerable, and unendurable. . . ."

4. Carrying out a conspiracy by means of:

(a) Gathering in large numbers near the places of business where complainants are employed and indulging in threatening gestures, insulting jeers and hisses, etc.

---

[9] Interview with Charles Lee Smith, president of Edwards and Broughton Printing Company, Raleigh, North Carolina.

(b) Shadowing or pursuing the complainants wherever they go; sometimes using abusive language.

(c) Surrounding complainants and humiliating them.

(d) Surrounding complainants and calling them "rats," "scabs," "runts," "bowery bums," and other abusive epithets.

(e) Making threats by saying: "We'll get them yet." "They had better not let us catch them walking home." "We will break his damn neck," etc.

(f) Calling young women who are complainants in this case "Kitty-cat," etc.

The printing companies, which were joint complainants with the non-union employees in this case, charged the defendant strikers with

1. Gathering in large numbers near their places of business.

2. Threatening to kill their officers and relatives and employees.

3. Taunting, hissing, and jeering at employees.

4. Bribing employees to break their contracts of employment.

5. Driving more than one hundred employees away from their jobs by threats, "hell-hackling," etc.[10]

The striking printers who were defendants in this case denied practically all of the charges listed above. They contended, through their attorneys, that they had engaged in lawful acts only. In support of this contention, they filed ninety-four affidavits. Bolstered up as they were by the affidavits of Josephus Daniels, of the Chief of Police

[10] Appendix II.

of the City of Raleigh, and others, they evidently had considerable weight with the Court.

As to the merits of the strike, *per se*, we shall not be concerned. Strikes for higher wages and fewer hours of labor have usually been upheld as lawful *in purpose*. The real controversy here is over *the means used* to accomplish the purpose.

The acts admitted by the union men interviewed are shadowing, peaceful picketing, persuasion, and securing jobs for strike-breakers in other cities. They contended that, in so far as threats and intimidation were used, they were the unauthorized acts of private persons and in no way connected with the strike itself.

Form of the Injunction.—The form of the temporary restraining order in this case may be noted. An exact copy is given in the Appendix.[11]

Careful examination will show that it is unusually well prepared. Nothing is said about "conspiracy" or "conspiring" or other meaningless expressions. The things prohibited are remarkably specific; i.e.,

1. Mass picketing in front of the establishments.
2. Intimidation of employees.
3. Shadowing, or dogging the steps of non-union employees.
4. Abusive epithets such as rats, scabs, runts, and bowery bums.
5. Endeavoring to induce non-union employees to break contracts of employment after they have received notice that the employees do not desire to break them.

A few of the familiar "catch-all" phrases do occur

[11] See Appendix III.

such as: "Calling the complaining employees ... *any other names*"; ". . . engaging in any conduct of any kind calculated to disturb, annoy, etc."

The use of such expressions makes strict enforcement difficult and places the defendant at a great disadvantage in case of contempt proceedings. However, the order is unusually clear in its terms and on most points a defendant could reasonably be expected to know whether he was violating it or not.

Procedure.—The points of procedure which are significant in this class of cases are as follows:

1. Was the action *ex parte;* i.e., without notice or hearing for the defendants?
2. What was the nature of the evidence submitted in the application for the injunction?
3. How soon, after the issuance of the temporary restraining order, was there a hearing?
4. How soon was there a final determination of the rights of the parties?
5. Were there special points in the pleading of the case which help to interpret the results?

The procedure in this case may well be described. Non-union employees were joined as plaintiffs with the employing printers. Counsel for the plaintiffs emphasized this fact by stating that in this case "labor at work begs protection from labor which is idle." The temporary restraining order was issued on affidavits and the bill of complaint filed by the plaintiff. There was no notice to the other side until the restraining order was served by the sheriff. The temporary restraining order was filed

August 19 and the date set for hearing was September 3.[12] The hearing was before a judge other than the one who had signed the original order.

At the preliminary hearing, the defendants had retained two law firms. One demurred to the pleading while the other answered the bill of complaint.[13] The court over-ruled the demurrer and, after hearing the evidence and argument, continued the injunction in practically the same form. Two differences may be noted. The second order restrains not only the defendants but also "their agents, associates, and abettors."[14] In section three of the original restraining order the phrase "any other names" is changed to "any other insulting names."[15] From this ruling, the defendants excepted and appealed. There were no contempt proceedings. Sixty-eight days elapsed between the issuance of the temporary restraining order and the final determination of the case.

The case was thoroughly argued before the Supreme Court of the state. A brief excerpt from the brief of counsel for defendants affords an interesting commentary on the whole proceeding: "They complain of irreparable injury without showing wherein they have not a remedy for every wrong alleged. The courts of the state have been open, and while plaintiffs complain of threats, no peace warrants have been issued; they allege assaults and no indictments have been asked. They allege disorderly conduct, and yet the police department of the city has never been called upon to suppress it."

[12] See Restraining Order, Appendix III.
[13] Interview with S. W. Eason, attorney for defendants.
[14] See Judgment, Appendix IV.
[15] Compare Judgment with Restraining Order, in Appendices.

The chief of police made affidavit to the effect that the conduct of the defendants had been peaceful and orderly at all times.[16]

The opinion of the Supreme Court, filed October 26, 1921, was characterized by ex-Governor Bickett[17] as "the shortest decision on the biggest question ever presented in the Supreme Court of North Carolina."[18] The opinion is indeed a model of brevity. It is a *Per Curiam* opinion of exactly seventy-four words:

"*Per Curiam.* Some serious and weighty questions of law are presented by the demurrer and the several motions filed in the cause; but we deem it unnecessary to pass upon them now; as we are convinced from a perusal of the record, that the evidence adduced and offered on the hearing was not sufficient to warrant a continuance of the injunction. It will therefore be dissolved without prejudice to the rights of any of the parties."

Effects of the Injunction.—Probably the most significant aspect of injunctions growing out of industrial disputes is their economic and social effect. In this and the following cases, we shall discuss effects under the following heads:

1. Effect on the outcome of the strike or other controversy.
2. Effect on the conduct of those enjoined.
3. Effect on the social attitudes of those enjoined.

In obtaining information as to the effects of this injunction, the writer examined the complete court record,

---

[16] Taken from the printed record of the case.
[17] Attorney for the Complainant.
[18] Interview with L. F. Alford.

including briefs of counsel and the file of affidavits, read newspaper reports, visited the City of Raleigh, where the strike had occurred, and interviewed a number of men who were familiar with the situation. Included in the list were the most important employers involved, the attorneys on both sides of the controversy, officers and members of the unions involved, and neutral parties.

1. *Effect on the Outcome of the Strike.*—The conflict in evidence which one finds in court is found here also. The Secretary of the Employing Printers Association (at that time) expressed the opinion that "if we hadn't had that injunction, we would all have had to go back to the union."[19] On the other hand, one of the attorneys for the defendants is convinced that it "had no effect on the outcome of the strike."[20] Certain objective facts help to clear the atmosphere. Some of the firms involved in the strike had already made an agreement with the unions before the injunction was issued. One of the larger firms remained non-union for a few years until the company was reorganized and the new management signed an agreement with the unions. Other firms have gone out of business. At the present time, all the commercial printing establishments originally involved, except one, are union shops.[21] Practically all the union men interviewed were of the opinion that an agreement with this firm could not have been reached even if there had been no injunction. Both sides were so determined to fight to a finish that agreement was impossible. The statement of the pres-

---

[19] Interview with R. J. Wilson. [20] Interview with S. W. Eason.
[21] Interview with L. E. Nichols, Assistant Commissioner of Labor and Printing, State of North Carolina (1921), Appendix VIII.

ident of the firm agrees with that of union men on this point. The shop superintendent of the *News and Observer* thought this injunction "more or less of a farce," and referred to the brevity of the Supreme Court decision.[22]

Summarizing this section, we may safely say the injunction did not break the strike. It would have been impossible to sign a trade agreement with the only firm which is now non-union even if there had been no injunction. In explaining the failure of the strike in this shop, the decline in prices, with the attendant business depression which characterized the year 1921, appears to be the most important factor.

2. *Effect on the Conduct of Those Enjoined.*—As we have already noted, the conduct of the defendants prior to the injunction is a matter of dispute. The Supreme Court did not think the acts charged were serious enough to constitute a cause of action. It is admitted, however, that there had been congregating in the vicinity of the struck establishments. Information from all sources indicates that there was less of this after the injunction than before. The president of the largest firm involved stated that the injunction "accomplished its principal purpose" in this respect.[23] Members of the union thought "it stopped congregating around the shops" or that "it broke up the crowd in front of Edwards and Broughton's."[24] One of the attorneys for the plaintiffs thought it "reduced the extent of picketing."[25]

The injunction seems to have had some effect on the

[22] Interview with L. F. Alford.
[23] Interview with Charles Lee Smith.
[24] See Summary of Interviews with Defendants, Appendix IX.
[25] Interview with Murray Allen.

use of epithets also. One of the plaintiffs thought it "was less marked afterward."[26] Another informant thought "it stopped the open and public use of epithets."[27] It appears that, outside the immediate vicinity of the shops involved, the use of epithets continued. Shadowing of non-union employees continued, but it was carried on more cautiously.

The most effective device of the strikers was meeting new employees at the railway station and sending them back. The union offered to pay their return fare if they would go. Those who were brought in without notice of the existence of a strike were frequently glad to have their return fare paid.[28] All the evidence indicates that the injunction had little effect on this system. New employees were sent out of town as rapidly as before. One of the plaintiffs stated that he spent a great deal of money bringing in employees who were sent back almost as soon as they arrived. Members of the union did not think it hindered them in keeping the "rats" run out of town.[29] It is noteworthy that the activities which appear to have been restricted by the injunction were those carried on in the open in the immediate vicinity of the shops involved. Police officers were able to enforce the injunction more strictly against these acts than against those which were less public.

3. *Effect on the Social Attitudes of Those Enjoined.* —The social effects of injunctions are definite in some respects but elusive and indefinite in others. Here we shall be concerned chiefly with *respect for law*, especially for courts, and *industrial strife*. The interviews contain

[26] Interview with Charles Lee Smith.
[27] See Summary of Interviews with Defendants, Appendix IX.
[28] *Ibid.* [29] *Ibid.*

many expressions which suggest the effect of the injunction on respect for the courts. In some cases the order of the court was not taken seriously. A few said they looked upon it as "a comic situation; a laughable matter."[30] In most cases, however, the idea of unfairness is emphasized. A few illustrations will bring this out more clearly:

"It kept us from doing things we had a right to do. ... We couldn't show a man our point of view."

"It doesn't give us a fair show. ... Without the injunction, management would be accessible and we could arbitrate."

"It went against the grain with me. I hadn't done a thing. ... If I had my way, there would never be another labor injunction issued. They are depriving a man of his constitutional rights without due process of law. *There is no jury trial. You are subject to the whim of a judge.*"

The effect on *industrial strife* is difficult to estimate in this case. There was much bitter criticism of the conduct of the management by members of the union and vice versa. The affidavits indicate that each side put forth a great effort to hunt up causes of offense. There was certainly a bitter feeling between the members of the printing trades unions and the management of the shop which is still non-union. The relative importance of the injunction and the other factors in producing this result cannot be determined.

Summary of Effects.—Summarizing the effects of the injunction in this case, the following conclusions seem to be justified: The injunction did not break the strike. It had little or no effect on the outcome of the strike. The

[30] *Ibid.*

injunction reduced the extent of picketing or congregating in the immediate vicinity of the plants. It made the defendants more cautious in the matter of shadowing. Otherwise, it had little effect on the conduct of those enjoined. It tended to decrease respect for courts. There is some evidence to show that it increased industrial strife.

CASE II

CITIZEN COMPANY V. ASHEVILLE TYPOGRAPHICAL UNION, ET AL.*

SUPREME COURT OF NORTH CAROLINA,
JANUARY 22, 1924

187 North Carolina 42, 121 Southeastern 31

This case is of unusual interest and significance in a study of the labor law of the State of North Carolina. It is the first injunction, growing out of an industrial dispute, to be sustained by the Supreme Court of the state. This case and that of the *Times Company v. Asheville Typographical Union* (187 N. C. 157), which grew out of the same controversy, are the only labor injunctions which have been sustained by the appellate court of the state up to the present time. The union involved represents one of the more highly skilled and better educated crafts in the labor movement.

The strike occurred on October 16, 1923. The occasion for the strike was a controversy over the renewal of the trade agreement which expired at that time.[1] The union asked for an increase in wages which the management refused in both cases. The union then asked that the matter be submitted to arbitration. Mr. Charles A. Webb, co-owner and manager of the *Citizen*, asked the union representatives:

---

* While there were technically two cases, the brief opinion of the Court in the case of the Times Company v. Asheville Typographical Union, 187 N. C. 157, 121 S. E. 37 (1924) indicates that the opinion in the case discussed here answers for both.

[1] Interview with Charles A. Webb, Appendix XIII.

"Do you mean arbitration up and down both?"

To this the union replied that there was really only one question to be arbitrated: "Shall wages be increased or remain the same?"

The management of each of the papers regarded this an unfair basis and refused to arbitrate.[2] The local union then applied to the International Typographical Union for strike sanction. Before granting strike sanction, the International Typographical Union sent a representative to investigate and attempt a settlement. After negotiations had failed, strike sanction was granted. The strike was called suddenly[3] and the publishers called upon Mr. Flagg of the Open Shop Division of the American Newspaper Publishers Association for a crew of temporary employees. In the meantime, linotype work was sent out to non-union shops in the vicinity. When the temporary crews arrived they took charge and thus gave each of the publishers a skeleton force. Printers from elsewhere were recruited as rapidly as possible. Members of the union picketed the premises of both establishments. The conduct of the pickets is in dispute. The plaintiffs contended and filed many affidavits to show that the picketing amounted to coercion and intimidation.[4] The union members interviewed and their attorneys contended that they had engaged in *peaceful* picketing only.[5]

---

[2] *Ibid.*

[3] Mr. Webb stated in his interview that the organizer had promised forty-eight hours notice. Instead, he gave fifteen minutes notice. On the other hand, union members claimed that the publishers had forfeited their right to notice by sending for printers from the open shop division before the strike had been called.

[4] Interview with Charles A. Webb, Appendix XIII.

[5] See Summary of Interviews with Defendants, Appendix XV.

The most important items in the complaint are reproduced in the Supreme Court opinion.[6] In summary form they are as follows:

(*a*) Organized picketing accompanied by threats, intimidation and violence.

(*b*) Attempts to cause employees to breach contracts and to compel the plaintiff to discharge employees.

(*c*) A systematic course of espionage, annoyance, intimidation, threats, abuse and insults.

(*d*) Gathering in large numbers near the place of business of the plaintiff and indulging in "threatening gestures, insulting jeers, and hisses"; using abusive, insulting, vile, and profane language when addressing the plaintiff's employees.

(*e*) Acts of violence in throwing bricks and other missiles into, upon, and against the building in which the plaintiff carries on its business.

(*f*) Threatening to do great bodily harm and to kill employees if they continued their present employment.

(*g*) Constant shadowing and pursuing employees.

. . . .

(*j*) Calling employees insulting names such as rats, scabs, runts, bowery bums, etc.

. . . .

(*m*) Threatening employees by saying, "We will get you yet." "We will mop up with you."

Perhaps the most serious charge against the strikers was an alleged plot to pour a large quantity of liquid ammonia down the vent pipe in the *Citizen* building.[7]

[6] Citizen Company v. Asheville Typographical Union, 187 N. C. 42, pp. 47-49, 121 S. E. 31, pp. 34-35 (1924).
[7] Interview with D. Hiden Ramsey, manager of the Asheville *Times*.

An affidavit to show that this was contemplated was introduced as evidence. A large can of ammonia was discovered in an adjacent building.

Certain acts are freely admitted by the union men. They admit endeavoring to persuade subscribers and advertisers to stop their subscriptions and their advertising.

"The committee of printers on this assignment endeavored to turn what advertising they could away from the struck papers to the so-called labor paper that was being printed weekly. As a further 'persuader,' union men of the city were urged to stay away from stores that patronized the struck papers. That seemed fair to me—the preachers caution their flock to stay away from blind tigers, etc."[8]

The union committee also endeavored to get each advertiser to insert this line in his advertisement: "We favor arbitration." One of them did but the papers refused to publish it.[9]

Some of the defendants admitted calling the non-union printers "scabs" and "rats" but they did not regard this as a basis for an injunction. Some of them were quite frank on this point. "Yes, we called them 'rats' but that's what they were. If you work in a printing shop when there's a strike on, that's what you are—a rat printer."[10]

Evidence from both sides indicates that the union members met new employees at the railway stations and succeeded in getting many of them to go elsewhere. They endeavored to induce or persuade them to join the union

---
[8] Personal letter from R. S. Meroney, Secretary of Asheville Typographical Union, January 4, 1930.
[9] Summary of Interviews with Defendants, Appendix XV.
[10] *Ibid.*

and take jobs in union shops which the International Typographical Union was finding for them in other cities.

As to the more serious charges, the union men interviewed entered a vigorous denial. Many charges of false affidavits were made. One of the members characterized the charge of "violence, threats of violence," etc., as a "lot of foolishness." A few verbatim quotations will bring this point out more clearly:

"I know the ammonia incident did not occur. The ammonia was planted there by the papers. They had to make out that there was a lot of disorder to get an injunction."[11]

"Part of an affidavit signed by ——— I know to be false. At certain times he swore I was around the ——— building I could easily prove I was in bed at home. One affidavit swore that a boy who was in Fruitland Institute studying for the ministry was picketing. He wasn't even in town."[12]

The charges of false affidavits were made just as vigorously by the other side. The manager of one of the papers involved said the union men "went around to the court and swore to a lot of lies."[13]

Form of the Injunction.—The restraining order in this case is very brief. It contains exactly thirty-eight lines of typewriting. While certain "catch-all" phrases such as "in any way or manner," and "doing any acts or things whatsoever," are used, in most cases they are modified by terms which restrict their content considerably. The defendants are enjoined from "in any way or manner

[11] *Ibid.*
[12] *Ibid.*
[13] Personal interview.

whatsoever, interfering with the plaintiff's business or employees by threats, personal injury, intimidation, suggestion of danger or threats of violence."[14]

Aside from threats, intimidation, and violence the acts enjoined are:

(a) Picketing or maintaining at or near the premises of the plaintiff or on the streets leading to the premises of the plaintiff, any picket or pickets, and from passing through, over and upon the private alley in the rear of the plaintiff's place of business.

(b) Doing any acts or things whatsoever in furtherance of any conspiracy or combination among themselves to interfere with the business of the plaintiff.

(c) Entering the grounds or premises of the plaintiff without permission.

(d) Injuring or destroying the property of the plaintiff.[15]

The parties enjoined are the local union, the named individuals and *all other persons.*[16]

The clauses relating to violence or threats of violence require little comment. There is no justification for such acts even in industrial warfare. Critics of the injunctive system can only argue that the criminal law is a more appropriate remedy, in such cases. The order restrains picketing without any qualification. This was probably intentional as part of the interview with the plaintiff in this case suggests: "One of the biggest farces in the whole business is what they call 'peaceful picketing.' There is no such thing as peaceful picketing. Any kind of picketing

---

[14] Restraining Order, Appendix XII.
[15] *Ibid.*   [16] Italics mine.

is a form of intimidation and interference with another man's business."[17]

A different view was expressed in the interview with one of the attorneys for the defendants: "Picketing has a legitimate object. The object of peaceful picketing is to find out who those still working are and advise them not to go back."[18]

The Supreme Court in 1921 had dissolved the injunction in the case of *McGinnis v. Raleigh Typographical Union*. In that case, the defendants admitted they had engaged in picketing but they contended that it was peaceful.[19]

The clause directed against acts in furtherance of a combination or conspiracy raises an important legal question which is discussed in greater detail elsewhere. It is sufficient to note here that the law of conspiracy is so vague and indefinite that it would be impossible for a person enjoined to know whether he was violating it or not.

It will be noted that the order is directed against "all other persons" as well as the named defendants. Critics have bitterly denounced this practice. The plaintiffs, on the other hand, contend that this is a necessary precaution for making the injunction effective. Otherwise, sympathizers might do the things which the named defendants are forbidden to do.

Procedure.—The procedure in this case, as in others, is of great significance. The temporary restraining order was issued on affidavits only. There was no hearing of

---
[17] Interview with Charles A. Webb.
[18] Interview with Gallatin Roberts.
[19] See McGinnis v. Raleigh Typographical Union, 182 N. C. 770, 108 S. E. 728 (1921).

the defendants. The local Typographical Union and all officers and members were named. The sheriff was ordered to serve each of the defendants with a copy of the order. This procedure is superior to the method of giving notice in the Tennessee case, which we shall examine later. *Actual* notice is certain. Each of the defendants was ordered to appear and show cause why the injunction should not be continued. The date set for this hearing was eighteen days after the issuance of the temporary restraining order.[20] Owing to the illness of the judge, the hearing was postponed one week and the temporary order was continued until that time.[21] The defendants objected to this procedure on the ground that it gave the publishers more time to break the strike while the defendants were throttled by the injunction.

At the preliminary hearing, the defendants demurred and asked that the restraining order be dissolved on the ground that the complaint did not set forth facts sufficient to constitute a cause of action.[22] The court granted this petition.

Attorneys for the plaintiff then excepted to the order of the court and prayed an appeal to the Supreme Court of North Carolina.[23] Thereupon the court decided that, in view of all the facts of the case, the injunction should be continued until the case was decided by the Supreme Court. The plaintiff was, of course, required to give sufficient bond.

The defendants were unusually fortunate in securing an early date for review of the case by the Supreme Court.

[20] See Restraining Order, Appendix X
[21] Court record.
[22] Judgment, Appendix XVI.
[23] *Ibid.*

The preliminary hearing was held November 24, 1923, and the opinion of the Supreme Court was filed January 22, 1924. Comparing this with Case IV below, a Tennessee case, in which a period of nearly two years was required for the appeal, the superiority of the procedure in this case is obvious.

Following established precedents, the Supreme Court held that the Typographical Union, which was an unincorporated Association, had not properly been made a party to the action.[24] As to the individuals, however, the court held that the facts set forth in the complaint did entitle the plaintiff to a continuance of the restraining order in modified form.

Since the defendants had demurred to the complaint, thereby admitting the facts set forth in the complaint to be true, the court did not pass on any factual controversy. This case was distinguished from the preceding case, *McGinnis v. Typographical Union*, on the grounds that in the McGinnis case nothing unlawful had been admitted. Upon reading that record, the court had been convinced that the evidence was not sufficient to warrant a continuance of the injunction.[25] In this case much that was unlawful—trespass, conspiracy, and assault—was admitted by the demurrer.

The order was modified to allow peaceful picketing involving only observation, watching, and persuasion.[26] The concurring opinion of Chief Justice Clark would re-

---

[24] Tucker v. Eatough, 186 N. C. 505; 120 S. E. 57 (1923) construing N. C. Consolidated Statutes (1919) sec. 457.
[25] Citizen Company v. Asheville Typographical Union, 187 N. C. 42, 50-51, 121 S. E. 31, 35-36 (1924).
[26] *Ibid.*

strict the injunction to "acts of violence or whatever may be equivalent thereto. . . ."[27] As modified, the order was continued to the hearing on the merits.

The final hearing has not been held. At each term of the court the case is placed at the foot of the docket. Consequently, the injunction is still in effect.

Effects of the Injunction.—In a case involving so many complex factors, it is by no means easy to set out clearly the effects of one factor alone. But the first-hand information, on which this section is based, is believed to give definite indications of the effects which are not already known.

1. *Effect on the Outcome of the Strike.*—Of most interest to students of the trade union movement is the effect on the outcome of the strike. In answer to the question "Did the injunction break the strike?" one of the publishers answered as follows:

"It broke the strike to this extent: it prevented terrorism. Then it was very easy for us to go ahead with our business. It forced them back upon the arguments of peace and reason and the thing failed."[28]

The sharp conflict of opinion is indicated by comparing the above statement with the statement made by one of the attorneys for the defendants: "I doubt if the injunction affected the outcome of the strike one way or the other."[29]

With a single exception, the defendants interviewed expressed the opinion that the injunction did not break the strike. A few of those who thought it did not, quali-

---

[27] *Ibid.*, 53.
[28] Interview with D. Hiden Ramsey.   [29] Interview with George Pennell.

fied their statements by saying, "It helped to break it," or "It slowed it up."[30]

The following comment indicates clearly that the injunction did not make the union entirely helpless:

"Injunctions make a lot of difference some places but they didn't here. After the injunction we just walked up to their employees, patted them on the back and said, 'Come on, join the union.' We got them to join, one after another. We got them jobs in other places. Today some of our best members are those who were brought in as scabs."[31]

In this connection it should be noted that "Flagg's Squad," from the Open Shop Division of the American Newspaper Publishers Association, came in and took charge of the shops. So long as the police gave them protection, they could get the papers out. This gave time to find a working force of non-union employees. There still remains the question as to how vigorous the police would have been in protecting the new employees in the absence of an injunction. The writer heard no complaint against the police department in this respect. It is a fact that both of the shops are still non-union so far as the Typographical Union is concerned. The *Citizen* still employs union pressmen and stereotypers.

Did the injunction have any effect on the outcome of the strike? In answering this question, an element enters

---

[30] Summary of Interviews with Defendants, Appendix XV.

[31] Appendix XV. This informant also explained that several of the printers brought in by the Open Shop Division were not professional strike breakers. They had been working on country papers where there was no union. These men did not know there was a strike on. "When they got here and found there was, they didn't like it."

here which is not significant in the other four cases. This element is the boycott. While the unions engaged in a boycott in the case of *McGinnis v. Raleigh Typographical Union* (see *supra*), it was not specified in the bill of complaint and does not appear to have been a factor of any importance in the proceedings. The union in the Asheville case was carrying on a campaign to induce subscribers and advertisers to stop their patronage. The effect is indicated by the following quotation:

"It [the injunction] broke up our campaign with the advertisers and subscribers. We were making a lot of headway before. When the injunction came out, the merchants took down the 'We believe in arbitration' signs."[32]

Other expressions on the point are in substantial agreement with this. It is not too much to say that the injunction weakened considerably the force of the boycott. It is significant in this connection that many of the men on strike became impatient and found themselves jobs in other cities. It has been suggested that this fact was partially responsible for the failure of the strike. One member thought the injunction "caused men to leave who would have stayed and helped."

The following conclusions seem to be justified by the evidence at hand: The injunction did not break the strike. It did frighten some of the members and most of the merchants who were in sympathy with the union. It probably caused some members of the union to seek work elsewhere sooner than they would have otherwise. The campaign to divert advertising and subscriptions from the struck

[32] *Ibid.*

papers would probably have been more successful if there had been no injunction. It certainly did not render the union entirely helpless as evidenced by the fact that it "pulled the whole crew out on Saturday afternoon before Thanksgiving" when the strike was two years old. "The papers had to send for Flagg the second time."[33]

2. *Effect on the Conduct of Those Enjoined.*—The effect of the injunction on the *conduct* of those enjoined is of vital interest to everyone. Did the injunction change the conduct of the strikers for the better?

In this case, the publishers are apparently certain that the injunction had the desired effect.

"It absolutely stopped the trouble. . . . Before that, they were engaged in all sorts of criminal acts. . . . It stopped the intimidation and picketing. After it was issued, our employees could go out at two o'clock A.M. and not be bothered."[34]

The interview with the other publisher is similar in tone:

Q. "Did the injunction give you genuine relief?"

A. "Yes. The law told them what they could do and what they couldn't do. Without the injunction, they could have wrecked our business."[35]

Most of the union men interviewed were of the opinion that the injunction restricted picketing. Some testified that they stopped picketing altogether. Others were simply more careful. Two of them indicated that they considered it a joke. However, this attitude seems to be exceptional.

[33] *Ibid.* [34] Interview with Charles A. Webb, Appendix XIII.
[35] Interview with D. Hiden Ramsey.

A number of affidavits, signed by employees who had taken the places of those on strike, contain the charge that before the injunction they had been threatened with violence, insulted, hissed at and called abusive epithets such as "scab," "rat," etc. Several of them close with this sentence: "Since the injunction was served we have not been molested or bothered in any way."

While it is easy to place too much confidence in such affidavits, it is a fact that they were signed. One of the more discriminating members expressed the opinion that the injunction did not affect the "rough-necks" but it did affect "those that thought they were sort of socially prominent, and such as were of a religious nature."[36]

It is quite evident from this discussion that the injunction restricted picketing. Just how unpeaceful the picketing was before the injunction is a matter of dispute. If we accept the view that picketing by any considerable number amounts to intimidation, the injunction did help to protect the property and the employees of the plaintiff.

3. *Effect on the Social Attitude of Those Enjoined.*—Did the injunction tend to increase respect for law, especially for courts? All of the union men interviewed regarded the use of the injunction as unfair. It is, of course, natural for a disappointed litigant to condemn the court. However, the reasons given for regarding it as unfair should be stated:

"I felt that it was unfair. I thought both sides should have a hearing."[37]

[36] Personal letter from R. S. Meroney.
[37] Summary of Interviews with Defendants, Appendix XV.

Several objected to the one-sided application of the injunction:

"It seems to me that working men should have as much right as the other side. Strike breakers tried to pick trouble with us. They violated the injunction they had against us."[38]

"The injunction does not apply to strike breakers. By having certain employees tantalize the pickets, they get them to violate the injunction."[39]

Several insisted that the injunction prohibited things which they had a lawful right to do. They laid special stress on peaceful persuasion:[40]

"We couldn't talk to the men who came in to take our jobs. It stepped on free speech."

"It kept us from talking to those other fellows. We had the same right to ask them to join the union that a preacher has to ask them to join the church."

"We couldn't approach a man and ask him not to go to work."

"We couldn't talk to any of the fellows to get them to join the union."

The absence of jury trial came in for strongest condemnation.[41] Denial of jury trial is "the reason union men are so afraid of injunctions. The power to punish for contempt lies with one man."

"It's a judge's personal law. It's harder to get justice. There is no jury trial."

[38] *Ibid.*
[39] Interview with W. B. Plemmons, vice-president of the State Federation of Labor.
[40] Summary of Interviews, Appendix XV.
[41] *Ibid.*

"It [jury trial] cuts down political influence. If you have jury trial, they can't try you before they take you up there."

As to the effect of the injunction on industrial strife we have only occasional clues. A few of the expressions are quite clear:[42]

"It made the union men more bitter."

"All it did was to antagonize the men and make them feel hard toward the management because of the false affidavits."

Statements from both sides indicate that before the strike, the relations between the union employees and the management had been exceptionally pleasant in both establishments. A careful review of the case certainly gives the impression that the injunction increased industrial strife.[43] However, it is difficult to distinguish between the effect of the injunction and the strike itself.

Summary of the Case.—The form of injunction is not unusual although some of the prohibitions are stated in very general terms. It enjoins "all other persons," as well as the named defendants. The temporary restraining order went farther in its prohibitions than allowed by the State Supreme Court. The rule that an unincorporated union could not be made a party defendant in an action as such or by an agent is confirmed. The procedure was typical for this class of cases. The temporary restraining order was granted on evidence which was wholly *ex parte*. Twenty-five days expired between the issuance of the temporary restraining order and the hearing. While

---
[42] *Ibid.*
[43] See Summary of Interviews, Appendix XV.

this is not exceptionally long, it might be regarded as enough time to break a strike. The decision of the State Supreme Court was filed eighty-three days after the issuance of the temporary restraining order. The Supreme Court ruled that the order should be continued with certain modifications. The right to peaceful picketing was specifically recognized. The injunction is still technically in effect. There were no contempt proceedings.

CASE III

MARION MANUFACTURING COMPANY V. UNITED TEXTILE WORKERS, AND OTHERS

SUPERIOR COURT, MCDOWELL COUNTY, NORTH CAROLINA, JULY 24, 1929

One of the simplest and clearest illustrations of the use and effects of injunctions in industrial disputes is found in the case of The Marion Manufacturing Company against Local Union Number 1659 of the United Textile Workers of America and one hundred twenty-seven named individuals. The plaintiff in this case is a corporation engaged in the manufacture of plain cotton cloth in the village of East Marion, which is on the outskirts of Marion, the county seat of McDowell County, North Carolina. The region is semi-mountainous and the laboring people are of the mountaineer type. Many of them have only recently come in from the hills. The standard of living has been low and the amount of formal education slight in most cases. The employees live in the compact mill village. Most of the houses are owned by the employer but some are owned either by the workers themselves or by private landlords. Most of the people are very religious and had previously been regarded as law-abiding citizens. Many of those who participated in the strike were active members in the local churches. In fact, the blow which seemed to hurt some of them worst was expulsion from the church on account of membership in the union and participation in the strike. As a means of building morale, the singing of religious songs, such as "Onward, Christian Soldiers," was found to be very effective.

The president of the company is a resident of Baltimore, Maryland, but spends a part of each week in the mill village. It is reported that the company is financed by Baltimore capital. The company involved had net assets of $1,141,495.21, as shown by the financial statement of December 31, 1928.[1] The number of employees on the payroll at the time the strike occurred was approximately six hundred fifty.[2]

Adjacent to the property of this company is the larger plant of the Clinchfield Manufacturing Company, which was involved in the same strike but not in the injunction proceedings. With one other cotton mill of considerable size, Marion may be called a mill town. The prosperity of the community is certainly dependent upon the cotton manufacturing industry. Soil and topography make agriculture relatively unprofitable. In many cases, two or more members of the same family work in the factory.

The strike, which began July 11, 1929, was indeed spectacular. The response to the strike call was so nearly unanimous that the management closed the plant and did not reopen until a settlement was agreed upon two months later. A discussion of the causes of the strike leads us into a field of sharp controversy. According to the management, the strike was due to the inflammatory speeches and activities of outside agitators who came in to stir up trou-

[1] *Information Service*, Federal Council of Churches, Vol. VIII, No. 47 (December 28, 1929), p. 9.
[2] Bill of Complaint, Appendix XVII.

ble. According to the strikers, it was due to low wages, long hours, the "stretch-out," and the discharge of union members. The following appear to be the facts: Wages were approximately fourteen dollars per week on the average.[3] Hours of labor were sixty per week. The management had endeavored to introduce an efficiency system which is known among the southern textile workers as the "stretch-out." In some cases, the number of looms to be tended by one person was doubled without any increase in pay.[4] The workers displaced by this change were given jobs at unskilled labor with a considerable reduction in wages.[5] Some employees were discharged when it was discovered that they belonged to the union.[6] It is also true that Mr. Alfred Hoffmann, an organizer for the United Textile Workers, was on the ground. He proved to be an enthusiastic worker. Mr. Tom Tippet and other unionists from the outside also helped with the work of organization. The struggle at Marion may be regarded as a part of the "Organize the South" movement. The question of wages and hours alone would probably not have been significant. To be exact, it appears that the "stretch-out" caused discontent; the organizer capitalized this; and the efforts of the company to break up the union precipitated the strike.

In its early stages, the strike was remarkably successful from the standpoint of the strikers. It has been estimated that 90 per cent of the employees on the payroll

---

[3] *Information Service*, Federal Council of Churches, Vol. VIII, No. 47 (December 28, 1929), p. 2.
[4] *Ibid.*, p. 3.
[5] Personal interviews.
[6] *Ibid.*

joined the union.[7] The strike had been in effect for about a week before the injunction was applied for.

The circumstances which led up to the application for the injunction appear to have been as follows: The company had several carloads of coal and cotton to unload and demurrage was piling up on them. Officials of the company were anxious to unload these cars in order to avoid the demurrage charges. Acting on the advice of counsel, President Baldwin of the Marion Manufacturing Company took a sufficient number of men to unload the cars and also the sheriff and some of his deputies to the mill gate.[8] The union pickets allowed the president of the company and officers of the law to enter but kept the others out, charging that they were strike-breakers.[9] The president explained that he merely intended to unload the cars and was not trying to reopen the mill. Apparently, this did not satisfy the pickets. There was a struggle, between the pickets and the men endeavoring to enter, and President Baldwin was struck upon the head and knocked down. The company claims that he was struck intentionally by one of the union pickets. The union members, on the other hand, claim that he was struck accidentally by the locking-pin on the gate. For our present purpose, the difference between these accounts is perhaps immaterial. Mr. Baldwin was struck on the head at this time. Whether it was intentional or accidental the reader may decide. Both sides agree that this incident was the immediate occasion for seeking the injunction.

[7] Interview with Elmer Cope, Emergency Committee for Strikers' Relief.
[8] Interview with G. F. Washburn, attorney for complainant.
[9] Letter from Alfred Hoffmann, organizer for United Textile Workers.

Form of the Injunction.—The form of the injunction is of considerable interest.[10] It covers slightly more than a page of double-spaced typewriting. All the defendants were named and personal service on each was ordered. Each and all of the defendants were restrained:

1. From entering upon or trespassing upon the plaintiff's mill property consisting of its cotton mill, offices, store, and grounds.

2. From interfering with, molesting, intimidating, or assaulting any of the plaintiff's employees.

3. From holding or participating in any unlawful assemblies on the property of the plaintiff, including the mill village, and from obstructing the gates to the mill.

Defendants Alfred Hoffmann and Tom Pettit (probably Tippet), their associates, agents and employees, are restrained from inciting or persuading the company's employees to maintain an espionage or picketing in or on any portion of the plaintiff's property and especially from holding unlawful assemblies on the plaintiff's property. Each of the defendants is required to appear before the court at a specified time and place to show cause why the order should not be continued until the final hearing.

A few explanations should be given at this point. The United States post office is housed in the company store. All the defendants are restrained from entering upon this property. The terms of the injunction prohibit the defendants from going after their mail.

The term "unlawful assembly" is not defined or explained. The defendants must rely upon their own resources in determining what constitutes an unlawful

[10] A copy of the Restraining Order is given in Appendix XVIII.

assembly. Other terms such as "picketing" and "intimidation" are not defined. Lack of understanding as to just what the injunction prohibited was quite general.[11]

Procedure.—The procedure followed the customary course in this class of cases. Relief was granted on the basis of a bill of complaint and affidavits filed by the plaintiff. The unlawful acts charged in the bill of complaint are:

1. Unlawful picketing and espionage, carried on by defendants, armed with sticks and other deadly weapons, whereby employees were kept from entering the plant.

2. Assaulting, molesting, threatening, and intimidating loyal employees.

3. Assaulting the president of the plaintiff corporation.

4. Trespassing on the premises of the plaintiff.

The defendants are charged with having "conspired, confederated, and agreed together" to interfere with plaintiff's employees. Irreparable damage is also alleged.

Defendants Hoffmann and Pettit (Tippet) are charged with inciting and inducing the other defendants to engage in the unlawful acts.

In a supporting affidavit, defendants Hoffmann and Tippet are charged with holding unlawful assemblies on the property of the plaintiff and with organizing small boys in the village into sling-shot gangs for the purpose of intimidating and injuring loyal employees.

The order was prepared by attorneys for the plaintiff and signed by the judge.[12] It was issued without notice

---

[11] Letter from N. A. Townsend, Appendix XX.
[12] Interview with G. F. Washburn.

or hearing to the defendants. In other words, it was wholly *ex parte*. No contempt proceedings were instituted.[13] The hearing, held twenty days after the original writ was served, was before a judge other than the one who had granted the injunction.[14] The case was argued by counsel for both sides. Each side filed a large number of affidavits. Counsel for the defendants asked the court to define the rights of the parties. The court did so under authority of a decision of the North Carolina Supreme Court, viz., *Citizen Company v. Asheville Typographical Union*, 187 N. C. 42.[15] The order was dissolved as to the union but sustained and modified as to the individuals. The judge continued the restraining order but modified it to allow access to the post office, peaceful picketing, and the right to use the highways and streets running through the village. The judge who modified the order in these respects stated that the original order infringed upon the constitutional rights of the defendants.[16]

Effects of the Injunction.—Because of the importance of this aspect of the case, information from many sources has been obtained. This includes interviews with the president of the company, the general superintendent of the plant, the attorneys for both sides, the union official who was in charge of the strike, the sheriff of the county, the solicitor for the state in the subsequent criminal proceedings there, and with thirty of the parties enjoined. We shall classify the effects according to the outline used in the preceding cases.

[13] Interview with D. F. Giles, attorney for defendants.
[14] *Ibid.*   [15] *Ibid.*
[16] Conversation with Judge Cameron MacRae, Asheville, North Carolina, December 23, 1929.

1. *Effect on the Outcome of the Strike.*—It seems to be conceded by all parties that the injunction had little or no effect on the outcome of the strike. While the detailed statements differ slightly, the general proposition seems to be abundantly supported. The fact should be noted that the plant did not open until an agreement was reached, although this was several weeks after the injunction was served on the defendants. Each of the defendants interviewed was asked if the injunction broke the strike. The replies were unanimously "No." This opinion is supported by interviews with the sheriff of the county, the attorneys for both sides, and by a letter from Mr. N. A. Townsend, Executive Counsellor to the Governor, who was on the ground when the events occurred. One of the best reasons for believing that it had little or no effect on the outcome of the strike is the fact that there is uniformity in the testimony that the strikers paid little or no attention to it. It is true that the strike appears to be broken at the present time, since most of the positions have been filled by non-union workers. However, this effect is attributable to factors other than the injunction.

After the settlement of what is called the first strike, on September 11, exactly two months after the strike began, the majority of the union members went back to work. However, some of them were not re-employed and there were many charges of discrimination against those who had been active in the strike. Vice-President Plemmons, of the State Federation of Labor, made an investigation and reported that there were one hundred ten people who had been refused re-employment. In the agreement, the president of the company reserved the right to refuse employment to "as many as twenty" who had "made themselves so objectionable" that he could not take them back. There is a dispute as to whether the "twenty" refers to individuals or families. Discontent over this situation led to the second strike, or informal walkout, which occurred on October 2. It was at this time that six of the union pickets were killed and several other union members and sympathizers were wounded by deputy sheriffs who were on guard. Bitterness aroused over this situation appears to have made a settlement impossible. Picketing was controlled, after the second strike, by the militia.

2. *Effect on the Conduct of Those Enjoined.*—It is apparent that this is one of the most significant points of inquiry with regard to the effect of an injunction. The interviews indicate that it caused some of the strikers to stop picketing for a short time and that possibly a few were kept away permanently. Only three out of the thirty strikers interviewed expressed the opinion that it made the pickets a little more peaceful. The interviews with the management indicate that this effect was negligible. The superintendent of the plant felt that it had some effect. "After the injunction was served, a good many of the outsiders left. A good many of those on picket dropped out for a few days immediately after the injunction was served but most of them came back. Others took the places of those who dropped out so *I couldn't tell the difference in the number on picket line.*"[17] A high official of the company expressed the opinion that "there was a slight difference in the number of pickets immediately after" but he

---
[17] Personal interview.

did not think it hindered any of the special movements inaugurated by the leaders.[18] This informant also called attention to the inadequacy of local police protection.

One of the attorneys for the complainant expressed his opinion as follows: "I think it had some restraining influence but its effect was destroyed by the union officials and organizers telling the people it was of no legal effect."[19]

An attorney who was not officially connected with this case, but who had observed it carefully, expressed a very definite opinion in these words: "It had no effect whatever. They went on picketing. They paid absolutely no attention to it. They said, 'To Hell with the injunction; to Hell with the courts.' ... It could have been made effective if the judge signing it had cited all those violating it for contempt and filled the jails full of folks."[20]

A similar opinion is expressed by the Executive Counsellor for the Governor: "The strikers did not pay any attention to the terms of the injunction.... The condition of the strikers after the injunction was, if anything, more unpeaceful than it was before."[21]

Of special interest at this point is the reaction of the women on strike. In a case investigated shortly before this one (Case IV, below), the writer found some reason to suspect that the reaction of the women was different from the reaction of the men. Special inquiry, as to the effect on women, was made in this case. Interviews with

---
[18] Personal interview.
[19] Personal interview.
[20] Personal interview.
[21] Personal letter from N. A. Townsend, Appendix XX.

two vice-presidents of the State Federation of Labor and with a number of the local strikers indicate that the women paid less attention to the injunction than the men.[22] The following remarks are illustrative:

"The men dreaded it a little the worst."

"All of those who quit picketing, so far as I know, were men. My wife laughed about it."

"My wife said, 'Pay no attention to it.'"

Some clue to the effects of the injunction on the conduct of those enjoined may be obtained by noting some of the remarks made by the defendants themselves. Some of the remarks indicate that the injunction had an effect in a few cases, at least:

"One man was scared so bad he left his family and joined the army."

"I stayed away from the post office one week. I was driven away by two of the men watching the gates."

"The injunction caused a few to crawfish out."

The attitude of the majority seems to be indicated by such remarks as:

"I thought it was a bluff," or, "I didn't pay no attention to it."[23]

3. *Effect on the Social Attitudes of Those Enjoined.*—Perhaps the most significant in this connection is respect for law. A few verbatim quotations will illustrate this point:

"I thought it was a bluff."

"I didn't think there was anything to it."

---

[22] The vice-presidents interviewed were W. B. Plemmons of Asheville, and John A. Peel of Durham. Mr. Plemmons explained that "in trade union work as in church work, women are more faithful."

[23] See Summary of Interviews, Appendix XXI.

"I knew, in reason, it wasn't wuth nothin'."

"I told the boys it wasn't wuth the paper it was wrote on."

Practically all of those who replied to the question regarded the use of the injunction in such cases as unfair. Some of the strikers interviewed volunteered the information that the attorney had advised them to continue peaceful picketing. He justified himself on the ground that the injunction went farther in abridging the rights of citizens than the law laid down in a previous decision of the Supreme Court.[24] This decision had specifically allowed peaceful picketing. The attorney was also of the opinion that they should be allowed to go to the post office to send or receive mail. These contentions of the defense were substantiated by the judge at the hearing.[25]

Under these circumstances, it is difficult to convince the working people involved that an injunction is law at all. In a previous chapter we have noted the criticism that preliminary injunctions are frequently made more drastic than the state of the law warrants. Here we have a concrete illustration. A striking illustration of the attitude of those enjoined toward the order of the court is indicated by the following "injunction song" which was produced by an amateur composer and sung with great fervor while the injunction was in effect:

> "Old injunctions are mighty fine.
> Pickets read 'em on the picket line.
> (Sing four times)."

[24] Citizens Company v. Asheville Typographical Union, 187 N. C. 42, 121 S. E. 31 (1924), Case II, *supra*.
[25] See modified order, Appendix XIX.

The effect on industrial strife cannot be accurately estimated on the basis of the material at hand. The Executive Counsellor to the Governor states that if "the injunction had any effect whatever upon the controversy, it was to make the tension between capital and labor more strained and deferred the day of settlement."[26]

Perhaps the most subtle effect is the tendency to encourage the martyr spirit. While this tendency was less marked here than in the case of *Glanzstoff v. Miller*, Elizabethton, Tennessee (Case IV, below), there is considerable evidence of it as illustrated by the following interview with one of the young women enjoined:

Question: "Weren't you afraid they would put you in jail for picketing after the injunction came out?"

Answer: "Mr. Hoffman said they might but I told him I didn't care. I told him if they hung me, it would be all the same; I was going to stay on picket."

There is one opinion as to the possible effect of this injunction which should be noted here. Several people, including one of the union organizers, felt that the charge of disobedience of the injunction was material evidence in the subsequent criminal proceedings in which four of the strike leaders, including Organizer Hoffmann, were found guilty of rioting and sentenced.[26a] This point is definitely cleared up, however, by information obtained in a brief interview with the solicitor for the state in these criminal proceedings. In answer to a question as to whether the injunction had any effect on the criminal proceedings, he

---

[26] Personal letter from N. A. Townsend, Appendix XX.
[26a] State v. Hoffman, 199 N. C. 328, 154 S. E. 314 (1930).

replied, "None whatever. The judge would not even admit evidence to show that an injunction had issued."[27]

Summarizing the effects of the injunction in this case, we are safe in concluding that the injunction did not break the strike. There is no reason to believe that the injunction had any effect on the outcome of the strike. As to the effect on the conduct of the strikers, there is evidence from both sides to indicate that it made a few of the strikers more timid about picketing. Beyond this, all the information indicates that the injunction had practically no effect upon the conduct of those enjoined. A possible exception might be noted in the letter from the Executive Counsellor for the Governor stating that it made them "more *unpeaceful* than they were before."

Some general questions of great importance are raised by this case. Are the theoretical arguments in favor of injunctions verified by what took place here? While the injunction did give some advice which was definite, it was definitely wrong on some points, if tested by a previous decision of the Supreme Court, and to this extent would probably have been modified if an appeal had been taken. The moral effect which an order from the court is supposed to have was not realized in this case. The explanation is somewhat difficult. The complainant and his attorneys are definitely of the opinion that the labor leaders counselled disobedience of the order. The labor leaders themselves, on the other hand, strongly maintain that they advised the strikers to stop picketing and obey the order of the court. The attitude of the strikers in this situation may be explained as a pursuit of their immediate

[27] Interview with Solicitor J. Will Pless, Marion, North Carolina.

economic interest. The order of the court was not clearly understood. The threat of punishment was indefinite. If punishment could be expected, it would be in the future. On the other hand, the menace of strikebreakers, who would enter the gates and take away the jobs of the strikers was immediate, definite and clearly understood. They were more inclined to protect their jobs from an obvious and immediate danger than to safeguard themselves against a *possible* punishment for disobeying an order of the court.

CASE IV

AMERICAN GLANZSTOFF CORPORATION AND AMERICAN BEMBERG CORPORATION V. GEORGE MILLER, UNITED TEXTILE WORKERS ET AL.

CHANCERY COURT OF CARTER COUNTY, TENNESSEE,
MARCH 18, 1929*

This is one of the most famous of recent cases in which the writ of injunction has been used in industrial disputes. It has been estimated that twelve hundred fifty people were arrested on the charge of violating the injunction.[1] Forty-three persons were convicted in the contempt proceedings.[2] The *Record of Evidence* in these contempt proceedings fills three massive volumes of typewritten manuscript containing one thousand fifty-eight pages.[3] The opinion of the Chancellor in the contempt proceedings covers forty pages. A large number of militia were ordered out to help enforce the injunction and preserve order.[4]

Technically speaking, these members of the National Guard were serving as state police and not as National Guardsmen. They were sworn in as deputy sheriffs. Since the legality of the proceeding seemed to be in ques-

---

* Reversed by Court of Appeals, 12 Tennessee Appeals Reports (Sept. 5, 1930). Certiorari denied by Supreme Court, Jan. 30, 1931.

[1] Personal letter from Alfred Hoffmann, organizer for the United Textile Workers.

[2] Opinion of the Chancellor.

[3] *Record of Evidence* on file in the office of the Clerk and Master, Chancery Court, Elizabethton, Tennessee.

[4] Article by Noel Sargent, *American Industries*, Vol. XXIX, No. 11 (June, 1929), pp. 7-32.

tion, the writer asked the War Department for information. The following excerpt from the Adjutant General's reply makes the situation clear:

No record has been found of any order or formal expression being issued from the War Department relative to the use of U. S. Army equipment in connection with the strike at Elizabethton, Tennessee, other than a communication on the general subject addressed by the Secretary of War, under date of June 17, 1929, to the Governor of Tennessee, to the effect that he had been informed that certain members of the Tennessee State Police, while engaged under the Governor's orders on active duty in the latter capacity, were allowed to wear U S. Army uniforms and to use arms and equipment belonging to the United States and issued to the State for the equipment and training of the National Guard and that, if so, such action involved an infraction of federal laws and regulations prohibiting the loan of such property to any other activity, or its use for any purpose other than those for which it had been issued to the State. It was therefore requested of the Governor that he take such action as might be necessary to prevent the unlawful use of federal arms and equipment in the hands of the Tennessee National Guard, there being no intention however to restrict the authorities of the State of Tennessee to employ the National Guard in any manner contemplated by the National Defense Act or State laws when legally called out by the State authorities.—Personal letter from the Adjutant General, May 14, 1930.

The plaintiffs in this case are two corporations engaged in the manufacture of rayon and artificial silk in the new, large plants near Elizabethton, Tennessee. At the time the first strike occurred, they employed three thousand two hundred employees. Thirty-eight per cent of these were women. The investment in the two plants was approximately fourteen and one-half million dollars.[4a] The

[4a] *Ibid.*

capital was originally furnished by German capitalists. Part of it is now furnished by New York investors.[5]

The nature of the community is significant. Prior to the advent of these mills, Elizabethton was a country town of less than three thousand inhabitants. It was the county seat for a rural county in eastern Tennessee. The people living in this county are chiefly native whites of the mountaineer type. They have had little opportunity for formal education. The plant of the American Bemberg Corporation began operations in 1926. The Glanzstoff plant came two years later.[6] The coming of large-scale industry to this section brought significant changes. It gave many of the mountaineers their first chance to earn "real money." It also made the prosperity of this city, with its mushroom growth, absolutely dependent upon these two manufacturing establishments. Laborers in the plants came daily from distances as far as thirty-two miles.[7]

While there have been several minor strikes at these establishments,[8] there are only two which are significant for our purpose. The first of these, which occurred March 12, 1929, started with a "walk-out" in the final inspection department of the Glanzstoff plant, but spread to the rest of this plant the following day and later to the Bemberg plant also. The original walk-out was brought about by dissatisfaction over existing wage rates. Those who participated in this walk-out demanded that the rate

[5] Interview with H. L. Taylor, American Bemberg Corporation.
[6] Interview with J. C. Donnelly, President of Local Union Number 1630, United Textile Workers (1929).
[7] *American Industries*, Vol. XXIX, No. 11, p. 11.
[8] Interview with J. C. Donnelly.

of pay for women workers in the Glanzstoff plant be made equal to the rate prevailing in the Bemberg plant for the same kind of work. The detailed story of the beginning of this strike is told by Miss Margaret Bowen, Secretary of the local union, in an address before the Women's Trade Union League.[9] On most points this account agrees with information gained on the ground. Both sides agree that a fight started. The employer group contends that the strikers were the aggressors[10] while Miss Bowen says it started when "a policeman struck a girl over the head with his billy."[11]

The strikers picketed the premises and the management was unable to reopen the plants. Dr. A. Mothwurf, president of both corporations, then sought relief, through his attorneys, from the Chancery Court. The "Original Writ of Injunction" is dated March 13, 1929.

The president of the corporations complained that "there was no protection given by the county authorities either to those willing to work or to the plants."[12]

Picketing continued and many charges of intimidation were made. Local companies of militia were called out. During the night of March 21-22, Sheriff Moreland and Mr. Charles G. Wood, Conciliator for the United States Department of Labor, arranged a meeting with the president of the companies in the John Sevier Hotel, Johnson City, at which a Captain of the National Guard, on duty there, the president of the Tennessee State Federation of Labor, and an organizer for the United Textile Workers

---

[9] *American Federationist*, June, 1929, pp. 666-67.
[10] See *American Industries*, Vol. XXIX, No. 11, p. 8.
[11] *American Federationist*, June, 1929, pp. 666-67.
[12] Hearings on Senate Resolution 49, May 9, 1929, p. 96.

were also present. The morning paper announced that an agreement had been reached and that the strike would be called off. By the terms of this agreement, satisfactory wage adjustments were made, the manager would meet with the committee representing the workers to discuss grievances, and would not discriminate against union labor; all injunctions were to be withdrawn.[13] The agreement was not signed, but Dr. Mothwurf said he would abide by it as a gentleman.[14]

Upon reading this newspaper story, Dr. Mothwurf immediately released a statement to the newspapers denying that he had been a party to any agreement.[15] This caused a great furor among the union people, and the sheriff called on Dr. Mothwurf to ask why he had issued this statement. He replied that these labor agitators were trying to take credit for something which they didn't do.[16] After some negotiation, the three disinterested parties at the meeting succeeded in assuring the union people that at least the wage adjustments had been agreed to and that there would be no discrimination on account of union membership. The strike was called off and many of the people went back to work. But complaints of discrimination against union members began to come in. Mr. Edward McGrady, secretary of the United Textile Workers, reported three hundred cases of discrimination in one week.[17]

This precipitated the second strike, which involved

---

[13] *Record of Evidence*, III, 859.
[14] *Ibid.*
[15] *Ibid.*
[16] Testimony of J. M. Moreland, *Record of Evidence*, III, 859.
[17] *American Federationist*, XXXVI (June, 1929), p.661.

THE EFFECTS OF INJUNCTIONS

considerable violence and damage of property.[18] Strikers and sympathizers from the Glanzstoff plant entered the Bemberg plant by force and took the employees out with them. Whether they "drove them out" or just "let them out," seems to be a matter of dispute. Those identified as committing unlawful acts on that occasion were cited for contempt of court and sentenced by the Chancellor.[19] It should be noted that many of those who took part in the disturbance were not employees of either of the plants.[20] This illustrates one of the most perplexing problems involved in strikes. The man who led the raid upon the Bemberg plant, at the time of the second strike, was neither a member of the union nor an employee at either of the plants. One of the attorneys for the plaintiffs remarked that the strike attracted a lawless element in the community composed of persons who are "no good" under ordinary circumstances but when an occasion like this comes up, "they come into their own."[20a]

It is also significant that sympathizers of the other side indulged in various lawless acts. Most spectacular was the kidnapping of Organizer Hoffmann and Secretary McGrady, of the United Textile Workers, from the hotel at Elizabethton. They were taken to the state line, released, and advised not to come back. On the same night, a large body of men attempted to kidnap Mr. J. B. Penix, the local organizer for the Textile Workers.[20b]

---
[18] *Record of Evidence*, I, 4, 58-59.
[19] Opinion of the Chancellor.
[20] Interview with Ben H. Taylor, Counsel for plaintiffs.
[20a] *Ibid.*
[20b] Interview with J. B. Penix. Also see *American Industries*, June, 1929, pp. 7-32.

The second strike was settled on May 25 through the good offices of Miss Anna Weinstock, Conciliator for the United States Department of Labor. Mr. E. T. Wilson, who was regarded as fair by the United Textile Workers, was employed as personnel manager. The following terms of agreement were announced by Miss Weinstock:

"There shall be no discrimination on account of union membership, but the company may refuse to re-employ any worker considered undesirable.

"If employees are not satisfied with conditions they find, they may appeal to Mr. Wilson.

"If an employee does not get his job back he will be told why.

"The company agrees to treat with a committee of employees if occasion requiring such action arises."[21]

On the strength of this settlement many of the union members applied for, and obtained, re-employment through the regular channels. A considerable number, including the local officers, were not re-employed. The situation was relatively quiet at the time the writer's investigation was made (November, 1929). Hours of labor had been reduced, wages had been increased—as much as three dollars per week in a number of instances. But production was much below capacity and a large number of employees had been laid off.

Form of the Injunction.—In this case, three writs of injunction were issued by the Clerk and Master of the Chancery Court. The original writ was issued the day following the first strike. The amended and supplemental order was issued a few days later. The writ which

---

[21] Greensboro *Daily News*, Greensboro, N. C., May 26, 1929.

was read by a deputy sheriff at a union meeting is a certified copy of the first two. The text of this writ appears below in Appendix XXII.

The first writ is against twenty-two individuals named as defendants "in their own right *and representing each and all employees of the American Bemberg Corporation and American Glanzstoff Corporation.*"[22] Some of the acts prohibited are clearly specified such as:

1. Entering upon the premises of the complainants;

2. Assembling in groups around the gates, or fences and property lines;

3. Molesting or damaging complainants' property;

4. Threatening complainants' plants, officers, employees, or those seeking employment.

5. Picketing is enjoined without any qualification. This appears to have been intentional since counsel for the complainants contend, in their brief, that there is and can be no such thing as peaceful picketing. Unlawfully procuring employees to breach their contracts of employment is also enjoined. It is unlikely that any considerable number of those enjoined knew the meaning of this term.

6. The order closes with a prohibition which is quite comprehensive. The defendants are enjoined ". . . from unlawfully *in any way interfering with complainants, their employees or those seeking employment, in a proper operation of their business, or the use and enjoyment of its plants, property and business, and all rights, benefits and privileges arising therefrom, incident thereto, etc.*"[23] Here we have a clear illustration of one of the things criticized above; namely, that the order is frequently so

---

[22] Italics mine.   [23] Italics mine.

worded that the parties enjoined do not know when they are violating it.

The amended and supplemental bill adds Elizabethton Local Number 1630, of the United Textile Workers of America, its leaders, officers, and members to the list of defendants. Seven officers are named. The prohibitions are similar to those contained in the first bill, but boycotting is specified as one of the unlawful purposes of interference. Various prohibitions, relating to the obstruction of the highways in front and along side of the plants of the complainants, are also added. The sheriff was ordered "by himself and deputies and such additional deputies as may be required, to carry out the terms of the injunction."

Procedure.—A few points of procedure in this case may well be noted. The order was wholly *ex parte*. There was no notice or hearing to the defendants until after the injunctions had issued. The case is similar to the others in this respect. The local union was made a party defendant by service upon its members and officers. This could not have been done in North Carolina.[24] Certain individuals are made parties defendant in their own right and as representing each and all employees of the complainants. It has been said that the latter clause could not lawfully be included in a North Carolina injunction. Although some language in the North Carolina cases tends this way, the question has not yet been presented for decision.[25] The fiat of the court here is similar to a tem-

---

[24] Citizen Company v. Asheville Typographical Union, 187 N. C. 42, Case II, *supra*; Tucker v. Eatough, Case II, *supra*, n. 24.

[25] See Tucker v. Eatough, Case II, note 24.

porary restraining order in other respects but *"it is an unlimited fiat and continues until modified or dissolved by the court."*[26] The temporary restraining order in North Carolina automatically expires in twenty days unless extended for cause by the court.[27]

The means of giving notice here is different from the North Carolina cases. In each of those cases, personal service on each of the named defendants was ordered. Here notice was given by reading the order at a union meeting. There was personal service on some of the leaders. The interviews with defendants indicate that many of them were not present at the union meeting. Some were notified of the injunction by enforcement officers, some read published or posted notices, while others were told about it by friends or relatives.

Tennessee has a dual system of courts; i.e., Law Courts and Chancery Courts. For cases in the Chancery Courts there is a Court of Appeals between the court of original jurisdiction and the Supreme Court. In this case twenty-two months intervened between the issuance of the original order and the final disposition of the case. In the two North Carolina cases we noted that there was an interval of only two or three months between the issuance of the temporary restraining order and the decision of the State Supreme Court.

This case is materially different from the North Carolina cases discussed above, in that contempt proceedings were instituted. While hundreds of persons were arrested on the charge of picketing the highway, most of the cases

---
[26] Interview with Paul Divine, Counsel for defendants.
[27] N. C. Code (1927), Sec. 848.

were disposed of in the Justice of the Peace courts. Only fifty were cited for contempt by the Chancellor. Forty of these were found guilty and sentenced. Three were given the maximum penalty allowed by statute, which is ten days in jail and a fine of fifty dollars. Thirty-one of the forty were fined $10.00 each and costs.[28] Counsel for the defendants argued that the contempt cases should be dismissed on the ground that the agreement reached in the meeting at the John Sevier Hotel rendered the injunction inoperative.

The case was reviewed by the Court of Appeals in May, 1930. Granting the appeal automatically gave a stay of sentence to the defendants who had been found guilty in the contempt proceedings.

The *Opinion* of the Court of Appeals was filed September 5, 1930. This Court reversed the decision of the Chancellor and set aside the convictions for contempt. The Court adopted the view that the meeting at the John Sevier Hotel, on March 21, amounted to a settlement of everything in dispute and thereby rendered the injunction inoperative. "It is, therefore, the opinion of this court that there was no injunction in force in this cause on April 15, 1929, and that, therefore, the petitions for contempt against the parties defendant will be dismissed."[29]

The Supreme Court of Tennessee refused to review the case on a writ of certiorari, January 30, 1931.[30]

Effects of the Injunction.—In a case which partakes of the nature of a civil war, it is obviously impossible to

---

[28] Opinion of the Chancellor.
[29] *Opinion*, Court of Appeals of Tennessee, Middle Section at Knoxville. September 5, 1930. 12 Tennessee Appeals Reports.
[30] Letter from Clerk of the Court.

ascertain and appraise all the effects. Only a few of the effects can be indicated here. We shall use the classification of effects indicated at the beginning of this chapter.

1. *Effect on the Outcome of the Strike.*—Did the injunction break the strike? Certain objective facts help to answer this question. The Glanzstoff plant remained closed in all departments and the Bemberg plant opened only one department with 30 per cent of the working force before the negotiation of what the strikers believed to be an agreement. By the terms of this agreement, wages were to be adjusted, according to the request previously made by the strikers, and there was to be no discrimination against members of the union.[31] After the second strike, an organization known as the "Loyal Bemberg Workers" was formed and partial production was resumed before the second agreement. However, this was very much below capacity production. A number of the employees did not return to work until after the negotiation of the second agreement through the good offices of Miss Anna Weinstock, Conciliator for the United States Department of Labor.[32] Wages were increased and hours of labor were shortened. It seems entirely safe to conclude that the injunction did not break the strike.

Would the strike have been more successful, from the standpoint of the strikers, if there had been no injunction? A conclusive answer to this question is difficult, if not impossible. An overwhelming majority of the defendants

---

[31] See *American Industries* (June, 1929), p. 8, and *Annual Report of Secretary of Labor* (June 30, 1929), pp. 86-88.

[32] *Annual Report of the Secretary of Labor* (June 30, 1929), p. 88.

interviewed were of the opinion that the strike would have been more successful if there had been no injunction.[33]

Some of the comments on this question are interesting. "We could have secured a better settlement without the injunction." "We could have secured a quicker settlement." "We could have picketed more." "The parties could have gotten together easier."

It should be noted at this point that a large force of national guardsmen were on duty at these two plants. The governor had as much authority to order the troops sent without the injunction as with it. Whether he would have done it or not is another question. It is impossible to say how effective the injunction would have been without the militia. Under the ordinary processes of law, it might have been more difficult to punish for all the cases of picketing involved here. Several of those found guilty and fined in the contempt proceedings were arrested for picketing on the public highway about four miles from the property of the complainant.[34] Careful reading of the record gives the impression that the injunction was used as a means of bringing pressure to bear upon the sheriff and inducing him to use more force against the strikers.

2. *Effect on the Conduct of Those Enjoined.*—Did the injunction prevent violence? It certainly did not prevent all violence. The record of evidence gives several examples of violence at the time of the second strike. Glass in doors was broken. One employee was knocked down, his eye-glasses broken and his head bruised.[35] Doors were pushed off their hinges, and other damage done.

[33] Summary of Interviews, Appendix XXIII.
[34] Opinion of the Chancellor. [35] *Record of Evidence*, I, 4, 58-59.

Would there have been *more* violence if there had been no injunction? No positive answer to this question can be given. Two questions asked in the interviews with those who had been in the strike are suggestive on this point, at least. The first of these is intended to discover the reaction which the injunction produced in the striker's mind. "How did you feel when you first read the injunction or heard about it?" The replies are extremely promiscuous in phraseology but can be classified in two approximately equal groups, namely,

1. "Felt that I'd better obey it."
2. "Didn't feel like obeying."

A few of the replies may be used for illustration:[36]

"I didn't think it was right but thought I'd better obey it."

"I didn't like it much, but there was danger of trouble, right or wrong."

"It was a dirty deal but I thought there would be trouble if we went against it."

On the other hand, some either regarded it with indifference or became more belligerent.

"I didn't care much about it."

"I wanted to fight that much harder."

"I thought it was . . . bull and I wasn't afraid of it."

The only safe conclusion we can draw from these replies is that the injunction impressed some and not others. Of the latter group there were some who were impelled "to fight that much harder." We found a situation similar to this in the case of *Citizen Company v. Asheville Typographical Union*, in which one observer expressed the

[36] See Appendix XXIII.

opinion that the injunction had no effect on the "roughnecks" and the "don't give a ———" class.

The defendants interviewed were also asked: "Do you think any of the workers were frightened by the injunction?"

Answers: Yes—Twenty.
             No—Eleven.
             Qualified—Eight.

Some of the comments are significant:

"It kept some off picket."

"It made the people more cautious."

"They laughed at it."

"It scared some of the boys but I don't think it scared any of the girls."

This last remark is in accord with a tentative conclusion reached in the Marion case; namely, that women pay less attention to injunctions than men.[37] The effect of the injunction on the extent of violence remains problematical.

Perhaps the most significant inquiry is the effect of the injunction on picketing. Was there less picketing, especially mass picketing, because of the injunction? As indicated above, several expressed the opinion that they could and would have picketed more if it had not been

---

[37] The writer was told the following story in the course of his investigation:
While the strike was on, the company would send men out from the office to get the names of those who were willing to come back to work. One of these fellows came up to a group of girls and said,
"Girls, wouldn't you like to come back to work?"
"Sure, we want to work."
"All right, please give me your names."
Two or three of the girls gave him their names. While he was busy writing, one of the girls snatched the paper out of his hands, others pulled his hair and kicked his shins and sent him back to the office.

for the injunction. Some plainly stated that "we could have kept the scabs out if it hadn't been for the injunction."

On the other hand, it is clearly shown by the record of evidence, in the contempt proceedings, that truck loads of pickets went out every morning and picketed the highways on which the non-union employees were being brought in. Many of the union people admit this but stoutly maintain that the picketing was peaceful. The following quotation from one of the interviews is in accord with the information gained from other sources, including the Record of Evidence in the contempt proceedings:

"We went on picket duty every day. We would get arrested, get bond, and go out on picket again."

Many were careful to explain that they did not go on company property or around the plants. Mr. William F. Kelly, vice-president of the United Textile Workers, expressed the opinion that "the injunction had the desired effect [on picketing] in the immediate vicinity of the plant and private roads leading to it. Picketing continued very much the same elsewhere."[38]

There still remains, however, the question of the relative importance of the injunction and the militia in this situation. It was obviously easier for the militia to maintain order in the immediate vicinity of the plant than to patrol the highways leading to all points within a radius of twenty-five or thirty miles.

3. *Effect on the Social Attitude of Those Enjoined.*—Did the injunction increase the respect for law in this case? In answering this question, it may be noted that

[38] Personal interview.

most of the defendants interviewed regarded the proceeding as unfair. The reasons for regarding it as unfair are numerous. Several of them imply the idea of the right of peaceful persuasion. Those interviewed were quite firmly of the opinion that the injunction deprived them of their constitutional rights in this matter. Others objected to the use of the writ because of what they consider the adverse prejudice or corruption of the courts. A lack of respect for the Chancery Courts is certainly evident in the community. A few of the statements are given verbatim:[39]

"It kept us off the public road where we had a right to be."

"We should have the right to advise them not to go in."

"It's a dirty law."

"It [the injunction] is generally issued by a man partial to the other side."

"The courts are so corrupt a man can't get justice."

"In case of another strike, I would picket anyway."

The opinion of one of the attorneys for the complainant is significant. The writer asked if the injunction gave the relief sought in this case.

Answer: "It would have if it hadn't been violated."[40]

Question: "Do you think it was violated only sporadically or quite generally?"

Answer: "I would say it was violated quite generally."[41] However, he attributed this to the strikers' lack of knowledge and experience with injunctions.

[39] See Summary of Interviews with defendants, Appendix XXIII.
[40] Personal interview.
[41] *Ibid.*

The effect of the injunction on the intensity of industrial conflict cannot be accurately estimated. We shall submit the information which is available for what it is worth. The following remarks were made by members of the union involved:[42]

"The injunction caused the sentiment of the people to be aroused against the management permanently."

"Soldiers won't carry yellow dogs in if they have another strike."

"It [the injunction] caused the workers to have less respect for the management."

"It stirred up strife otherwise non-existent."

Many expressed the opinion that the injunction made enemies for the management. One of the local leaders expressed his belief that the injunction caused a bitter feeling toward the management, which still continues. These statements reinforce the impression gained in general conversation that the injunction tended to stir up strife and bitterness.

We noticed in the Marion case above that the injunction had the effect of encouraging a martyr spirit. In this case, such a tendency is more marked. One of the young women on strike stood on the railway track when a train, bringing in non-union employees, was coming. The engineer blew the whistle but she refused to move. He stopped the train and one of the military officers ordered her to get off. She stood there until she was picked up bodily and removed from the track.[43] On another occasion, strikers were picketing the highway. A truck

---

[42] Interviews with Defendants, Appendix XXIII.
[43] Interview with J. Clyde Donnelly.

carrying non-union employees with guards came up and stopped. The guards ordered a girl who was standing in front of the truck to get out of the way. She refused to move. The officer then gave orders to drive over her. The truck ran over her and dragged her several yards, causing serious bodily injury.[44]

In one other instance, the strikers were picketing the highway. One of the officers drew a pistol on one of the young women on picket. Instead of obeying his order, she snatched the pistol from his hand saying, "That —— thing won't go off."

In March, 1930, trouble broke out anew. A strike was ordered as a protest against the inauguration of a company union. Picketing on the highways was renewed. The sheriff and his deputies were again ordered to enforce the injunction. In a few days the sheriff tendered his resignation. At the same time he released to the press a statement saying he had been forced out by a group who insisted on his going out on the highways and shooting down pickets.[45]

We have here an illustration of a labor injunction in all its phases. The issuance of the order, attempts at enforcement through local police authorities, a heroic attempt at enforcement by the militia, and finally contempt proceedings. The paper prohibition meant very little. Even with the militia, picketing on the highways continued. Only forty-three persons, out of the hundreds who picketed the highways daily, were convicted in the

[44] See Summary of Interviews, Appendix XXIII.
[45] Greensboro *Daily News,* March 10, 1930.

contempt proceedings. Most of these were sentenced to pay a fine of only ten dollars. The convictions were set aside by the Court of Appeals. When we consider the expense of this remedy and the results obtained, it affords an interesting contrast to the absolutely free services of the Conciliator from the Department of Labor.

CASE V
RIVERSIDE AND DAN RIVER COTTON MILLS, INCORPORATED, V. FRANCIS J. GORMAN AND OTHERS

Corporation Court of Danville, Virginia,
September 30, 1930[1]

This case grew out of the recent spectacular strike in the mills at Riverside and Dan River Cotton Mills, Incorporated, at Danville and Schoolfield, Virginia. The mills, when working at capacity, employed approximately five thousand workers.[2] At the close of the year 1930 this was the only large strike going on under the jurisdiction of the American Federation of Labor.[3]

The open conflict, which gave rise to the strike and the injunctions, began January 9, 1930, when the management announced a 10 per cent reduction in the wages of all employees of the company.[4] The real struggle, however, goes back much farther. In the year 1919, a dispute between the management and a local organization of Loom Fixers led to the introduction of a system called Industrial Democracy.[5] This system comes in for severe criticism in the *Answer* of the defendants to the Bill for Injunction. It is charged that this "vague, theoretical

---

[1] This is technically composed of two cases since the Corporation Court of the City of Danville had jurisdiction within the corporate limits of the City of Danville while the Circuit Court of the County of Pittsylvania had jurisdiction outside these limits.

[2] Bill of Complaint, see Appendix XXIV.

[3] Address of President William Green, Danville, Virginia, December 30, 1930.

[4] Raleigh (N. C.) *News and Observer*, October 26, 1930.

[5] Answer to Bill for Injunction, Appendix XXVI, and interview with Francis J. Gorman, vice-president, United Textile Workers.

system . . . deluded the workers into the belief that they would have some sort of voice in the management of said mills"; and "that if any worker was bold enough to suggest improvements which did not meet with the approval of the management, . . . that worker was, on some slight pretext, discharged and placed on the 'black list.' "[6]

The management defended the wage reduction on the ground that "a wage differential of more than 20 per cent above the average of the entire South . . . created an unsound economic condition which neither the company nor the operatives could afford."[7]

Soon after the wage reduction was announced, a delegation of Loom Fixers met President William Green of the American Federation of Labor at Richmond and asked for help in organizing a local union. Mr. Green notified the United Textile Workers, and Mr. Francis J. Gorman, vice-president of the union, was sent to Danville.[8] The first public meeting for organization purposes was held February 9, 1930, at the Majestic Theatre in Danville. The meeting was addressed by Francis J. Gorman, O. E. Woodberry, publicity representative of the American Federation of Labor, and Miss Matilda Lindsay, representative of the Women's Trade Union League. Membership increased rapidly, and by March 26 the local union

---

[6] *Ibid.* "The purpose was," said Mr. Gorman, "to substitute this form of organization for bona fide trade unionism and if possible to abolish the loom fixers' union which at that time was the only outside organization. The loom fixers still maintained their independent union after the establishment of industrial democracy and were also represented in the company union under industrial democracy."

[7] Letter Poster No. 192, February 12, 1930, signed by H. R. Fitzgerald, president and treasurer. This wage differential is disputed by the union.

[8] Raleigh *News and Observer*, October 26, 1930. Confirmed by William Green in Danville address, December 30, 1930.

claimed a membership of three thousand.[9] By the end of the summer, unionization of the plants was practically complete. Local officers and committees were functioning and dues were being paid regularly.[10]

There is a sharp disagreement as to the causes of the strike. According to the management, the trouble was caused by paid agitators from the outside who appealed to prejudice, stirred up strife, and made promises which neither they nor anyone else could fulfil.[11]

According to the union, the strike was caused by the abuses of the Industrial Democracy system, the "stretch-out," the wage cut, and, most of all, by the discharge of union members who occupied key positions.[12]

The strike was called September 29, 1930. The gates at both the Riverside and the Dan River Mills were closed. Organized picketing was conducted by the union. The Bill for Injunction was filed and the temporary orders granted by both courts on September 30, 1930. The action was wholly *ex parte* in both cases. The defendants did not ask for an immediate hearing.[12a]

[9] *Memorandum on Danville Situation* by Francis J. Gorman and Matilda Lindsay, March 26, 1930.
[10] Interview with Francis J. Gorman.
[11] H. R. Fitzgerald in Letter Poster No. 192, February 12, 1930.
[12] Answer to Bill for Injunction Riverside and Dan River Mills, Incorporated v. Francis J. Gorman *et al.*, Circuit Court, Pittsylvania County, Virginia.
[12a] On October 2nd., Governor Pollard offered mediation in the following telegram to President Fitzgerald:

"On account of important public interests involved, I hereby offer to appoint a committee of mediation for the purpose of seeking to bring about an amicable settlement of the pending controversy between your corporation and its former employees, to whom I am addressing the same offer." (*Danville Register*, October 3, 1930.)

To this offer President Fitzgerald, with authority from the Board of Directors, sent the following reply:

"Many thanks for your fine telegram.

In the bill of complaint the defendants are charged with assembling in large numbers (as many as 25 or more) at the gates of entrance to the plants, standing in front of and obstructing the gates and, by force and intimidation, preventing persons from passing in and out. Details of specific instances of intimidation and interference with employees wishing to enter are recited. Trespassing on the property of the complainant, unlawful assembly, and assault are also charged.

In legal terms the charges are trespassing on private property, unlawful assembly, assault, intimidation. The complaint also alleges that the defendants are "unlawfully constituting an unlawful conspiracy to do an unlawful act and that the damage to your complainant will be irreparable and that it is without adequate remedy at law."[13]

The defendants did not answer the bill presented in the case in the Corporation Court of Danville. The reason given was that the injunction was not used in such a way as to interfere with the conduct of the strike.[14] They did file an answer in the Circuit Court of Pittsylvania County denying all the equities in the bill and setting forth in considerable detail the grievances of the strikers.[15]

Form of the Injunction.—The form of the injunction is strikingly unusual. It begins by stating what the de-

"We believe that if you knew the mill situation and the history of our Company you would realize that, so far as our Company and its employees are concerned, there is absolutely nothing to mediate. . . ."
The officers of the Local Union, on the other hand, expressed their willingness to accept the Governor's offer. *(Ibid.)*

[13] Bill for Injunction, by Malcolm K. Harris, Counsel.
[14] Interview with H. T. Williams, Counsel for defendants.
[15] See Answer to Bill for Injunction, Appendix XXVI.

fendants have a lawful right to do.[16] This is followed by a detailed statement of what is unlawful. The statement of the law is based upon the opinion of the State Supreme Court in the case of *Everett Waddey v. Richmond Typographical Union.*[17] Following this general statement of the law, the restraining clauses enjoin Francis J. Gorman, Local No. 1685, United Textile Workers of America *and the members thereof,*[18] B. F. Nash, as President, J. C. Blackwell, its Secretary, *and all other persons:*[19]

1. From congregating in large numbers in front of the gates leading to said plants and interfering with the free passage of persons lawfully desiring to pass therethrough;

2. From entering upon and trespassing upon the private property of the complainant;

3. From congregating on the private steps of the property;

4. From in any way, by force, threats, intimidation, coercion, or otherwise, preventing free passage of the agents and employees of the Riverside and Dan River Cotton Mills and of all other persons in and out its gates over and along its property.[20]

It is apparent that this order is quite different from those which have been criticized so severely on account of their drastic nature. Even the labor leaders described the order as "mild" in its terms.[21] Care seems to have been

---

[16] See copy of Order, Appendix XXV.
[17] Everett Waddey Company v. Richmond Typographical Union, 105 Va. 188, 53 S. E. 273 (1906).
[18] Italics mine.   [19] Italics mine.
[20] See copy of Order, Appendix XXV.
[21] Interview with Matilda Lindsay.

taken to keep the prohibitions within the limits set by the Supreme Court in the ruling case. However, some of the criticisms presented in Chapter IV, above, are applicable here. The parties enjoined include not only named defendants but also the members of the union and "all other persons." It is not to be supposed that all members of the union and all other persons would have notice of the order. Counsel for complainant recognized the necessity for proof of actual notice in contempt proceedings.[22]

The prohibition of "congregating in large numbers" was found to be so indefinite as to be practically useless. The parties could not agree as to what constituted large numbers.[22a] On November 27 the Police Commissioners in the City of Danville fixed an arbitrary limit of six pickets at any one gate.[23] This gave the police definite orders which were literally carried out.[24] In the county this uncertainty proved to be more serious. The sheriff and his deputies had no definite rule as to what constituted "large numbers." The mill management and the local authorities feared the situation might get out of their hands and asked the governor to send the militia, which he did on November 26.[25]

Procedure.—The injunctions were issued simultaneously by the Corporation Court of Danville and the Circuit Court of Pittsylvania County. Neither court required notice or hearing for the defendants. The bill of

---
[22] Interview with Malcolm K. Harris, Counsel for Riverside and Dan River Mills, Incorporated.
[22a] Interview with Commonwealth Attorney.
[23] Resolution adopted by Police Commission of Danville, November 27, 1930.
[24] Interview with John W. Carter, Commonwealth Attorney.
[25] Greensboro (N. C.) *Daily News*, November 29, 1930.

complaint, signed by counsel for the complainant and certified by a mill official in each case, was supported by affidavits signed by interested parties. The restraining order was prepared by counsel for the complainant and signed by the judge in each case. Officers of the union and the named individual defendants were personally served with copies of the order.

Judge J. T. Clement of the Circuit Court of Pittsylvania County was criticized for sitting in the case, in view of the fact that he owned stock in the complainant corporation.[26] On October 10 this judge asked the Governor to be relieved of presiding at the trial of the case, and Judge J. L. McLemore of Suffolk was appointed to serve in his place. On October 15 the case in the Circuit Court of Pittsylvania County came up for hearing on the motion of the defendants to dismiss. The bill of complaint, the answer, and many affidavits on each side were presented at this time. The motion to dissolve was argued by counsel.

The court ruled that the injunction was not improvidently awarded and continued the order in accordance with its original terms, i.e., until December 1, 1930.[27]

In the Corporation Court of the City of Danville, a supplemental bill was filed November 20, 1930, naming thirty-one additional individuals who were made parties defendant.[28] On November 28, the order was continued until January 19, 1931.[29] At the final hearing held on

[26] The *Danville Register,* October 14, 1930.
[27] Taken from the court records of the case.
[28] Record in office of Clerk of Corporation Court of Danville, Va.
[29] Order in vacation.

January 17, 1931, the injunction was made perpetual on the ground that "none of the defendants demurred, pleaded, or answered" the bill.[30] The order issued by the Circuit Court of Pittsylvania County has also been made perpetual.

Effects of the Injunction.—It should be made clear at this point that this is a double case. While there was only one strike, the plants involved were in different jurisdictions. The most significant point of difference is the degree of police protection. Within the corporate limits of the City of Danville, there was a fairly large, well-disciplined police force. In the village of Schoolfield, there were only the half-dozen private policemen, paid by the Company, and the county peace officers including the sheriff and his deputies. The writer's conclusions are based upon a personal investigation and upon interviews with informed persons who were on the scene. The courtesy shown by representatives of both sides of the controversy and by public officers of the City of Danville and Pittsylvania County was commendable.

1. *Effect on the Outcome of the Strike.*—The effect of the injunction on the outcome of this particular strike is easily stated and, so far as the writer has been able to discover, is undisputed. It appears to have had *no effect* on the outcome of the strike. A newspaper reporter, who had covered the strike daily, expressed the opinion that it it had "no effect whatever." A public officer of the City of Danville who had intimate personal knowledge of the situation, thought the strikers had "just as good a chance to win with the injunction as without." An officer of

[30] Greensboro (N. C.) *Daily News*, January 18, 1931.

Pittsylvania County, equally familiar with the situation, "couldn't see where it had much effect." One of the active leaders in the strike stated that the injunction "wouldn't have hurt anything without the soldiers and special deputies." It should be noted that the troops were ordered out to preserve peace and not to enforce the injunction.[81]

Officers of the union were also of the opinion that the injunction "didn't hinder much here." As we have noted above, the union officers and their counsel regarded the injunction in the City of Danville so lightly that they did not even answer the bill of complaint.

A statement made by the counsel for the complainant is significant in this connection.

Q. "How would you describe the effect of the injunction in this case?"

A. "As a general proposition, it [an injunction] has considerable effect. So far as individual cases are concerned, it has little or no effect.

"An injunction which properly defines and sets out those rights [of the defendants] puts an end to any conflict as to what their rights are. Ninety per cent of the people will voluntarily respect the order of any court. . . . Take the man who says he will violate the injunction regardless . . . you have a more expeditious remedy under the criminal law."[82]

No effort was made to enforce the injunction in either jurisdiction. No contempt proceedings were instituted.

[81] Interview with John W. Carter, Commonwealth Attorney.
[82] Interview with Malcolm K. Harris, Counsel for Complainant.

The complainants were convinced that they had a more expeditious remedy in the criminal law.[33]

In many cases the injunction may be said to have an indirect effect on the outcome of the strike because of the financial burden involved. It is apparent that the diversion of funds from strike benefits (or the feeding of starving strikers) to court costs is a serious matter in some cases. In this case, however, the union put forth so little effort in fighting the injunction, that the cost was not a large item. The cost of the criminal proceedings is a different matter.

2. *Effect on the Conduct of Those Enjoined.*—At this point we must proceed with caution. There is some conflicting evidence which makes a clear-cut statement difficult. According to one informant, "the civil authorities were helpless. . . . After the injunction was served, gatherings on private property dispersed and all pickets abandoned private property."[34] Information from various other sources indicates that trespassing on company property practically ceased after the injunction was served. However, one informant suggested that the police would probably have stopped this anyway. There is some divergence of opinion as to the effect on mass picketing. It certainly did not stop all mass picketing. It does appear, however, that after the injunction was served, it was easier for the police to keep pickets from physically blocking the gates. This applies especially to the village of Schoolfield. That the effect in this respect was slight, is evidenced by such statements as the following:

[33] *Ibid.*   [34] *Ibid.*

"It made no difference in the way people acted."[35]

"The injunction order was never observed by workers generally. . . . The public authorities, entirely independent of the injunction and without reference thereto, proceeded against members of the crowd under the common law with reference to unlawful assemblies."[36]

"Picketing in large numbers did not stop until after the order of the Police Commissioners [City of Danville] limited the number of pickets to six at each gate. . . . There was no decrease in the number of pickets after the injunction but they did get back from the gate."[37]

"They said they [injunctions] didn't amount to anything. Some of them laughed."

A deputy sheriff was of the opinion that strikers didn't gather in such large crowds at the picket stands, at Schoolfield, after being served with copies of the injunction.

The difficulty of determining what constitutes picketing "in large numbers" has been referred to above. Before the troops were sent to Schoolfield, there was argument and friction between the officers and the pickets on this point. Upon the arrival of the troops, Colonel Opie, the commanding officer, was instructed by the sheriff to stop unreasonable picketing. He objected to the indefiniteness of this order and the sheriff amended the instructions to read *"stop all picketing."* This order was literally enforced for a time, but the union people protested so vigorously that Governor Pollard made a personal investigation and modified the order to allow reasonable pick-

---
[35] Interview with one of the strike leaders.
[36] Interview with Commonwealth Attorney.
[37] Interview with a police lieutenant, City of Danville.

eting.[38] Later an informal agreement between the commanding officer and the captain of the pickets fixed eight as the maximum number of pickets at one gate.[39]

The effect on violence is difficult to estimate. There was relatively little violence in either jurisdiction before the injunction was served. The bill of complaint and other affidavits cite instances of "rough hands" being laid on men who attempted to enter. Other affidavits charge defendants with physically blocking the gates and prohibiting employees from entering. These charges are vigorously denied by other affidavits. Here, as elsewhere, it seems unsafe to draw any conclusions from an examination of affidavits. After the injunction had been served, there were numerous arrests on charges of assault and intimidation. Dynamite explosions were frequent in the strike area. As usual, each side charges the other with responsibility for this nefarious business. However, in view of the numbers involved and the bitterness of the struggle, it must be admitted that the strike was carried on in a remarkably peaceful manner. To say it would have been less so if the injunction had not been used, would be little more than a guess. Competent, unbiased observers, who were on the scene before and after the copies of the injunction were served, informed the writer that they couldn't tell any difference in the way people acted except that they kept off company property and did not physically block the gates. Since no attempt was made to enforce the injunction, by either court, this opinion seems to be in accord with the facts.

[38] Interview with John W. Carter, Commonwealth Attorney.
[39] Interview with Matilda Lindsay, vice-president, Women's Trade Union League.

3. *Effect on the Social Attitude of Those Enjoined.*—Evidence on this point is not so complete here as in the previous cases. Such information as we have indicates clearly that the effect was unfavorable. One of the leaders was firmly convinced that "it made the strikers more bitter." In other cases it seems to have impressed them lightly. Some of the strikers laughed when the injunction was served on them. Such expressions as "To Hell with injunctions" and "To Hell with the courts" were not lacking. One competent witness emphasized the point that the injunction caused the defendants to put politics into the strike immediately. There was much talk about the government of the county and the city being run by one man.

A press reporter who covered the strike found abundant evidence of bitterness against the court as a result of the injunction. This informant was of the opinion that the Danville cases afforded excellent evidence in support of Senator Pepper's argument that the use of injunctions in this class of cases weakens the prestige of the courts.

Widespread unemployment and the cost of feeding a city of fifteen thousand people proved to be serious difficulties.

The strike came to an end January 29, 1931, when a statement, ratified by the local union, was read by Mr. Gorman. According to this statement, the management, in taking back former employees without raising the question of unionism, had made continuance of the strike unnecessary.[40]

---

[40] *The Bee*, Danville, Va., January 29, 1931.

Comparison and Summary of Cases

We have examined five cases in considerable detail. So far as these cases are concerned, some fairly definite conclusions can be drawn. On other points, however, we cannot speak with certainty. The injunction did not break the strike in any of these cases. In three of these cases, *McGinnins v. Raleigh Typographical Union, Marion Manufacturing Company v. United Textile Workers,* and *Riverside and Dan River Cotton Mills v. Gorman et al.,* the injunction had no effect on the outcome of the strike. This might be qualified in the Marion case by stating that it may have delayed the day of settlement. In the Asheville case, it appears that the injunction dampened the ardor of some of the defendants and was probably a contributing factor in the failure of the strike.

In the Elizabethton case, most of the union members interviewed believed that a quicker and more satisfactory settlement could have been reached if there had been no injunction. Since it is impossible to separate the effects of the injunction and the militia, the evidence on this point is inconclusive.

Did the injunctions prevent violence and intimidation and thus give genuine protection to the property rights of the complainants? Confining our attention first to violence, we find a wide diversity of facts in the five cases. In the Raleigh case it was not shown that violence occurred either before or after the injunction. Since the State Supreme Court dissolved the injunction, it appears that violence was not seriously threatened. In only one of the five cases, namely, the one at Elizabethton, was there any considerable amount of violence. There was more violence at the opening of the second strike, *after* the injunction had issued, than at the opening of the first strike *before* the injunction had issued. However, no causal relationship is implied. In an absolute sense, the injunction did not prevent violence. There is evidence to show that the more belligerent element either ignored the injunction or felt like fighting that much harder. In the Asheville case, the Supreme Court was convinced that violence was threatened. However, the decision is based primarily upon the fact that counsel for the defendants demurred to the complaint, thereby admitting that the things charged were true. Observers on the ground say the effect of the injunction at Marion, on the conduct of those enjoined, can be summed up in six words: "They paid no attention to it." As we have noted above, this statement needs some qualification. However, the evidence tending to show that it had little or no effect is undisputed.[1]

The effect of the injunction on intimidation is one of the most important points of inquiry. At Marion it had little or no effect. The Executive Counsellor to the Governor believes it made the situation worse in this respect. The complainant dropped the injunction and resorted to the militia and the criminal law instead. When the militia came the pickets stood back.[2] The complainant also succeeded in the criminal prosecutions. These facts suggest an answer to one of our questions in the Elizabethton

---

[1] One of counsel for complainant thought it had some effect although it was slight.

[2] Interview with a high official of the Marion Mfg. Co.

case. Was it the injunction or the militia that restricted picketing and intimidation in the immediate vicinity of the plants at Elizabethton? The militia and the injunction did not keep as good order at Elizabethton as the militia alone did at Marion. No further generalization on this point is attempted. In the Elizabethton case, the injunction did not stop picketing in large numbers on the highways outside the immediate vicinity of the plants.

In the other two North Carolina cases, both of which were in the printing trades, it appears that the injunction had some effect on picketing. In the Raleigh case it was slight. The strikers stopped congregating near the entrances to the struck establishments. According to the decision of the Supreme Court, the extent of intimidation before the injunction was negligible. In the Asheville case, it appears that the injunction had a noticeable restraining influence.

At Danville it seems that there was less trespassing after the injunction was served. There is evidence to indicate that there was less physical blocking of the gates at Schoolfield after the injunction was served. Observers have suggested that the police could, and probably would, have stopped this without an injunction. Two of the most competent witnesses, when asked what effect the injunction had, replied "No effect whatever" and "Practically no effect," respectively.

As to the effect on industrial strife, the weight of evidence in all these cases inclines to the view that injunctions intensify it. Bitterness against the management, which had previously been dormant or non-existent, became very strong. There is no denying the fact that a strike without an injunction has this effect. However, the efforts to fight the case out in the courts probably had the effect of still further stirring up strife. Closely related to this is the effect of the injunction on respect for our legal system. It is admitted by defenders of the injunction that respect for the law and the courts is one of the essentials of success. In all five cases, the result, in this respect, appears to be bad. The procedure for obtaining the injunction seems to have impressed the defendants as being unfair. We found more evidence of this in the printing trades cases than in the textile cases. This is probably due to the fact that the former are better educated and know more about the procedure.

We have also noted the argument that the injunction keeps the disputants apart and thus prevents adjustment of differences. In a technical sense this is certainly true. By the terms of the injunction, the defendants are ordered to stay away. Even if the parties enjoined are willing to make concessions, the management is not accessible. Written communications are likely to be thrown into the waste basket. There is, of course, the possibility of negotiating through third parties, but it is sometimes difficult to find a third party acceptable to both sides. Overtures by the management are suspected also, where there is an injunction. The strikers are afraid this is a trick to get them on company property and prosecute them for contempt.[8] It appears from a study of these cases that injunctions tend to retard rather than hasten peaceful settlement of industrial disputes.

[8] Interview with Paul Aymon, President, Tennessee State Federation of Labor.

CHAPTER VI

GENERAL SUMMARY AND CONCLUSIONS

IN THE preceding cases, selected for detailed study, we have had an opportunity to observe the injunction in operation. The thing which must impress anyone who is intellectually honest is the baffling complexity of the whole problem. Conflicting economic philosophies, and claims to rights which are irreconcilable, present a problem to the court, as well as to the student, which cannot be solved in a manner satisfactory to all parties.

At this point, it becomes pertinent to ask how our observations in these cases coincide with, or depart from, the prevalent theories on the subject. In Chapters III and IV, we reviewed briefly the theoretical arguments pro and con. As all students know, this is a field of sharp controversy.

The arguments, presented in Chapter III, make out a strong case for the beneficent influence of injunctions in industrial disputes. The injunction protects property by preventing unlawful acts which would cause irreparable injury. It does this by peacefully determining the rights of the parties and then giving definite advice, as to what acts would be unlawful. Those who threaten the injury are placed upon notice and, because of respect for the integrity and impartiality of the court, or because of fear of punishment for contempt, the defendants obey.

It must be apparent that the thing described here is an ideal situation. While the courts in North Carolina, as the writer believes, are nearer the ideal than equity courts in many other jurisdictions, we have found that, even in this state, the ideal conditions described above are not likely to exist. While the orders examined above gave definite advice on some points, they contained terms which were either too technical for a layman to understand or were couched in such indefinite language that it was impossible to know what acts were prohibited. This is especially true of the prohibitions against "combining" or "conspiring" to injure the business of the plaintiff, interfering with the property or business of the plaintiff "in any way," and "unlawfully in any way interfering with complainants, their employees or those seeking employment, in a proper operation of their business . . . and all rights, benefits, and privileges arising therefrom, incident thereto, etc." Since these clauses left so much ground for interpretation, the parties enjoined seem to have given themselves the benefit of the doubt. Closely related to this matter of definite advice is the matter of notice. North Carolina courts have been very strict on this point. The same is true of the Virginia courts involved here. The individual defendants are named and personal service on each of them is ordered. In the Elizabethton, Tennessee, case, however, we found that notice on many of the defendants was little more than hearsay. The moral restraining influence of an order coming from a respected tribunal cannot be denied. In these cases we have found reason to doubt if the courts command the respect which is necessary to make their orders a strong moral force. Many individual defendants in these cases expressed the opinion that the courts issuing the orders were either corrupt or biased.

Injunctions have been defended as a means of reinforcing the criminal law. The most obvious reason for this is the inadequacy or indifference of the local police authorities. In all the textile strike cases investigated, the local police protection was inadequate.[1] Indifference was charged in one of the cases. The only objection here relates to a matter of policy. Is this a judicial function or an executive function?

The efficiency of the injunctive remedy in reaching strike leaders and those who participate in conspiracies, even though they commit no overt acts which would afford a basis for criminal prosecution, cannot be estimated from a study of the North Carolina cases since no contempt proceedings have been instituted. It is a peculiar fact that the organizer involved in the Marion case was prosecuted and convicted under the criminal law instead of being cited for contempt. As we have noted in the preceding chapter, the Supreme Court of North Carolina has been cautious in applying the conspiracy doctrine because of its "distressing uncertainty."

In the contempt proceedings, which were instituted in the Elizabethton, Tennessee, case, all persons convicted were charged with overt acts. However, there is no presumption that this is generally true.

The injunctive remedy has been defended on the ground that the procedure is more expeditious. So far as the temporary restraining orders are concerned, the proposition is not debatable. In the cases examined here, as in others, the order was issued promptly upon the *ex parte*

---

[1] Outside the city limits in the Danville case.

application of the plaintiff, supported by affidavits. The procedure at law would have been much slower in this respect. If the parties enjoined comply with the order as soon as it is issued, the relief is immediate. We have found varying degrees of effectiveness in this respect. In two of the cases, at least, it appears that the complaining party obtained a measure of genuine relief more quickly than he would have otherwise. If we turn our attention to the contempt proceedings, we find that the greater speed is not so apparent. The examination of witnesses was long and tedious. The only noticeable difference between these proceedings and the ordinary criminal trial was the absence of a jury. In view of the fact that it is often difficult to find an impartial jury, some saving of time may be admitted. But even the expeditious procedure in obtaining restraining orders is objected to on the ground that it endangers liberty.

In defending equity against the criticism that it restricts one's liberty without notice or hearing, it has been contended that this is not a serious invasion of liberty. The injunction *restrains only unlawful acts*. The defendants are still at liberty to do that which is lawful. Here again we find the contrast between the real and the ideal. If the line between lawful and unlawful were always sharply drawn, and if the courts applied a uniform standard, much of the trouble would be removed. In practice, however, we find the widest divergence in the standards of lawfulness which the courts apply. If we take the statutory law and the decisions of the courts of final appeal as our standard of lawfulness, we find that this argument breaks down completely. In all three North Carolina cases, the temporary restraining orders prohibited acts which either upon hearing or upon appeal to the Supreme Court were found to be lawful. In the Tennessee case, it now appears that the Chancellor was punishing for violation of an injunction which did not exist.

The question of the inappropriateness of jury trial leads us into the sharpest kind of controversy. The trade unionists find that the greater certainty of conviction in proceedings for contempt is the strongest possible reason for desiring jury trial. Feeling, as many of them do, that judges are likely to be biased in favor of the employing group, they bitterly resent the evasion of jury trial.

There remain two important arguments for the retention of injunctions which cannot be easily dismissed. These relate to the oppressive practices and the violence engaged in by trade unionists. Some of the illustrations cited in Chapter III are doubtless extreme. Statements and affidavits charging violence are of varying degrees of reliability. But, when due allowance for all these factors has been made, this basis for criticism still remains.

The superiority of the injunction over the ordinary criminal law as a remedy for this situation is not easy to demonstrate; but the fact that violence and other forms of lawlessness are indulged in makes the removal of admitted abuses exceedingly difficult. Violence is most likely to occur in connection with picketing. In the course of these investigations, the writer has been told repeatedly that there is no such thing as peaceful picketing.

In Chapter IV we reviewed the case against injunctions. Much that is contained in the argument there presented cannot be either affirmed or denied on the basis of the cases investigated. On other points, however, the facts observed in these cases shed some light. It should be made clear at this point that injunctions have played a very small part in the history of industrial relations in North Carolina and Virginia.

Government by injunction, as described above, was not found in any of the North Carolina and Virginia cases. No considerable police force has been placed at the disposal of the court in any of the cases. Two orders are directed against "all other persons" but the others restrain only the named defendants. The whole problem of injunctions used to prevent organization of employees who have signed individual anti-union "contracts" is not touched in these cases. While contempt proceedings were involved in the Tennessee case only, defendants in the other cases were found to have definite beliefs on the subject.

One of the most serious bases for criticism has been avoided to a very large extent in North Carolina by the unwillingness of the Supreme Court to apply the *conspiracy doctrine*. According to at least one authority, this is the heart of the whole controversy.[1] So far as these cases are concerned, the effectiveness of injunctions in "throttling" strikers does not seem to be very great. In the cases growing out of textile strikes the activities of the unions went forward very much as before. In the Marion case, where the injunction was not supplemented by the use of physical force, the parties enjoined paid practically no attention to it. In the Elizabethton, Tennessee, case *(Glanzstoff v. Miller)* military force was extensively

---

[1] A. T. Mason, *Organized Labor and the Law*, Introduction.

used but even then picketing continued. Outside the immediate vicinity of the plants involved, the combined force of the injunction and the militia had little effect. In the printing trades strikes we find more indications of some effect attributable to the injunction alone. But in one of these cases, as explained in Chapter V, the injunction had no effect on the outcome of the strike. In only one of the five cases did we find good reason to believe that the injunction had any material effect on the outcome of the strike. The injunction seems to have been most effective in reducing the force of the boycott. A trade unionist of long experience and considerable knowledge expressed the opinion that "strikes break themselves." By this he seems to have meant that strikes are sometimes called under conditions, especially economic conditions, which make their success impossible.

On the other hand, it should be made clear that present practice in issuing injunctions is peculiarly objectionable to trade unionists. Strikes depend for their success largely upon the ability of those who participate in them to make use of a strategic opportunity. Temporary restraining orders, issued without notice or hearing, may prohibit acts which are necessary for the effective prosecution of the strike. If these orders were confined to unlawful acts, the objection would not be important. But we have found that in all three North Carolina cases the temporary order imposed restraints which, upon hearing or appeal, were declared to be excessive or improper. In one case the Supreme Court found that no injunction should have issued. Some of the prohibitions contained in these orders, such as those prohibiting all picketing, might be the decisive factors in the success or failure of the strike, if literally obeyed. On this point our findings are in accord with the argument presented in Chapter IV.

The time which may elapse between the issuance of the *ex parte* order and the final disposition of the case is a matter of great practical significance. In the Tennessee case, the original order was issued March 13, 1929. The case was not heard by the Court of Civil Appeals until May 5, 1930. The reversal of the decision of the Chancellor by this court was of little more than academic interest. The issues involved in the strike had long since been settled. The only practical effect was that the court costs were levied upon the complainant instead of the defendants. The defendants claimed that they have been restrained for more than a year by the improper use of an injunction. In the case of *McGinnis v. Raleigh Typographical Union*, approximately three months elapsed between the issuance of the temporary restraining order and the decision of the Supreme Court which held that no injunction should have issued.

Reference has already been made to the fact that, in the absence of a statute on the subject, trial for contempt is without jury. The petition of counsel for defendants for jury trial was denied by the Chancellor in the case of *Glanzstoff v. Miller,* discussed in the preceding chapter. The strongest legal objection to allowing the judge to try cases for contempt of his own order is that he is really trying his own case. The judge is really a party to the action and therefore should not be allowed to try the case. A compromise, which would meet the legal objection, is to have contempts tried by another judge. However, this would not satisfy the trade unionists who are likely to be defendants in these cases. The light, if any, which the present study throws on this problem, is the evidence to show that the rank and file of trade union members interviewed in these cases were conscious of the absence of jury trial in contempt cases and protested bitterly against it.

The economic and social arguments against present equity practice in these cases are less definite than the legal objections. Because of this fact, an objective basis for testing them is more difficult. It is patent, however, that, at the present time, there is no adequate machinery for obtaining significant economic facts in industrial disputes.

It may be logically argued that, regardless of the underlying economic facts which brought about the controversy, striking employees have no right to use unlawful methods. But, as we have already indicated, the line which separates lawful and unlawful, in industrial disputes, has not been clearly defined by the decisions of equity courts. In view of this fact it would seem doubtful policy for the government to throw itself on one side of the conflict or the other without ascertaining facts which might be decisive on the question of the appropriateness of relief by injunction.

One possible effect of injunctions, which has not been emphasized in the literature of the subject, is that it tends to keep the disputants apart and delay settlement. This point was emphasized by the Executive Counsellor to the Governor in the case of Marion Manufacturing Company against the United Textile Workers. He went so far as to say that if the injunction had any effect on the controversy it was this effect. The same idea, in strikingly similar words, was expressed by Mr. Donald Richberg, counsel for the railway shop crafts in the case of *United States v. Railway Employees Department*.[2] Frequent reference to this point was made in the course of the interviews. Before condemning the injunction on this ground, we should seriously consider the argument for it. It has been contended, and demonstrated in some cases, that the union is dominated by a small group who happen to hold strategic positions and who indulge in grossly unlawful and oppressive practices. Negotiation has been refused on the ground that any recognition of these men or their organization, even for purposes of conciliation, would amount to an indorsement of their course of action. Here again the complexity of the problem is apparent. In criminal cases, such a condition cannot be assumed, even after formal indictment. It must be established by proof. The procedure for obtaining temporary restraining orders does not permit satisfactory proof of such a situation. Before proof of the anti-social character of the union or its leaders has been established, the court should hesitate to place obstacles in the way of a peaceful settlement.

In the discussion of Case IV, above, certain differences between the procedure in that case and the procedure in North Carolina cases were noted. It was indicated that the North Carolina cases showed greater strictness in safeguarding the rights of the parties enjoined. It may be noted that in the formative period of labor law in North Carolina, the Supreme Court was composed of men who were hesitant to apply loose historical doctrines in labor

[2] Personal letter dated March 8, 1928.

GENERAL SUMMARY AND CONCLUSIONS 141

cases. Evidence of this is found in the famous case of *State v. Van Pelt.*[3]

Our conclusions, as to the effects of the injunctions in the cases studied, have been stated in the preceding chapter. The cost of injunction proceedings has been mentioned. While considerable information on this point has been collected, most of it was confidential in character. However, it is certain that the cost of injunction proceedings is enormous. This is true of at least three of the cases included in the present study.

There remains the question of the amount of actual relief obtained by an injunction. Our findings in these cases indicate that this effect has been greatly exaggerated. To what extent are these findings confirmed by other available information? A few illustrations may be cited. In the case of *International Tailoring Company v. Hillman* (Unreported. See New York County Clerk's office, file number 29908 [1925]. Brissenden and Swayzee found conditions strikingly similar to those we found at Elizabethton.[4] "On occasions when great numbers were thrown into jail, the jails 'would ring with the songs of the Amalgamated.' The women, many of whom were arrested more than once, would return to the picket line as soon as they had been released."[5]

In the forty-eight cases in the New York needle trades, investigated by Brissenden and Swayzee, there were only three motions to punish for contempt and only one contempt case proved in court.[6]

---
[3] 136 N. C. 633, 49 S. E. 177 (1904).
[4] 45 *Political Science Quarterly* (March, 1930), 87, 98.
[5] *Ibid.* *Cf.* Chap. V, Case IV above: ". . . we would get arrested, get bail, and go out on picket again."
[6] 45 *Political Science Quarterly* (March, 1930), 101.

It has frequently been pointed out that an injunction from a court of equity does not physically prevent an unlawful act.[7] Dr. Witte has illustrated this by the case of *Coronado Coal Company v. United Mine Workers.* The acting attorney general, Honorable John W. Davis, who had recently been president of the American Bar Association, advised the United States Marshal that his deputies could not lawfully be used as strike guards. A leading stockholder wrote a letter to the Attorney-General to the effect that if such is the law then the injunction is not worth the paper it is written on.[8]

The testimony of Mr. Debs, that the injunction broke the Pullman strike of 1894, has frequently been quoted. Careful investigation, however, has shown that the strike was broken by military force.[9] The following excerpts are taken from a telegram sent to the Attorney-General by the United States Marshal on duty at the strike:

"I read the injunction writ to this mob and commanded them to disperse. The reading of the writ met with no response, except jeers and hoots. Shortly after, the mob threw a number of baggage cars across the track, since when no mail trains have been able to move.

"I am unable to disperse the mob, clear the tracks, or arrest the men who were engaged in the acts named...."[10]

These cases illustrate clearly the danger of purely deductive reasoning. One may start with the premise that a majority of the people are law-abiding. The injunction

---

[7] See 16 *Harvard Law Review,* 400-1.
[8] 32 *Journal of Political Economy* (June, 1924), 335.
[9] See Frankfurter and Greene, *op. cit.,* pp. 17-19 especially n. 71, p. 17.
[10] Report of the Attorney General, 1894, p. xxxiii. Quoted by Frankfurter and Greene, n. 71, p. 17.

notifies them that it is unlawful to picket. Therefore they will stop picketing. On a similar basis of reasoning, practically all drivers of motor vehicles would come to a full stop at all railway crossings in the state of North Carolina. In actual practice, very few pay any attention to the law. Two important practical questions are involved. Is there a strong incentive for violating the law or the injunction? Is there enforcement machinery which makes punishment for violation certain? In the case of an injunction which orders striking workers to stop picketing when their jobs are about to be taken away from them, there is a very strong incentive for violating the order. If the injunction is not backed by adequate enforcement machinery, we are likely to find widespread violation. This is especially true if the order of the court is not supported by public opinion. A good police force can keep order without an injunction. The reverse does not appear to be true in these cases.

It is obvious that an injunction, if used without an extra police force, would be less expensive and less disturbing to the community than the militia, if it gave genuine relief. But our findings suggest that an injunction is likely to increase the need for the militia rather than *diminish* it. The real problem is to make both unnecessary.

While diagnosis is the primary purpose of this work, a few remedies may be suggested. Much could be accomplished within the present system by the reform of procedure, especially by narrowly restricting or abolishing *ex parte* orders.[11] The practice of throwing the force of the state on one side of a controversy before hearing the other

[11] For a thorough discussion of remedies, see Frankfurter and Greene, *op. cit.*, chap. V, and Appendix IX. For the recent Wisconsin Act on this subject see Appendix XXVIII.

is a poor compromise between compulsory arbitration and a hands-off policy. In some jurisdictions, the need of a more expeditious appeal is apparent. The indefiniteness and uncertainty of the law underlying injunctions could be reduced by the adoption of an industrial code.

Much dissatisfaction and unrest could be avoided by allowing jury trials in indirect contempt cases. This plan has been favored by a number of students of the subject including former Chief Justice Clark of the North Carolina Supreme Court.

Under a system which frankly recognizes the supremacy of the judiciary, the personnel of our courts is of great importance. Means should be adopted to assure the selection of judges with social vision as well as an accurate knowledge of the law.

Most important of all is a new attitude on the part of the disputants. So long as one side or the other prefers war to peace, undesirable conditions will continue. A conciliatory spirit on both sides, coupled with an organized plan for putting this spirit into operation, would go a long way toward solving the problem. There is great need for the "mutual confidence, forbearance, patience and concession, accompanied by a free, frank interchange of thought and feeling" which was advocated by the Supreme Court of North Carolina in 1904.[12]

[12] State v. Van Pelt, 136 N. C. 633, 49 S. E. 177 (1904).

APPENDIX I

LIMITING THE JURISDICTION OF EQUITY COURTS

71st CONGRESS
2d Session S. 2497

IN THE SENATE OF THE UNITED STATES

December 4 (calendar day, December 9), 1929
Mr. Shipstead introduced the following bill; which was read twice and referred to the Committee on the Judiciary

---

A BILL

To amend the Judicial Code and to define and limit the jurisdiction of courts sitting in equity, and for other purposes.

Be it enacted by the Senate and House of Representatives of the United States of America in Congress assembled, That chapter 2 of an Act entitled "An Act to codify, revise, and amend the laws relating to the Judiciary," approved March 3, 1911, be amended by adding thereto the following:

"SEC. 28. Equity courts shall have jurisdiction to protect property against irreparable injury arising from definite destructive action, when there is no remedy at law; for the purpose of determining such jurisdiction the expression 'remedy at law' shall be held to be any remedy, criminal or civil, provided by legislation, and nothing shall be held to be property unless it is exclusive, tangible, and transferable; and section 4 of the Antitrust Act of 1890, together with all amendments thereof and all laws and parts of laws inconsistent herewith, are hereby repealed."

SENATE SUBSTITUTE FOR SHIPSTEAD BILL[1]

May 19, 1930

71st CONGRESS
2d Session   S. 2497

IN THE SENATE OF THE UNITED STATES

A Bill to amend the Judicial Code and to define and limit the jurisdiction of courts sitting in equity, and for other purposes.

Be it enacted by the Senate and House of Representatives of the United States of America in Congress assembled,

Section 1. That no court of the United States as herein defined, shall have jurisdiction to issue any restraining order or temporary or permanent injunction in a case involving or growing out of a labor dispute, except in strict conformity with the provisions of this Act; nor shall any such restraining order or temporary or permanent injunction be issued contrary to the public policy declared in this Act.

Sec. 2. In the interpretation of this Act and in determining the jurisdiction and authority of the courts of the

---

[1] The best discussion of this proposal is Frankfurter and Greene, "Congressional Power over the Labor Injunction," 31 Col. L. Rev. 385 (1931).

United States, as such jurisdiction and authority are herein defined and limited, the public policy of the United States is hereby declared as follows:

Whereas under prevailing economic conditions, developed with the aid of governmental authority for owners of property to organize in the corporate and other forms of ownership association, the individual unorganized worker is commonly helpless to exercise actual liberty of contract and to protect his freedom of labor, and thereby to obtain acceptable terms and conditions of employment, wherefore it is necessary that he have full freedom of association, self-organization, and designation of representatives of his own choosing, to negotiate the terms and conditions of his employment, and that he shall be free from the interference, restraint, or coercion of employers of labor, or their agents, in the designation of such representatives or in self-organization or in other concerted activities for the purpose of collective bargaining or other mutual aid or protection; therefore, the following definitions of, and limitations upon, the jurisdiction and authority of the courts of the United States are hereby enacted.

Sec. 3. Any undertaking or promise, such as is described in this section, or any other undertaking or promise in conflict with the public policy declared in section 2 of this Act, is hereby declared to be contrary to the public policy of the United States, shall not be enforceable and shall not afford any basis for the granting of legal or equitable relief by any court of the United States, including specifically the following:

Every undertaking or promise hereafter made, whether written or oral, express or implied, constituting or contained in any contract or agreement of hiring or employment between any individual, firm, company, association, or corporation, and any employee or prospective employee of the same, whereby—

(a) Either party to such contract or agreement undertakes or promises not to join, become, or remain a member of any labor organization or of any employer organization; or

(b) Either party to such contract or agreement undertakes or promises that he will withdraw from an employment relation in the event that he joins, becomes, or remains a member of any labor organization or of any employer organization.

Sec. 4. No court of the United States shall have jurisdiction to issue any restraining order or temporary or permanent injunction in cases involving or growing out of any labor dispute to prohibit any person or persons participating or interested in such dispute (as these terms are herein defined) from doing, whether singly or in concert, any of the following acts:

(a) Ceasing or refusing to perform any work or to remain in any relation of employment;

(b) Becoming or remaining a member of any labor organization or of any employer organization regardless of any such undertaking or promise as is described in section 3 of this Act;

(c) Paying or giving to, or withholding from, any person participating or interested in such labor dispute any strike or unemployment benefits or insurance or other moneys or things of value;

(d) By all lawful means aiding any person participating or interested in any labor dispute who is being proceeded against in, or is prosecuting, any action or suit in any court of the United States or of any State;

(e) Giving publicity to the existence of, or the facts involved in, any labor dispute [whether by advertising, speaking, patrolling, or by any other method not involving fraud or violence];[2]

(f) Assembling peaceably to act or to organize to act in promotion of their interests in a labor dispute;

(g) Advising or notifying any person of an intention to do any of the acts heretofore specified;

(h) Agreeing with other persons to do or not to do any of the acts heretofore specified; and

(i) Advising, urging, [or otherwise causing] or inducing without threat, fraud, or violence the acts heretofore specified, regardless of any such undertaking or promise as is described in section 3 of this Act.

Sec. 5. No court of the United States shall have jurisdiction to issue a restraining order or temporary or permanent injunction upon the ground that any of the persons participating or interested in a labor dispute constitute or are engaged in an unlawful combination or conspiracy because of the doing in concert of the acts enumerated in section 4 of this Act.

Sec. 6. No officer or member of any association or organization, and no association or organization participating or interested in a labor dispute, shall be held responsible or liable in any court of the United States for the unlawful acts of individual officers, members, or agents, except upon clear proof of actual participation in,

[2] Matter in brackets proposed to be omitted.

or actual authorization of, such acts, or of ratification of such acts after actual knowledge thereof.

Sec. 7. No court of the United States shall have jurisdiction to issue a temporary or permanent injunction in any case involving or growing out of a labor dispute, as herein defined, except after hearing the testimony of witnesses in open court (with opportunity for cross-examination) in support of the allegations of a complaint made under oath, and testimony in opposition thereto, if offered, and except after findings of fact by the court, to the effect—

(a) That unlawful acts have been threatened or committed and will be executed or continued unless restrained;

(b) That substantial and irreparable injury to complainant's property will follow;

(c) That as to each item of relief granted greater injury will be inflicted upon complainant by the denial of relief than will be inflicted upon defendants by the granting of relief;

(d) That complainant has no adequate remedy at law; and

(e) That the public officers charged with the duty to protect complainant's property have failed or are unable [or unwilling] to furnish adequate protection.

Such hearing shall be held after due and personal notice thereof has been given, in such manner as the court shall direct, to all known persons against whom relief is sought, and also to those public officers charged with the duty to protect complainant's property: Provided, however, that if a complainant shall also allege that unless a temporary restraining order shall be issued without notice, a substantial and irreparable injury to complainant's property will be unavoidable, such a temporary restraining order may be issued upon testimony under oath, sufficient, if sustained, to justify the court in issuing a temporary injunction upon a hearing after notice. Such a temporary restraining order shall be effective for no longer than five days, and shall become void at the expiration of said five days. No temporary restraining order or temporary injunction shall be issued except on condition that complainant shall first file an undertaking with adequate security sufficient to recompense those enjoined for any loss, expense, or damage caused by the improvident or erroneous issuance of such order or injunction, including all reasonable costs (together with a reasonable attorney's fee) and expense of defense against the order or against the granting of any injunctive relief sought in the same proceeding and subsequently denied by the court.

This undertaking herein mentioned shall be understood to signify an agreement entered into by the complainant and the surety upon which a decree may be rendered in the same suit or proceeding against said complainant and surety, the said complainant and surety submitting themselves to the jurisdiction of the court for that purpose. But nothing herein contained shall deprive any party having a claim or cause of action under or upon such undertaking from electing to pursue his ordinary remedy by suit at law or in equity.

Sec. 8. No restraining order or injunctive relief shall be granted to any complainant who has failed to comply with any obligation imposed by law which is involved in the labor dispute in question, or who has failed to make every reasonable effort to settle such dispute either by negotiation or with the aid of any available governmental machinery of mediation or voluntary arbitration, but nothing herein contained shall be deemed to require the court to await the action of any such tribunal if irreparable injury is threatened.

Sec. 9. No restraining order or temporary or permanent injunction shall be granted in a case involving or growing out of a labor dispute, except on the basis of findings of fact made and filed by the court in the record of the case prior to the issuance of such restraining order or injunction; and every restraining order or injunction granted in a case involving or growing out of a labor dispute shall include only a prohibition of such specific act or acts as may be expressly complained of in the bill of complaint or petition filed in such case and as shall be expressly included in said findings of fact made and filed by the court as provided herein.

Sec. 10. Whenever any court of the United States shall issue or deny any temporary injunction in a case involving or growing out of a labor dispute, the court shall, upon the request of any party to the proceedings, and on his filing the usual bond for the costs, forthwith certify the entire record of the case, including a transcript of the evidence taken, to the circuit court of appeals for its review. Upon the filing of such record in the circuit court of appeals the appeal shall be heard [and temporary injunctive order affirmed, modified, or set aside] with the greatest possible expedition, giving the proceeding precedence over all other matters except older matters of the same character.

Sec. 11. In all cases where a person shall be charged with indirect criminal contempt for violation of a restraining order or injunction issued by a court of the United States (as herein defined), the accused shall enjoy, upon demand, the right to a speedy and public trial by an impartial jury of the State and district wherein the contempt shall have been committed: Provided, That this requirement shall not be construed to apply to contempt committed in the presence of the court or so near thereto as to interfere directly with the administration of justice or to apply to the misbehavior, misconduct, or disobedience of any officer of the court in respect to the writs, orders, or process of the court.

Sec. 12. The defendant in any proceeding for contempt of court is authorized to file with the court a demand for the retirement of the judge sitting in the proceeding, if the contempt arises from an attack upon the character or conduct of such judge and if the attack occurred otherwise than in open court. Upon the filing of any such demand the judge shall thereupon proceed no further, but another judge shall be designated in the same manner as provided in case of the approval of an affidavit of personal bias or prejudice under section 21 of the Judicial Code. The demand shall be filed prior to the hearing in the contempt proceeding.

Sec. 13. When used in this Act, and for the purposes of this Act—

(a) A case shall be held to involve or to grow out of a labor dispute when the case involves persons who are engaged in the same industry, trade, craft, or occupation; [or have direct or indirect interests therein;] or who are employees of the same employer; or who are members of the same or an affiliated organization of employers or employees; whether such dispute is (1) between one or more employers or associations of employers and one or more employees or associations of employees; (2) between one or more employers or associations of employers and one or more employers or associations of employers; or (3) between one or more employees or associations of employees and one or more employees or associations of employees; or when the case involves any conflicting or competing interests in a "labor dispute" (as hereinafter defined) of "persons participating or interested" therein (as hereinafter defined).

(b) A person or association shall be held to be a person participating or interested in a labor dispute if relief is sought against him or it and if he or it is engaged in the same industry, trade, craft, or occupation in which such dispute occurs, [or has a direct or indirect interest therein,] or is a member, officer, or agent of any association of employers or employees engaged in such industry, trade, craft, or occupation.

(c) The term "labor dispute" includes any controversy concerning terms or conditions of employment, or concerning the association or representation of persons in negotiating, fixing, maintaining, changing, or seeking to arrange terms [and] or conditions of employment, or concerning employment relations, or any other controversy arising out of the respective interests of employer and employee, regardless of whether or not the disputants stand in the proximate relation of employer and employee.

(d) The term "court of the United States" means any court of the United States whose jurisdiction has been or may be conferred or defined or limited by Act of Congress, including the courts of the District of Columbia.

Sec. 14. If any provision of this Act or the application thereof to any person or circumstance is held invalid, the remainder of the Act and the application of such provisions to other persons or circumstances shall not be affected thereby.

Sec. 15. All Acts and parts of Acts in conflict with the provisions of this Act are hereby repealed.

APPENDIX II

Number 252   Seventh District

MARGUERITE McGINNIS AND OTHERS

against

RALEIGH TYPOGRAPHICAL UNION, NUMBER 54, AND OTHERS

Complaint and Affidavit

The plaintiffs above named, complaining of the defendants above named, allege:

First. That the individual complainants above named are residents and citizens of the State of North Carolina and are all engaged in doing work for the printing houses above named in the city of Raleigh, North Carolina.

Second. That the printing houses above named are all corporations organized under the laws of the State of North Carolina, with their principal places of business in the city of Raleigh, North Carolina, with the exception of M. J. Carroll & Son, which is a co-partnership, engaged in the printing business in the city of Raleigh, North Carolina.

Third. That the Raleigh Typographical Union, the Raleigh Printing Pressmen's Union and Raleigh Bookbinders Union are labor Unions with headquarters in the city of Raleigh, North Carolina, and the individual defendants above named are officers and members of said unions.

Fourth. The individual complainants above named, in behalf of themselves and all other employees of the several printing houses above named, respectfully show unto the Court:

(1) That the labor unions above named and their officers, members and associates above named have entered into a conspiracy to drive these individual complainants from their positions as employees of the several printing houses above named, and to make it impossible for these complainants to work and live in peace in the city of Raleigh while they are engaged in their present employment.

(2) That these individual complainants have done the defendants no wrong and the said defendants have no grievance of any kind against these complainants. Some time in May 1921, the unions above named demanded of the printing houses above named (which were then running as closed shops) that the number of hours for a week's work be reduced from forty-eight to forty-four. Upon the refusal of the printing companies to accede to this demand, the members of the several labor unions above named quit work and went on what is popularly known as a "strike." The printing companies offered in writing to submit all differences between themselves and their employees and the unions to an impartial board of arbitration, but this proposition was summarily rejected by the unions. Thereupon, the printing companies gave notice that they would be compelled to run their shops with whatever labor they might be able to obtain, whether the laborers belonged to a printers' union or not, but also gave notice that the jobs of all former employees would be open to them if they returned within a given time. The defendants above named refused to return to work and

have since then been making war on the printing houses and their employees.

(3) That in pursuance of the plan, purpose and conspiracy mentioned in sub-section 1 above, the defendants have devised and are executing a systematic course of espionage, annoyance, intimidation, threats, abuse and insults which are intended to make, are calculated to make, and are making the lives of these complainants and all other employees of the several printing houses above mentioned miserable, intolerable and unendurable, and unless the defendants are compelled to desist from such conduct these complainants will be forced to give up their jobs and become objects of charity or else leave the city of Raleigh to seek employment elsewhere, and these complainants allege that they are informed and believe that it is well nigh impossible for one who loses his job to obtain another in the present economic condition of the country.

(4) In pursuance of said plan, purpose and conspiracy, the said defendants *(a)* gather in large numbers around the places of business where complainants are employed, and when complainants finish their day's work and emerge from their places of employment, the defendants indulge in threatening gestures, insulting jeers and hisses, and in many ways annoy, disturb, humiliate and put in fear these complainants. *(b)* After complainants leave their several places of employment, the defendants constantly "shadow" them. As soon as complainants leave their work, two or more of the defendants will trail them wherever they go. On the streets, in the stores, to their homes, to their work, in the day, in the night, always and everywhere they are pursued and persecuted by these de-

fendants, sometimes with abusive language, sometimes with threats, sometimes in such numbers as to cause complainants to fear for their lives. *(c)* The defendants whenever and wherever they can find one or more of these complainants surround them and by words and gestures humiliate them and put them in fear. *(d)* The said defendants constantly and systematically call these complainants insulting names, such as rats, scabs, runts, Bowery bums, and other epithets calculated to humiliate and distress, and which do humiliate and distress these complainants, and have a tendency to bring on breaches of the peace, and but for the forbearance of these complainants bloodshed and probable loss of life would result. *(e)* Said defendants are constantly and systematically threatening these complainants by saying in their presence: "We'll get them yet." "There are plenty of us to do it." "They had better not let us catch them walking home." "We will break his damn neck." "If this thing goes on, I will be in the penitentiary soon," meaning that they would perpetrate some crime against these complainants. *(f)* The young girls above mentioned as complainants are not free from the insult and abuse set forth above but have been subjected by the defendants to all sorts of embarrassment and humiliation. As they pass along the streets they are jeered and hissed and scraped at and called "kitty-cat." In the drug stores they are sneered at and called cats. In the picture-shows they are disturbed and annoyed. They are yelled at by defendants when they are a block away. They are shadowed and pursued as they pass along the streets, and unless they are afforded protection they will be compelled to leave the city of Raleigh.

Fifth. This course of conduct has been so persistently and relentlessly pursued by the defendants that already more than one hundred employees of the printing houses above named have been literally driven from their work and been forced to leave the city.

Sixth. These individual complainants have no object or purpose in bringing this action other than to secure for themselves and all their associates the right to work and live in peace, as free American citizens, desirous of the privilege of doing an honest day's work for a fair day's pay, and to this end they invoke the protection of the law.

Seventh. The printing houses above named complain and allege:

(1) That they have read the complaint of their employees, and from observation and reliable information they know the same to be true.

(2) That the defendants above named have planned and conspired to destroy the business of these printing companies for no other reason than they decline to accede to the unreasonable and unrighteous demands of the labor unions and are now exercising the right of every American citizen to run their business on the American plan and to give employment to any man who applies for the same, this right being odious to and utterly denied by the defendants herein.

(3) In furtherance of their said plan, purpose and conspiracy to utterly destroy the business of these complainants, the defendants have gathered in large numbers in front of and near the places of business of these complain-

ants, have used threatening words and gestures, have threatened to kill the officers and relatives and employees of these complainants, have pursued and taunted and hissed and jeered the employees of these complainants, and have endeavored to render burdensome and intolerable the life of every man and woman who dares to work in the employ of these complainants.

(4) In further pursuance of said plan, purpose and conspiracy to utterly destroy the business of these complainants, the said defendants have induced and bribed many of the employees of complainants to break their contracts that they have made to work for these complainants.

(5) In further pursuance of said plan, purpose and conspiracy to destroy the business of these complainants, the defendants have literally driven, by threats, annoyances, pursuits, and a relentless policy of "hell-hackling" more than one hundred employees of these complainants from their jobs and away from the city of Raleigh.

The complainants have this day commenced a civil action against the defendants in the Superior Court of Wake County for the purpose of obtaining a perpetual injunction, and summons has been issued therein.

Wherefore, these complainants pray the Court that an injunction be issued against the labor unions above named and against all officers, members, aiders, abettors, and associates, compelling them to desist from indulging in any of the conduct set forth above, and to leave these complainants free to work and to carry on their business without molestation or annoyance of any kind.

T. W. BICKETT,
Attorney for Plaintiffs.

NORTH CAROLINA—WAKE COUNTY.

O. R. Moore, an employee of Edwards & Broughton Printing Company, Robert Hall, an employee of Commercial Printing Company, R. H. Bryan, an employee of H. S. Storr Company, Charles Lee Smith, president of Edwards & Broughton Printing Company, Robert J. Wilson, business manager of Commercial Printing Company, V. C. Moore, vice-president of H. S. Storr Company, and M. J. Carroll . . . of M. J. Carroll & Son, each for himself being duly sworn, says that the foregoing complaint and affidavit is true of his own knowledge, except as to such matters stated therein on information and belief, and as to such matters he believes it to be true.

>O. R. MOORE
>ROBERT H. HALL
>R. H. BRYAN
>CHARLES LEE SMITH
>ROBERT J. WILSON
>V. C. MOORE.

Subscribed and sworn to before me, this 18th day of August, 1921.
[Seal]
>BESSIE C. WHEELER,
>Notary Public.

My commission expires January 18, 1923.

APPENDIX III
McGINNIS ET AL. V.
RALEIGH TYPOGRAPHICAL UNION ET AL.

Restraining Order

This cause coming on to be heard before me at chambers in Smithfield, North Carolina, on the 18th day of August, 1921, on the application of the plaintiffs herein for a temporary injunction, and it appearing from the complaint that the plaintiffs are entitled to the relief demanded and that the acts and conduct complained of would work irreparable injury to the plaintiffs if allowed to continue pending the litigation, it is considered, ordered and adjudged by the Court that defendants be notified to appear before the Honorable W. M. Bond, judge holding the courts of the Seventh Judicial District, at Raleigh, North Carolina, on Saturday, the third day of September, 1921, at two o'clock P.M., and show cause where the injunction herein prayed for should not be granted until the final hearing of this cause.

In the meantime, upon the plaintiffs giving bond in the sum of two hundred dollars, the Clerk of the Superior Court of Wake County shall issue a restraining order requiring each and every one of the defendants named in the complaint to refrain from:

1. Assembling in large numbers before or near the places of business of the complainants or any of them and engaging in any conduct or using any words or gestures calculated to annoy, disturb or intimidate any of the complainants herein, whether employers or employees, and to

prevent them from going about their work with a quiet mind;

2. From "shadowing," pursuing or following after the complaining employees or any of the officers of the complaining printing companies as they move from place to place in the city of Raleigh, from dogging the steps, surrounding the complainants, or any of them;

3. From calling the complaining employees rats, scabs, runts, Bowery bums, or any other names, or from intimidating, disturbing or annoying the complainants in any way;

4. From following after the complaining employees of the printing companies for the purpose of worrying, harassing or disturbing them, or for the purpose of talking to them on the subject of their employment if said employees shall notify the defendants that they do not wish to be talked to on this subject;

5. From using any threats, gestures, or from engaging in any conduct of any kind calculated to disturb, annoy or put in fear any of the complainants herein;

6. From following after the complaining employees or any other employees of the complaining printing companies for the purpose of inducing them to break their contracts to work for the printing companies after they have been informed by such employees that they have made contracts with the printing companies and do not desire to break them.

(Signed) E. H. CRANMER,
Judge holding the Courts of the
Fourth Judicial District.

Bond of $200.00 given by
 Edwards & Broughton Printing Company,
 by Charles Lee Smith, President.
  Robert J. Wilson, Surety.
Filed August 19th, 1921.

APPENDIX IV

McGINNIS ET AL. V.
RALEIGH TYPOGRAPHICAL UNION ET AL.

Judgment

North Carolina } In the Superior Court
Wake County

Marguerite McGinnis, Rosa McGinnis, Dorothy Tomlinson and others, vs. Raleigh Typographical Union, Number 54; Raleigh Printing Pressmen's Union, Number 120; Raleigh Bookbinders' Union, Charles H. Jones, C. F. Koonce, and others.

This cause coming on to be heard at Raleigh, North Carolina, on September 3rd, 1921, on motion of plaintiffs to continue restraining order to the hearing, both sides having filed affidavits and being represented by counsel, defendants moved to dismiss the action as to the defendants, Labor Unions, upon the ground that they are not corporations, which motion the Court overruled and defendants excepted; and certain of the defendants moved to dismiss the action as to them for that they were minors, which motion the Court overruled and said minors excepted, and the demurrer in the record being filed and overruled by the Court and exception noted, after hearing the evidence and argument, it is adjudged, ordered and decreed as to each and all defendants properly before the Court as follows:

Said defendants, their agents, associates and abettors are forbidden to and restrained from:

1. Assembling in large numbers before or near the places of business of the complainants or any of them and engaging in any conduct or using any words or gestures calculated to annoy, disturb or intimidate any of the complainants herein, whether employers or employees, and to prevent them from going about their work with a quiet mind;

2. From "shadowing," pursuing or following after the complaining employees or any of the officers of the complaining printing companies as they move from place to place in the city of Raleigh, from dogging the steps, surrounding the complainants or any of them;

3. From calling the complaining employees rats, scabs, runts, Bowery bums, or any other insulting names, or from intimidating, disturbing or annoying the complainants in any way;

4. From following after the complaining employees or any other employees of the printing companies for the purpose of worrying, harassing or disturbing them, or for the purpose of talking to them on the subject of their employment if said employees shall notify the defendants that they do not want to be talked to on this subject;

5. From using any threats, gestures or engaging in any conduct of any kind calculated to disturb, annoy or put in fear any of the complainants herein;

6. From following after the complaining employees or any other employees of the complaining printing companies for the purpose of inducing them to break their contracts to work for the printing companies after they have been informed by such employees that they have

made contracts with the printing companies and do not desire to break them.

That the restraining order issued in this cause, as modified herein, is continued to the hearing.

W. M. BOND,
Judge holding the Courts of the
Seventh Judicial District.

September 3rd, 1921.

To this judgment defendants except at the time of its rendition and appeal to the Supreme Court; notice in open court, further notice waived; appeal bond fixed at $100.00. The pleadings, restraining order, affidavits, motions and judgment to constitute case on appeal for Supreme Court.

W. M. BOND, Judge.

September 3rd, 1921.

To the foregoing judgment the defendants except.
This is the defendants' EIGHTH EXCEPTION.

R. N. SIMMS,
DOUGLASS & DOUGLASS,
EVANS & EASON,
Attorneys for Defendants.

APPENDIX V
ARGUMENT OF COUNSEL FOR PLAINTIFFS

North Carolina }
Wake County } In the Superior Court

Marguerite McGinnis and others
vs.
Raleigh Typographical Union and others.

Ex-Governor T. W. Bickett, of Raleigh, was of counsel for the plaintiffs seeking the injunction, and the following is a synopsis of his argument made before Judge Bond:

When this case was called this morning, your Honor said it was the duty of all good men to do everything possible to decrease rather than increase irritation between different classes of our citizens. I am in hearty accord with that statement. The man who stirs up strife between the white man and the black man, between the man who lives in the country and the man who lives in the town, between the man who works with his head and the man who works with his hands, is an enemy to the peace and prosperity of us all.

Differences can never be permanently settled until each side to the controversy arrives at an intelligent and sympathetic understanding of the other side. My heart's desire is, and my hope is, that my remarks here tonight may contribute something to such an understanding. Every beat of my heart is kindly towards the men who are dependent upon their daily work for their daily bread.

... I am deeply and irrevocably in sympathy with the aspirations of working men to better their condition by pooling their resources. ...

But the surest way to lose a right is to abuse it. ...

Two years ago we had in this city a flourishing carpenters' union. Today we hear nothing of it. No outside hand wrought its destruction. It committed suicide. It built up and imposed upon the public a system of tyrannies and extortions, and places that knew it once know it no more forever. The printing unions have started down the same broad road, and unless they halt, or are halted, a like fate awaits them.

... I weigh my words when I say there is not a single fact in the economic world upon which this strike can stand. Every wind and tide in human affairs is against it. The wages of the tillers of the soil went down 400 per cent when cotton plunged from 42 to 10c., and tobacco from 50 to 8c. a pound. The workers in the cotton mills voted upon themselves or cheerfully accepted wage reductions from 25 to 33 per cent., and complained only when the employers cut the wage 60 per cent. The merchants are everywhere marking down the prices of their goods, the whole world is in the grip of the worst financial depression ever known. The grim and ghastly spectre of bankruptcy stalks through the land, and every man trembles lest it knock at his door. In the face of all this distress and disaster, although they were getting the highest wages ever paid their craft in all the world's history, they "struck" for less work and more pay. I repeat that this strike is the unlovely and abortive child of autocracy and greed, and was born to die.

In the beginning, they struck for four hours less work per week and $12.00 more pay. This was the complexion of the baby on the day it was born. Finding that they were up against a stone wall, they abandoned the claim for more pay per hour, but insisted on making forty-four hours the standard week's work, with "time and a-half for over time." The employers offered in writing to submit all differences to the arbitration of an impartial board, and back came the world-old reply of the autocrat: "There is nothing to arbitrate."

But a man has a legal right to quit work for a bad reason, or for no reason at all. But when he does quit, he has no sort of right, legal or moral, to make everybody else quit.

This case is something new under the sun. For the first time in legal history a band of working men come into a court of equity and pray for protection in their right to work. Heretofore injunctions have been sought by capital against labor; here labor, at work, begs for protection from labor that is idle. Therefore, the one big and burning question in this case is, has a man who wants to work in North Carolina the right to do so with a quiet mind? Let us not get away from that, your Honor: has a man, who is able and willing to work, the right to do so, and be at peace?

. . . .

The defendants in this case believe in their hearts, and have been acting on that belief, that no man has a right to work in a print shop in Raleigh without their permission.

I have said that labor has a right to organize, the right to sell its skill and energy collectively in open market. For that right I will fight with organized labor to the last ditch. But I will turn and fight against it just as hard when it dares to say that the humblest non-union worker in all the land hasn't as much right to sell his labor to whom and for what he may see fit, as a union whose membership girdles the earth. The right to work is as sacred as the right to worship and the law is quick and powerful to protect this right.

. . . .

The point that I am trying to burn into the conscience of the court is that a man has a God-given right to work, a right that can neither be denied or impaired by his refusal to join any organization.

. . . When organized labor says a man shall not work unless he belongs to a union, it puts it into the mouth of capital to say that a man shall not work if he *does* belong to a union. Both propositions are bastards, outside the blood of the covenant in a republic founded on equal and exact justice to all and special privileges to none.

. . . .

I regret the necessity for taxing your Honor's strength in such killing weather as this, but I congratulate you upon the opportunity before you to render your generation an immortal service. I have an unclouded faith that the judgment of your Honor will be a ringing proclamation that in this dear State the humblest citizen can go to his work in the blessed assurance that none will dare to molest or make him afraid.

T. W. BICKETT
Counsel for Plaintiffs.

APPENDIX VI

McGINNIS V. RALEIGH TYPOGRAPHICAL UNION

Interview With Dr. Charles Lee Smith, President, Edwards and Broughton Printing Company.

Q. Did the injunction have any effect on the strike in this case?

A. Yes, the injunction had the desired effect. After it was secured, our employees could come and go without being molested. The injunction had accomplished its principal purpose before the Supreme Court Decision. It caused the strikers to come to the conclusion that they could not use terroristic methods. It probably forestalled violence and brought the strike to an end sooner.

Q. Was the injunction better than the criminal law for dealing with this situation?

A. Yes. It would have been hard to find the guilty ones after the acts of violence had occurred.

Q. Had the strikers been guilty of all the acts enjoined in the temporary restraining order?

A. (Looking at copy of order)
  (1) Assembling in front of our place of business? Yes.
  (2) Shadowing our employees? Yes.
  (3) Calling our employees "rats" and "scabs"? Yes.
  (4) Harassing our employees? Yes.
  (5) Threatening and annoying our employees? Yes.
  (6) Trying to induce our employees to break their

contracts? Yes. They had been doing all these things.

Q. Did these things stop after the injunction was served?

A. They stopped assembling out in front here. The shadowing was not so marked afterward. The use of epithets did not continue to any marked degree. It was less open afterward. It stopped them from harassing our employees. It stopped them from threatening our employees. They still tried to get our men to leave but they did it in a more genteel manner.

(Signed)   CHARLES LEE SMITH.

APPENDIX VII
EXCERPTS FROM BRIEF OF DEFENDANTS, APPELLANTS*

Marguerite McGinnis *et al.*
        against } From Wake
Raleigh Typographical Union No. 54, *et al.*

So far as we can learn, this Court in passing upon this question is in new ground. Never before in the history of the State has an employer resorted to an injunction to fight a strike of his employees; and never before have our courts been asked to restrain acts of individuals which ordinarily, and in every other field save a strike zone, have been considered harmless. . . .

They (the complainants) complain of irremediable injury without showing wherein they have not a remedy for every wrong alleged. The courts of the State have been open, and while the plaintiffs complain of threats, no peace warrants have been issued; they allege assaults, and no indictments have been asked. They allege disorderly conduct, and yet the police department of the city has never been called upon to suppress it. Complaints that have been made were found by the officers to be without foundation. See affidavit of A. E. Glenn, chief of police, page 37 of the record.

. . . .

As heretofore stated, the use of the injunction in labor

* Supreme Court of North Carolina. *Records and Briefs* Fall Term, 1921, No. 252, Seventh Judicial District. Pages 3-9 of the Brief.

disputes is a new thing in North Carolina. That it has made advance in other states of the Union we do not deny; but the principles and remedies of equity applied to the restraint of epithets, abuse, threats and the like, even in the jurisdictions which have gone to the farthest lengths, are only said to be applicable when the Court finds as a fact that force, fraud or actual intimidation has been practiced. And no such facts are found or could justifiably be found, in the case at bar.

... Our constitution has guaranteed the citizen a trial by jury and equal protection of the laws.

These constitutional guaranties ... are not to be swept aside by an equitable invention which would turn crime into contempt, and enable a judge to declare innocent acts a crime and punish them at his discretion.

... This court ... has declared that abusive language is of itself not an assault. But under this judgment the use of the term 'Kitty Cat' addressed to some of the complaining parties would subject the guilty party to contempt proceedings to answer for an act not otherwise criminal except through the injunction process, and to be tried therefor without a jury, with a possibility of being fined or imprisoned more largely than could be inflicted in a criminal case.

The plaintiffs have attempted to justify a misjoinder of parties and causes of action by alleging, in a general way, a conspiracy among the members of the several unions, and have thereby attempted to allege facts sufficient to constitute a cause of action.

A careful perusal of the record will disclose that there are not sufficient facts appearing in the affidavits to support the broadside charges of "threats, intimidation, and insults" appearing in the complaint. Such charges are but mere conclusions; they are not concise statements of fact. The specific overt acts complained of are attributable to the conduct of a few minors—boys and girls.

When the great mass of generalities and conclusions are dissected from the complaint and affidavits of the plaintiffs, and the action dismissed as to the unions as such and as to the minors referred to—as it should be—the remaining specific allegations of overt acts and statements are wholly insufficient to invoke the injunctive power of the Court.

... the plaintiffs did not offer any affidavit as to the alleged conclusion of conspiracy, unless the allegations of overt acts on the part of the minors and a very few isolated acts on the part of three or four persons—who happened to be members of the unions—should be found sufficient, which we earnestly insist is insufficient.

Surely the allegations and proof should be as specific in an effort to invoke the injunctive power of the court as that required for the issuance of an ordinary peace-warrant. The affidavit in obtaining such warrant which states a mere conclusion, i.e. fear of death or great bodily harm, is insufficient. The facts should be specifically alleged in order that the Court may determine whether a person of reasonable prudence would entertain such fear, and whether such charges are well founded. ...

We earnestly contend that the order of his Honor should be revised.

Respectfully submitted,

EVANS & EASON

R. N. SIMMS

CHARLES U. HARRIS

DOUGLASS & DOUGLASS

Attorneys for Defendants.

SUPPLEMENTAL BRIEF FOR DEFENDANTS, APPELLANTS

... It would appear from the affidavits that the employing printers and their foreign strike-breakers are the aggressors. This is an appeal to the law to place the situation in the hands of the so-called strike breakers. ... Nothing has been done that ordinary firmness would not and has not fully met and overcome. It looks like the clamoring and complaints of children on a playground. And in sum and substances the offenses consist in the following: "She called me 'Kitty Cat'," "He followed me," "He hollered 'rats' on the street." ... The defendants who made affidavits in this case are men of high character who by their long residence amongst us through industry, sobriety and right-living have thoroughly established themselves and are entitled to be heard, and if heard, what becomes of the conspiracy upon which the plaintiffs admit this injunction must depend? As to these so-called strike-breakers, we do not know them; they come from the four quarters of the land. ... What is to be done as to these good men a large number of whom swear that they and their Unions as bodies have counselled gentlemanly conduct and peace, whose sworn testimony is unimpeached. ... Every material allegation in the case has been fully met. No conspiracy has been established. ...

The very language of the order is an insult to 95% of the members of these three unions, and yet it is said that, if these men do not intend to violate this order, why should they resist it? The answer is certainly apparent to every thinking man. No man wants a court record enjoining him from an unlawful act; and especially from an indictable conspiracy. These printing establishments want trouble, they want somebody to shadow, they were nervous and had their girls and men put themselves in the way of interference. . . .

If the police force of Raleigh and the constabulary have failed in this great hour of danger, why not impeach the Chief of Police, the Sheriff, call out the State Guard, declare martial law, arrest the Unions and save the country.

Respectfully submitted,

EVANS & EASON
R. N. SIMMS
CHARLES U. HARRIS
DOUGLASS & DOUGLASS
Attorneys for Defendants.

APPENDIX VIII
McGINNIS V. RALEIGH TYPOGRAPHICAL UNION

Interview with L. E. Nichols, Assistant Commissioner of Labor and Printing, State of North Carolina (1921), and member of Typographical Union.

Q. Did the injunction break the strike?

A. No. The strike was a success in all shops except Edwards & Broughton.

Q. Did the injunction have any effect on the outcome of the strike?

A. I doubt it. The Edwards and Broughton Company were so determined not to continue contractual relations with the union that we couldn't have won in that shop anyway.

Q. What effect did the injunction have on the strikers?

A. It didn't scare them or lower their morale. It made them determined to fight harder in a legitimate way. They took pains to keep from violating the injunction. The union ordered the men to strictly obey the injunction.

Q. Had the things prohibited in the injunction been going on before?

A. There had been some congregating across the street in front of Edwards & Broughton's. There were reports of individual instances of shadowing and the use of epithets but no union sanction or order to that effect. The union had been sending as many strike breakers as possible out of town when they arrived at the depot, but claimed the right to do that. Offers were made to pay their way back home.

Q. Did the injunction turn public opinion against you?

A. No, it brought to the surface the fact that a large per cent of the public sympathized with us. I don't think the mere issuing of an injunction would alienate public opinion. When, and if, followed by bombing and other forms of violence, public opinion would unquestionably be forfeited.

Q. What effect did it have on the attitude of the union men toward the court?

A. It caused a feeling of resentment. The attempt to enforce the injunction comprehends more than the terms of the injunction itself. In this case they tried to stop all picketing.

There are injunctions so strict and so utterly in conflict with constitutional rights that they are openly violated. The purpose of an injunction has usually been served before a hearing is given.

(Signed) LAWRENCE E. NICHOLS.

APPENDIX IX
SUMMARY OF INTERVIEWS WITH DEFENDANTS

McGinnis v. Raleigh Typographical Union et al.

Q. Were you served with a copy of the injunction?
A. Yes—9.
   No—2.
Q. How did you feel about it when a copy of the injunction was served on you?
A. "I thought it was a comic situation; a laughable matter."
   "I laughed at it."
   "I thought they were fools."
   "It didn't scare me."
   "I didn't think anything about it."
   "I didn't think it would get me into trouble."
   "I thought I would have to comply with it."
   "I thought I had to obey it. It's contempt of court if you don't.'
   "I thought they would get me in trouble."
   "I thought I had better look out or the judge would take all my savings in a fine."
Q. Did the injunction break the strike?
A. Yes—3.
   No—12.
   In a way it did—1.
Q. Did the injunction have any effect on the outcome of the strike?
A. Yes—3.

No—8.

"It might have had some effect."

"We might have been able to get the forty-four hour week without an increase in pay if they hadn't had the injunction."

Q. Could you have signed an agreement with Edwards & Broughton if there had been no injunction?

A. Yes—1.

No—7.

"Dr. Smith [the President] had his head set."

"Dr. Smith had his mind made up."

"We would have signed them or broke them."

Q. Did the injunction have any effect on the conduct of the men on strike?

A. "We had to quit everything."

"We had to stop picketing."

"It stopped standing around in front of Edwards and Broughton's."

"It kept pickets away from Edwards & Broughton's side of the street."

"We couldn't do public picketing afterward."

"There was not so much picketing afterward."

"It did quiet down some of the harum-scarum younger element."

"It stopped the open and public use of epithets."

"Epithets continued away from the shops."

"It might have stopped epithets in the immediate vicinity. It made them stronger elsewhere."

"It had no effect on epithets."

"It didn't stop the shadowing."

"It didn't hinder us much in keeping the rats run out of town." [Unanimous.]

Q. Did the injunction have any effect on public opinion with reference to the strike?

A. No—2.

"It did not alienate public sentiment"—2.

"If any difference, it made public opinion more favorable to us."

Q. Are you opposed to the use of injunctions in labor cases?

A. Yes—8.

"A printer knows he must obey a court order but he can see the injustice of it."

"It doesn't give us a fair show. It makes the other side bull-headed."

"Without the injunction *management would be accessible and we could arbitrate.*"

"It takes a man's right to reason with another man away from him. We couldn't show a man our point of view."

"It kept us from doing things we had a right to do."

"Courts haven't anything to do with it so long as you live within the law. It is wholly a matter between the employee and employer."

"It didn't give the people their rights."

"It took away our only weapon."

"If I had my way there would never be another labor injunction served. They are depriving a man of constitutional rights without due process of law."

"There is no jury trial."

"You are subject to the whim of a judge."

"It would be easier to keep scabs out if they didn't use injunctions."

General Remarks:

"This injunction didn't do either party any good."

"Some were weak-kneed and were scared of the injunction. Most of us were not. They have no effect on those of higher intelligence."

"————'s bull-headedness broke the strike."

"They brought strike breakers in here under misrepresentation. Lots of them were not told there was a strike on. They told them business expansion was the reason for high wages."

APPENDIX X

NORTH CAROLINA
BUNCOMBE COUNTY } IN THE SUPERIOR COURT

THE CITIZEN COMPANY, PLAINTIFF

vs.

ASHEVILLE TYPOGRAPHICAL UNION, NUMBER 263, ET AL., DEFENDANTS

Complaint and Affidavit

The Plaintiff complaining of the Defendants and each and every one of them says:

1. That THE CITIZEN COMPANY is a corporation, created by and existing under the laws of the State of North Carolina, with its principal office and place of business in the City of Asheville, in the said State, and, at the time hereinafter mentioned was, and still is, engaged in the business of printing and publishing of a daily newspaper in the City of Asheville of general circulation in said City and in the State of North Carolina, and known as THE ASHEVILLE CITIZEN and the SUNDAY CITIZEN.

2. That Frank J. Torlay is the organizer of the International Typographical Union, and shortly before the time of the matters herein complained of came to the City of Asheville for the purpose of advising his Co-Defendants as to calling and conducting a strike, and, as the Plaintiff is informed and believes, has advised, encouraged and procured the commission of the unlawful acts hereinafter alleged.

3. That Asheville Typographical Union Number

263 is a Labor Union, composed of members whose vocation is that of printers.

4. That [forty-three named Defendants] are officers and members of said Asheville Typographical Union Number 263.

5. That ———— is an apprentice, who is working as such, in order to qualify himself for carrying on the business of a printer.

6. That the Plaintiff, in carrying on its business hereinafter mentioned, employed and still employs about fifty men and women, and, of these, a large number are printers and proof readers.

7. That the Plaintiff has done the Defendants no wrong, and the Defendants have no grievance of any kind against this Plaintiff.

8. That on or about October 16th, 1923, and subsequent thereto, the Defendants, with malice and absence of lawful excuse, performed and have executed organized picketing, accompanied by threats, intimidation and violence towards persons employed or seeking employment at the place of business of the Plaintiff, and have done actual injury to said employees and the Plaintiff in an effort to cause said employees to breach their contracts with the Plaintiff and to compel the Plaintiff to discharge said employees through intimidation; that the Defendants, pursuant to said conspiracy, have devised and are executing a systematic course of espionage, annoyance, intimidation, threats, abuse and insults, which are intended to make, or calculated to make, and are making the lives of said employees miserable, intolerable and unendurable, and, unless the Defendants are compelled to desist from

such conduct said employees will be forced by intimidation to abandon their contracts with the Plaintiff and quit working for the Plaintiff, and the Plaintiff will be unable to carry on its business; that in pursuance of said conspiracy, plan and purpose, the Defendants gather, and have gathered in large numbers around and about the place of business of the Plaintiff, and when said employees are entering said place of business to perform their work, or are emerging and have emerged therefrom after their day's work, the Defendants indulge in threatening gestures, insulting jeers and hisses, using abusive and insulting, vile and profane language when addressing said employees, and in many ways annoy, disturb, humiliate and put said employees in fear; that the Defendants are also guilty of acts of violence in throwing bricks and other missiles into, upon and against the building in which the Plaintiff carries on its business, and have made threats of great bodily harm, and to kill said employees if they continue in the employment of the Plaintiff or remain in the City of Asheville; that while said employees are away from the place of employment the Defendants constantly shadow them, following them on the streets, in the restaurants and stores, and to their homes, to their work, in the day, in the night, always and everywhere, they are pursued and persecuted by the Defendants, sometimes in such numbers as to cause said employees to fear for their lives, that the Defendants frequently surround said employees, whenever and wherever they can find one or more of them, and by words and gestures humiliate them and put them in fear, that the Defendants constantly and systematically call said employees insulting names, such as "rats," "scabs," "runts," "bowery bums" and other epithets, calculated to humiliate and distress and which do humiliate and distress said employees and have a tendency to bring on breaches of the peace, and, but for the forbearance of said employees, bloodshed and probable loss of life would have resulted, that they have also used opprobrious epithets and insulting language in addressing those of said employees who are ladies and, while in the presence of said ladies have used profane and indecent language, all with like purpose and intent.

9. That the Defendants are constantly and systematically threatening, and have constantly and systematically threatened said employees by saying in their presence, "We will get you yet," and "We will mop up with you," and "You had better leave Asheville or you will be killed," and "If you come out again you will be carried back a corpse."

10. That the Defendants above named have planned and conspired to destroy the business of the Plaintiff for no other reason than that it declines to accede to the unreasonable and unrightful demands of the Defendants and is now exercising the right of every American citizen to run their business on the American plan, and to give employment to any man who applies for the same, this right being odious to and utterly denied by the Defendants herein, and solely because of their malice and without any lawful excuse.

11. In further pursuance of said plan, purpose and conspiracy to utterly destroy the business of the Plaintiff, solely because of the malice and without any lawful excuse, the said Defendants have induced many of the em-

ployees of the Defendant to break their contracts, that they have made with the Plaintiff to work for the Plaintiff, and to quit work for the Plaintiff.

12. That the said Defendants are still engaged in the acts herein complained of and threaten to continue the commission of the said acts to the irreparable damage and injury of this Plaintiff, and that by reason of and by consequence of the said acts herein set forth the Plaintiff has already been damaged from said cause in the sum of Ten Thousand Dollars ($10,000.00), and, unless the Defendants are restrained and enjoined, the Plaintiff will be irreparably damaged and its business will be irreparably damaged and its business will be greatly injured, if not destroyed.

13. That by reason of said acts of the Defendants the Plaintiff has no adequate remedy at law.

14. The Plaintiff has this day commenced a civil action against the Defendants in the Superior Court of Buncombe County, North Carolina, for the purpose of obtaining a perpetual injunction and a summons has been issued therein.

15. WHEREFORE, the Plaintiff prays the Court that an injunction be issued against the Defendants and each of them, and all other aiders, abettors and associates, compelling them to cease from indulging in any of the conduct above set forth and to leave the Plaintiff free to carry on its business in its own way, without molestation or annoyance of any kind from the Defendants.

(Signed) JONES, WILLIAMS & JONES,
MARK W. BROWN,
Attorneys for Plaintiff.

APPENDIX XI

NORTH CAROLINA
BUNCOMBE COUNTY } IN THE SUPERIOR COURT

THE CITIZEN COMPANY, PLAINTIFF
VS.
ASHEVILLE TYPOGRAPHICAL UNION, NUMBER 263, ET AL. DEFENDANTS

Summons for Relief

THE STATE OF NORTH CAROLINA
TO THE SHERIFF OF BUNCOMBE COUNTY—*Greetings:*

You are Hereby Commanded to Summon Asheville Typographical Union Number 263, Frank J. Torlay, [and the other] Defendants above, if they be found within your County, to be and appear before the Clerk of the Superior Court, at the Court House in Asheville, North Carolina, on the 17th day of November, 1923, and answer the complaint which will be deposited in the office of the Clerk of the Superior Court of said County, on or before said date, and let the said Defendants take notice that if they fail to answer to the said complaint within the time required by law, the Plaintiff will apply to the Court for the relief demanded in the complaint.

Herein fail not, and of this summons make due return.

Given under my hand, this the 29th day of October, 1923.

> J. B. CAIN,
> Clerk Superior Court, Buncombe County.
> Per Ethel S. Rickman, D. C.

FEES PAID $————
To use of————————————
——————————————C. S. C.

* * * * *

We acknowledge ourselves bound to Asheville Typographical Union Number 263, and the other Defendants in this action, in the sum of two hundred dollars. To be void, however, if the Plaintiff shall pay to the Defendants all such costs as the Defendants may recover of the Plaintiff in this action.

WITNESS our hand and seal this 30th day of October, 1923.

> THE ASHEVILLE CITIZEN COMPANY (Seal)
> Per CHARLES A. WEBB (Seal)
> Vice-President and Treasurer.

APPENDIX XII

North Carolina
Buncombe County } In the Superior Court

THE CITIZEN COMPANY, PLAINTIFF
VS.
ASHEVILLE TYPOGRAPHICAL UNION, NUMBER 263, FRANK J. TORLAY AND OTHERS
DEFENDANTS.

Restraining Order

This cause coming on to be heard before His Honor, P. A. McElroy, Judge of the Superior Court for the 19th Judicial District, on motion of the Plaintiff for an order requiring the Defendants to show cause, if any cause they have, why the Plaintiff is not entitled to the relief demanded in its complaint, and the Court being of the opinion that the Defendants should be required to show cause, and that in the meantime they should be enjoined, restrained, and forbidden from further unlawful interference with the property, business, and employees of the Plaintiff.

IT IS NOW on motion of Jones, Williams & Jones, and Mark W. Brown, Attorneys for the Plaintiff:

ORDERED, ADJUDGED AND DECREED that the Defendants and each of them show cause before the undersigned Judge at his chambers in Asheville on Saturday, the 17th day of November, 1923, at ten o'clock A.M., why the injunction herein applied for should not be continued until final hearing of this action.

And that in the meantime the Defendants, and each of them, and all other persons, are hereby restrained, and enjoined from, in any way or manner, whatsoever, interfering with the Plaintiff's business or employees by threats, personal injury, intimidation, suggestion of danger, or threats of violence of any kind, interfering with, hindering, obstructing or stopping any person engaged in the employ of the Plaintiff in connection with its business in the city of Asheville or elsewhere, and from interfering by violence, or threats of violence in any manner, with any person desiring to be employed by the Plaintiff in or about its place of business; and from inducing or attempting to compel or induce by threats, intimidation, force or violence, or putting in fear, or suggestions of danger, any of the employees of the Plaintiff or persons seeking employment with it, so as to cause them to refuse to perform any of their duties as employees of the Plaintiff; and from preventing any person by threats, intimidation, force or violence, or suggestions of danger or violence, from entering into the employ of said Plaintiff; and from protecting, aiding, or assisting any person or persons in committing any of said acts; and from assembling, loitering, or congregating about or in the proximity of the place of business of the Plaintiff; for the purpose of doing, or aiding or encouraging others in doing any of said unlawful or forbidden acts or things and from picketing or maintaining at or near the premises of the Plaintiff or on the streets leading to the premises of the Plaintiff, any picket or pickets, and from passing through, over and upon the private alley in the rear of the Plaintiff's place of business, and from doing any acts or things whatsoever in furtherance of any conspiracy or combination among themselves or any of them to obstruct or interfere with the Plaintiff or its business, agents or employees, in the free and unrestricted control and operation of its plant and property and in conducting its business and from entering upon the grounds and premises of the Plaintiff without first obtaining its consent, and from injuring or destroying any of the property of the Plaintiff.

This, the 30th day of October, 1923.

P. A. MCELROY,
Judge of the Superior Court for the 19th
Judicial District of North Carolina.

A TRUE COPY:
(Signed) J. B. CAIN,
Clerk of the Superior Court.
Per Ethel S. Rickman, D. C.

APPENDIX XIII
CITIZEN COMPANY V. ASHEVILLE TYPOGRAPHICAL UNION

Interview with Charles A. Webb, Co-Publisher and Co-Owner (1923) of the *Asheville Citizen*.

Q. What was the effect of the injunction in this case?

A. It absolutely stopped the trouble. The Typographical Union would have put us out of business if we hadn't secured the injunction. Before that the strikers were engaged in all sorts of criminal acts. They even tried to pour five gallons of liquid ammonia down the vent pipe into our composing room, which would have probably killed twenty-six people. They would have done it, too, if we hadn't found out about it beforehand and stopped them.

Before the strike we were paying our printers $48.00 per week for six days work with time and a half for overtime. Each printer was making from $50.00 to $55.00 per week with a few exceptions. They forced us to put in Union proofreaders. The Advertising Manager nor Managing Editor couldn't even proof-read advertising matter or news stories.

The Typographical Union had a rule that if the foreman discharged an employee, the employee had the right to appeal to the Chapel and the Chapel had a right to tell the foreman to put the employee back. There was then the right of appeal to the whole local Union and finally to the whole International Typographical Union. The decision of the I. T. U. was final. If it ordered a man put back, even if he had been put off six months before, the owner of the paper had to pay the discharged wages for the intervening time.

I issued an order that no employee could come in the building under the influence of liquor. That was posted in all departments. A few weeks after this order was posted, one Saturday night ─────, President of the local Typographical Union, came in the composing room drunk. The foreman pulled his slug off of the board (which meant that this employee had been discharged) and notified him of it. The discharged employee got mad and called a meeting of the Chapel. The Chapel ordered reinstatement. There was a terrible row about it. The foreman refused to put the discharged one back and appealed to the full meeting of the Union and to the I. T. U. The man, however, got another job and the case was dropped. Under that rule a foreman might catch a man stealing and still the man had all these rights of appeal.

Our agreement was about to expire. I offered to renew the old contract. The Union demanded $55.00 per week and the 45 hour week. I was already paying them more than they could get anywhere else and I couldn't give them the increase. Then they wanted arbitration. I asked if it was arbitration up and down both. They said no; it was arbitration as to whether wages should go up or stay the same. I said "I won't agree to any such arbitration, it is not a fair arbitration" and they walked out on fifteen minutes notice.

Q. Do you have any union men now?

A. None in the typesetting department. We have Union men in the press room and stereotype departments.

They asked for Union sanction and the I. T. U. sent an organizer by the name of Torlay. Torlay was an obstinate, hot-headed fellow. Torlay talked to me. He said he would give me 48 hours notice of a strike in case they called one. They finally got strike sanction. I was in touch with the American Newspaper Publishers Association. They wired me about 6:00 P.M. that strike sanction had been granted. I got in touch with the mayor of the city and the chief of police. At 6:45 I got to my office and they gave me fifteen minutes' notice of the strike.

I got in touch with the Open Shop Division of the American Newspaper Publishers Association (Mr. Flagg). He got in touch with his crew of printers and told them to come to Asheville. We got out an eight-page paper the next morning. That first night the strikers tried to cut the light wires. The police stopped it. We got type set in an open shop here in town.

On Friday Mr. Flagg's men came and took charge. There were fifteen or sixteen of them. Then the Union men started their devilment. They behaved so badly that I had to get an injunction to stop it. They resorted to the usual methods of intimidation, violence and interference with our new printers. They tried to get people to stop their subscriptions and to stop advertising with us. They threatened to stop trading with business firms if those firms didn't stop advertising with us.

That night when they told me they were going to strike in fifteen minutes I said to them, "If you go out of here tonight, you'll never work for me again." And I've stuck to it.

One of the biggest farces in the whole business is what

they call "peaceful picketing." There is no such thing as peaceful picketing. Any kind of picketing is a form of intimidation and interference with another man's business. My position on this question is very simple and very plain: Laboring people have a right to organize themselves into a union. Those that don't want to join have a right to stay out. Nobody has a right to force them in. An employer has a right to employ union or non-union men as he sees fit. If he prefers non-union men, it is his business. A non-union worker has a right to work anywhere and under any condition which he prefers. So does the Union man. No Union organizer or union laborer has any right to interfere with him. The right to work is as sacred as the right to worship. No union has a right to tell a man how, when or why he shall work. When a non-union man wants to work, it's the duty of the state to protect him from picketing.

The injunction is still in effect.

Q. How would you summarize the effects of the injunction?

A. It stopped the intimidation and picketing. After it was issued, our employees could go out at 2:00 A.M. and not be bothered.

The Typographical Union is the most arbitrary and unreasonable union in the world. There is not a newspaper publisher in America today who would deal with it if they could avoid it. The trend is away from the Typographical Union shops among newspaper publishers. As I stated in an address before the Newspaper Publishers Association, only about twenty-five per cent. of the typesetters belong to the Union.

Q. How was the injunction enforced?

A. We had police stationed here and three or four special deputies. Those fellows were scared because they knew if they violated that injunction they would go to jail for contempt.

If I should ever have another strike, I wouldn't try to operate as we did in this case. I would simply close up until they were willing to come back and sign a contract to work non-union. On the other hand, a man feels an obligation to the men who want to keep on working.

Q. What is the procedure for obtaining an injunction in this state?

A. We file a petition before the Court setting forth the facts and ask for an injunction. The Court issues a citation directing the defendants to come before the court and show cause. The sheriff serves it on the defendants. The judge takes testimony.

Q. Was there personal service on each defendant in this case?

A. Yes.

Q. Were there any contempt proceedings?

A. No; they just quit.

If we hadn't secured this injunction the strikers would have ruined us. Three or four days after the strike most of them came around and begged me to let them come back.

Q. Who could give me the correct information at the *Times* office?

A. D. Hiden Ramsey, the Manager. He stood right with me all through the fight.

I want it distinctly understood that I have no fight against organized labor as an organization. My fight has been and is against only one union and that is the International Typographical Union. We still employ members of the Pressmen's Union and the Stereotyper's Union.

(Signed) CHARLES A. WEBB.

APPENDIX XIV
EXCERPTS FROM OPINION OF THE SUPREME COURT

Citizen Company v. Asheville Typographical Union, 187 N. C. 42.

CLARKSON, J. . . . There is no allegation in the complaint that the Asheville Typographical Union is a corporation, and it is not a natural person. It is an unincorporated association and cannot be sued. . . .

As we understand the law to be, an individual or group of individuals have a right to organize and use all peaceful means to see that their rights and liberties . . . are protected. . . . Ordinarily, any individual or group have a right to quit work when he or they see fit, and, by peaceful means, use their influence and argument with other individuals and groups (to keep them) from filling or taking their places. The quitting work by individuals or combinations must be peaceful, and their conduct in persuasion of others must be peaceful. . . .

In the instant case, we do not finally pass on the facts. Their probative value is for another tribunal. For the purposes of this action they are admitted to be true. . . .

The complaint in this cause alleges, with certainty and definiteness, much that is unlawful—continuous trespass, conspiracy, assault, etc. (which is admitted by the demurrer). There are sufficient allegations and specific facts stated that are definite and certain enough to continue the restraining order against the individual defendants to the hearing, subject to certain modifications. The defendants have a legal right to have a reasonable number for peaceful picketing, but this cannot be attended by any disorder, intimidation or obstruction, but only by observation, watching, and persuasion.

APPENDIX XV

SUMMARY OF INTERVIEWS WITH DEFENDANTS

Citizen Company v. Asheville Typographical Union

1. Were you in the Typographical Union strike here in Asheville in 1923?
   Yes—7.
   No—2 (Members of the union but worked in other shops.
2. Were you served with a copy of the injunction?
   Yes—8.
   No—1.
3. How did you feel when it was served on you?
   "Very depressed."
   "I thought we were obliged to obey it."
   "I thought it was law."
   "I thought it was unjust."
   "I thought it was uncalled for."
   "I took it as a joke."
4. Did the injunction break the strike?
   Yes—1.
   No—8.
   "It helped to break it."
   "It slowed it up."
   "It was a temporary set-back."
   "It did break up some of our plans."
   "I don't think it had any effect at all in any way."
   "No, sir. It's not broken yet."
   "The Typographical Union never gives up. We

won a strike in Savannah, Georgia, after thirteen years."

5. What were the effects of the injunction?

"I doubt if we could have won sooner without the injunction. We couldn't meet their rats on the street and call them names. We had to be more careful."

"It kept us all off picket duty. It made the sympathizers stop picketing, too. If the injunction had not been used, we might have got a good settlement in a few months. It gave themselves a leverage to pry themselves up until the public had forgotten it."

"It kept us separated. They wouldn't allow more than two together on the street. We had to stay away from the building."

"It taught us all a great lesson."

"It broke the morale and caused men to leave who would have stayed and helped. It broke up our campaign with the advertisers and subscribers. We were making a lot of headway before that. When the injunction came out, the merchants took down the 'We believe in arbitration' signs."

"All it did was antagonize the men and make them feel hard toward the management because of the false affidavits."

"It demoralized the whole thing."

6. Do you think the injunction had any effect on public opinion?

       Yes—4.
       No—2.

"It tended to turn public opinion against us."
"Not noticeable."

"The public paid little attention to it."

"It put us in the wrong light. This is one of the greatest effects."

"They believed the false testimony. It tended to throw public sentiment on the other side."

"With the masses it was in our favor. It probably caused the unbiased public to brand the strike as lawless."

7. Do you think the injunction kept you from doing anything which you had a right to do?

Yes—6.

No—2.

"It kept us from talking to those other fellows. We had the same right to ask them to join the union that a preacher has to ask them to join the church. It kept us from going anywhere around the place of employment."

"We couldn't approach a man and ask him not to work. We couldn't congregate near the place of business."

"Absolutely, I do. It stepped on free speech. We couldn't talk to the men who came in to take our jobs. We could have got many of them to join the union if we had been allowed to talk to them."

"It ordered us to stay off the street."

"I hadn't been doing anything out of the way so I went on the same as before."

"It stopped us from going to boarding houses. Johnson, one of the strikers, owned half of the alley back of the *Citizen* building. He was forbidden to be on it."

Remarks:

"We would have been more likely to win if the injunction had not been used. There's no law for the working man to use. You caint buck the law. You'll lose in the long run by trying. The purpose of an injunction is to make the strikers helpless. It puts you on the defensive. We wanted arbitration. They wouldn't arbitrate. We tried to get all the advertisers to insert the line, 'We favor arbitration.' One man did and they refused to publish it.

Q. Did the union men use epithets in talking to the strike breakers?
A. "Yes, we called them rats. If you work in a printing shop when there's a strike on, that's what you are—a 'rat printer.' We have the word rat in the dictionary."
Q. Do you remember Chief Justice Clark?
A. "Yes, he was one of the best friends labor ever had."

. . . .

"A scab fears the contempt of union men. I had talked to fellows to keep them from taking our places. When the injunction came out, we stopped peaceful picketing. I felt that I had to obey the order of the court. I didn't think it was fair. I couldn't even talk to former Foreman Stallings who came back from the hospital and scabbed on us. One of the greatest disappointments of my life was ————'s affidavit that I had used a stick and threatened him. I had a sprained ankle and was using a window stick for a cane. We had talked for a long time in the most friendly and peaceful manner and had parted as the best of friends. I had always thought a lot of ————. Then he came out with this fake affidavit.

"No injunction was needed for the ammonia incident. The law takes care of intimidation and things like that. The union should not be held responsible for the outlaw act of one member. I think there are times when injunctions are needed to protect property. There is no excuse for injunctions in cases like this. I knew nothing about the epithets. We would hear that a fellow was coming to town, talk to him, try to get him to join the union, get him a job and offer to pay his way to it."

. . . .

"Part of an affidavit signed by ———— I know to be false. At times he swore I was around the ———— building I could easily prove I was in bed at home. One affidavit swore that a boy who was in Fruitland Institute studying for the ministry was picketing. He wasn't even in town."

Q. Do you favor jury trial in contempt cases?
A. "Absolutely. That's the reason union men are so afraid of injunctions. The power to punish for contempt lies with one man."

. . . .

"Strike breakers tried to pick trouble with us. They violated the injunction they had against us. It seems to me a working man should have as much right as the other side. We should have jury trial."

. . . .

"We wanted arbitration. They wouldn't arbitrate so we came out. They had to sign yellow dog contracts at both places at one time. This 'threats of violence, etc.' is a lot of foolishness. We didn't threaten them. After the injunction, we just walked up to their employees, patted them on the back, and said, 'Come on, join the union.' We got them to join one after another. Today, some of our best members are those who were brought in as scabs. We made the few roughnecks cut out the jeering, hissing, etc. A lot of the strike breakers didn't know they were being brought into a strike. A lot of them were from country papers. When they saw what they were in, they didn't like it.

"The papers had to send for Flagg and his strike breakers the second time when the strike was two years old. We pulled the whole crew out on Saturday afternoon before Thanksgiving.

"Torlay (the organizer sent by the International Typographical Union) was too much of a fighter for the place."

Q. Do you think there is legitimate ground for criticism of injunctions as now used in labor cases?

A. "I certainly do. It's a judge's personal law. It's harder to get justice. There's no jury trial.

"I can't see much to yellow dog contracts. The employer binds you but you can't bind him.

"Injunctions make a lot of difference some places but they didn't here. The boys did quiet down some when the injunction came out. The injunction probably gave the papers a feeling of security."

. . . .

"Mr. Webb and I are still the best of friends. Some of the strike breakers are now good union men. No picketing was permitted by union officers. The injunction has a depressing effect on families.

"To the best of my knowledge the printers did not engage in violence."

Q. Do you think there is legitimate ground for criticism of injunctions as now used?

A. "Yes, sir. They are greatly abused. I hope to see the time when they will be harder to get. The injunction is largely responsible for causing the men to lose their homes and leave town. They do have a tendency to cripple the movement but it's only temporary. They take away a strategic opportunity."

. . . .

"They made us sign a contract to arbitrate before. This time they wouldn't arbitrate. They kept putting the hearing off and putting it off. They said the judge was sick. Putting off the hearing on the injunction gave them a longer time to break the strike. Delay in getting the trial is the worst thing. They sent me down to Marshall to see if Judge McElroy really was sick. He may have been sick but he wasn't in bed. I saw him sitting in a chair reading.

"I know the ammonia incident did not occur. I'm the man they accused of it. ———— and I were accused. Nobody from our crowd was up there with ammonia. It would have been impossible to get it over the roof. The ammonia was planted there by the papers. They had to make out there was a lot of disorder to get an injunction. I like Mr. Webb otherwise. Torlay (the organizer) was too hot-headed."

Q. Do you favor jury trial?

A. "Yes; it cuts down political influence. If you have jury trial they can't try you before they take you up there."

APPENDIX XVI

State of North Carolina } In the Superior Court
Buncombe County } November Term, 1923

THE CITIZEN COMPANY
VS.
ASHEVILLE TYPOGRAPHICAL UNION
NO. 263 AND OTHERS

Judgment

This cause coming on to be heard before his Honor, P. A. McElroy, Judge presiding, at this term, upon the complaint, answer and evidence offered by the respective parties in support of their claims and contentions, and at the close of all of the evidence and defendants having demurred *ore tenus* on the ground that the complaint does not state facts sufficient to constitute a cause of action and move to dismiss said action on that ground and after argument of counsel the court stated in open court that he was of the opinion that the restraining order should be continued to the final hearing if the complaint states facts sufficient to constitute a cause of action for injunctive relief, but that he was further of the opinion that the complaint did not state facts sufficient to constitute a cause of action for injunctive relief, and would dissolve the injunction heretofore issued in this cause for that reason, but would allow said injunction to remain in full force and effect until the appeal could be heard in the Supreme

Court, provided the transcript would be docketed at this term of said court and on the further condition that the plaintiff should execute a bond in the sum of Seventy-five Hundred ($7500.00) dollars, conditioned as required by Chapter 58 of the Public Laws of 1921:

It is now on motion of J. W. Haynes, George Pennell, Gallatin Roberts and Guy Weaver, Attorneys for the defendants,

ORDERED, ADJUDGED and DECREED that the restraining order issued herein and dated October 30th, 1923, returnable on the 17th day of November, 1927, be and the same is hereby dissolved.

Thereupon the plaintiff in open court having prayed an appeal to the Supreme Court from the foregoing order and judgment, and the court finding that an injunction is the principal relief sought by the plaintiff, and upon all of the facts in the case said injunction should be continued and remain in full force and effect until said appeal has been finally disposed of, it is ordered by the court that upon the filing by the plaintiff in the office of the Clerk of the Superior Court, entitled as in this cause, a written undertaking with sufficient sureties, in the sum of Seventy-five Hundred ($7500.00) dollars, approved by the Clerk of the Court, and conditioned as required by said statute, that said restraining order hereinbefore issued and dissolved shall remain in force and effect pending the said appeal of plaintiff to the Supreme Court of North Carolina, and until the hearing and determination thereof.

That it is understood and agreed that this appeal shall be perfected, docketed and heard in the Supreme Court during the week for hearing appeals from the 19th Judicial District, present term, unless the same is continued on motion of the defendants or on motion of the Supreme Court. Should the appeal be not heard by reason of the motion of the plaintiff, then the restraining order hereinbefore dissolved and continued herein shall be dissolved.

It is further ordered that if the Supreme Court shall hold that the complaint states facts sufficient to entitle the plaintiff to injunctive relief, that said restraining order hereinbefore issued shall be continued until the final hearing.

It is further ORDERED that the summons, complaint, judgment and appeal entries shall constitute the record to the Supreme Court.

     (Signed)   P. A. MCELROY,
           Judge Presiding.

To the foregoing Judgment the Plaintiff excepts and appeals to the Supreme Court. Notice of appeal given and waived in open court. Appeal bond in the sum of $50.00 is adjudged sufficient.

APPENDIX XVII

North Carolina
McDowell County

MARION MANUFACTURING COMPANY
VS.
THE LOCAL UNION OF UNITED TEXTILE WORKERS OF AMERICA OF EAST MARION, NORTH CAROLINA, BEING UNION NO. 1659, AND ALFRED HOFFMAN, TOM PETTIT, ET AL.

Complaint and Affidavit

And now comes the plaintiff, who complaining of the defendants, alleges:

1. That the plaintiff is a corporation, created, organized and existing under and by virtue of the laws of the State of North Carolina, with its principal office at East Marion, North Carolina, and as such is engaged in the manufacture of cotton goods known as print cloths, from raw cotton; and until within the last few days has had in its employ about Six Hundred Fifty (650) persons operating this plaintiff's mill.

2. That on or about the 11th day of July, 1929, that portion of this plaintiff's employees known as the day shift, at about 3:00 o'clock P.M. on said date walked out of the mill and refused to work longer for this plaintiff, and since that time the greater portion of this number, to-wit: about Two Hundred Fifty (250) persons together with the greater portion of the night shift, consisting of

an equal number of the employees, have refused to return to work, have armed themselves with deadly weapons, to-wit: sticks, bludgeons and other implements, and have been unlawfully picketing this plaintiff's premises, including the building used in the manufacture of said goods, and the grounds of this plaintiff surrounding the same.

3. That the defendants above named in this complaint, together with their associates, many of whose individual names this plaintiff cannot now give, have steadily and continuously since the 11th day of July, 1929, maintained an organized espionage and picketing upon the works, place of business and office of this plaintiff, and have unlawfully, wrongfully, willfully and intentionally, prevented the employees of this plaintiff who are willing to do so, to go upon this plaintiff's premises to look after this plaintiff's property and protect it from injury.

4. That on the 18th day of July, 1929, as well as on divers and sundry prior occasions, the defendants above named, together with a great many other persons whose names are not now known to the plaintiff, other than Alfred Hoffman and Tom Pettit, being armed with deadly weapons, consisting of clubs, sticks and bludgeons, were engaged in and did maintain an organized espionage and picketing upon the work, office and place of business of this plaintiff; that this plaintiff had on said date three car loads of cotton on its side track in its mill yard, near its mill, and also two car loads of coal on said yard; that when this plaintiff, with certain of its loyal employees, had designated its intention and desire to unload the said cotton and coal in order to prevent demurrage from accumulating, the time for unloading same already having

expired, through its agents notified the defendants, or many of them, other than Alfred Hoffman and Tom Pettit, that they desired to unload the said cotton and coal; that the company did not intend to start up its works with other employees, whereupon the defendants herein named, other than said Alfred Hoffman and Tom Pettit, announced that the same could not be unloaded, declaring "To Hell with the Law," "To Hell with the Courts," and thereupon voices in the crowd of defendants then and there assembled, shouted "Close the Gates," meaning thereby as plaintiff is informed and believes and now alleges, to prevent any of the employees of this plaintiff from going into, or out of this plaintiff's premises.

5. That the defendants and their associates, have as plaintiff is informed and believes and now alleges, conspired, confederated and agreed together that they will prevent the plaintiff's employees who are willing to do so from entering upon the plaintiff's grounds for the protection of plaintiff's property and any and all purposes, and when plaintiff's employees attempted to discharge their duties about plaintiff's premises they were and have been continually assaulted, molested and prevented by force from entering plaintiff's grounds; and said plaintiff's loyal employees are continually and constantly harassed and intimidated by the defendants and large numbers of their associates, numbering in all Two Hundred and more, who stand by day and by night armed, as hereinabove mentioned, and constantly and continually intimidate, threaten, and assault, plaintiff's loyal employees, who would discharge their duties to this plaintiff and who would look after plaintiff's property and prevent its injury and dam-

age, but for such hindrance and obstruction; that by reason of the large numbers of these defendants assembling in such numbers, heavily armed, and thus preventing plaintiff's employees who are willing to do so, from entering plaintiff's grounds and property, have practically confiscated the property of the plaintiff, in that it is no longer permitted to manage its property and use it in a lawful and rightful manner, to this plaintiff's great and irreparable damage.

6. That the defendants, Alfred Hoffman and Tom Pettit with others have been organizing, influencing and directing the co-defendants for the purpose of intimidation, as plaintiff is informed and believes, and now alleges, and for the purpose of compelling any persons who are willing to work for the plaintiff to remain outside of plaintiff's premises; and said Hoffman and Pettit, as plaintiff is informed and believes and now alleges, have on divers and sundry occasions influenced the minds of this plaintiff's employees, have charged that this plaintiff was cruelly treating its employees, and have so influenced this plaintiff's employees as to induce them to quit work for this plaintiff, and to organize an unlawful espionage and picketing on, about, and around this plaintiff's premises.

7. That the defendants above named, have and do now maintain an unlawful espionage and picketing around, about and on this plaintiff's premises and by intimidation and unlawful persuasion, and by compulsion do not allow this plaintiff's employees who are willing to do so, to enter upon this plaintiff's premises to look after and care for this plaintiff's property; that when said employees walked

out of this plaintiff's mill, and refused longer to work for this plaintiff, they left this plaintiff's looms with the yarns upon same; left the spinning frames in a dirty condition, and all other machinery in the mill did at that time and does now need cleaning and shaping up if it shall stand idle; and the plaintiff also shows that in order to maintain insurance it is required under the terms of its policies to keep one boiler in active service at all times for the purpose of operating pumps and apparatus necessary for quenching any fire that might occur; that the defendants herein above named by reason of their conduct in willfully and unlawfully preventing such of this plaintiff's employees as are willing to do so, from entering this plaintiff's premises and place of business to look after its machinery, property and grounds, are irreparably damaging this plaintiff's property.

8. That the defendants, with their accomplices and associates, unlawfully and wrongfully and willfully trespassed upon this plaintiff's property and grounds, and continue to so trespass upon said property and grounds.

9. That the defendants, as plaintiff is informed and believes and now alleges, has created and maintains unlawful assemblies, being heavily armed and thereby becoming a public nuisance, threatening and intimidating any of this plaintiff's employees who are willing to assist in taking care of this plaintiff's property.

10. That on the 18th day of July, 1929, when the president of this plaintiff was attempting in a peaceable and conciliatory manner to persuade the defendants and their associates to permit the plaintiff, through its loyal employees to unload the coal and cotton hereinbefore

referred to from the cars, standing on its side track, and inside its mill-yard, the defendants, other than the said Hoffman and Pettit, together with divers and sundry other persons, whose names are not now known, and in the presence of the High Sheriff of McDowell County who was present undertaking to maintain peace and good order of the community, assaulted and beat this plaintiff's president with a deadly weapon, and assaulted other of this plaintiff's loyal employees, shut the gates of this plaintiff by force, and thus prevented the plaintiff's employees from entering plaintiff's premises in a quiet manner to look after plaintiff's property.

11. That as plaintiff is informed and believes and now alleges, each and all of the defendants are wholly and totally insolvent and no sum whatever can be recovered in this or any other section against them.

WHEREFORE plaintiff prays the Court: for a Temporary Restraining Order, which Temporary Restraining Order this plaintiff prays the Court may upon the hearing be continued and made perpetual, restraining the defendants, and each of them, their agents, officers, associates and employees, from: FIRST: Entering upon this plaintiff's grounds, or in any manner trespassing upon this plaintiff's property, consisting of its cotton mill, offices, store and grounds; SECOND: That each and all of the defendants be restrained from interfering with, intimidating, or in any manner molesting or assaulting any of the plaintiff's employees in their homes, or while working for, or in the employment of this plaintiff; THIRD: That the defendants and each of them be restrained from in any manner holding or participating in any unlawful assembly or assemblies on or in property belonging to this plaintiff, including the mill village and the highways and streets passing through same, and particularly from obstructing this plaintiff's gates or modes of ingress and egress, to, upon, around or about its mill; FOURTH: That the said Alfred Hoffman and Tom Pettit, their associates and agents be enjoined and restrained from inciting this plaintiff's employees, or former employees, or persuading them to maintain an espionage or picketing, on or in any portion of this plaintiff's property, and that they especially be enjoined and restrained from holding unlawful assemblies in, on, or about this plaintiff's property, including its mill village; FIFTH: That the Court set a day for the hearing before referred to and prayed for, and granting of a Temporary Restraining Order; SIXTH: For the cost of this action and for such other and further relief as to the Court may seem just and equitable; and that this complaint may be treated as an affidavit upon which application may be made for an Injunction or Restraining Order.

   (Signed) E. F. WATSON & W. T. MORGAN
   (Signed) G. F. WASHBURN
          Attorneys for Plaintiff.

NORTH CAROLINA
McDOWELL COUNTY

 Rignal W. Baldwin, first being duly sworn, deposes and says:

 That he is the President of the Marion Manufacturing Company, the plaintiff above named; that he has read the foregoing Complaint and Affidavit and knows the contents of same; that the same is true of his own knowledge, except as to such matters and things as are therein stated upon information and belief, and as to such matters and things he believes it to be true.

(Signed) RIGNAL W. BALDWIN,
Affiant.

Sworn to and subscribed before me, this the 19 day of July 1929.

(Signed) J. L. LAUGHRIDGE,
Clerk Superior Court.

APPENDIX XVIII

MARION MANUFACTURING COMPANY V. UNITED TEXTILE WORKERS

North Carolina
McDowell County } In the Superior Court

Restraining Order

THE LOCAL UNION OF THE UNITED TEXTILE WORKERS OF AMERICA OF EAST MARION, NORTH CAROLINA, BEING UNION NUMBER 1659, ET AL. [defendants named]:

This cause coming on to be heard, and being heard upon the application of the plaintiff for a Restraining Order in this cause,

IT IS NOW ORDERED, ADJUDGED AND DECREED by the Court that the defendants above named, and each and every one of them, be, and they are hereby enjoined and restrained, FIRST: from entering upon the plaintiff's grounds, or in any manner trespassing upon the plaintiff's property, known as the Marion Manufacturing Company's Mill property consisting of its cotton mill, offices, store and grounds; SECOND: that each and all of the defendants be restrained from interfering with, intimidating or in any manner molesting or assaulting any of the plaintiff's employees in their homes or on the grounds of the plaintiff; THIRD: That the defendants, and each of them be, and they are hereby enjoined and restrained from holding or participating in any unlawful assembly or assemblies on or in the property belonging to the plaintiff, including the mill village, the ways and streets passing through the same, and particularly from obstructing the plaintiff's gates or modes of ingress and egress, to, upon, around or about the mill; FOURTH: That the said Alfred Hoffman and Tom Pettit, their associates and agents and employees, be, and they are hereby enjoined and restrained from in any manner inciting the plaintiff's employees, or former employees, or persuading them to maintain an espionage or picketing in, or on any portion of this plaintiff's property, and that especially they be enjoined and restrained from holding unlawful assemblies in, on or about this plaintiff's property, including its mill village; FIFTH: That the defendants and each of them are hereby required to appear before Judge James L. Webb, or any other Judge who may be holding the Courts in the Town of Burnsville, North Carolina, on the 12th day of August, 1929, and show cause, if any they can, why this restraining order should not be continued to the final hearing.

IT IS FURTHER ORDERED BY THE COURT that upon the plaintiff's filing a bond in the sum of $1,000.00 sufficiently justified, that the Sheriff of McDowell County shall thereupon immediately serve a copy of the Bill of Complaint and this Restraining Order, on each of the defendants, requiring them to appear at the time above stated.

Given under my hand, this the 19th day of July, 1929.

(Signed) J. H. HARWOOD,
Judge Presiding and Holding the Courts
of McDowell County.

APPENDIX XIX

MODIFIED ORDER

North Carolina } In the Superior Court
Yancey County   } August Term, 1929

MARION MANUFACTURING COMPANY
V.
ALFRED HOFFMANN, JOHN WILKIE, ET AL.

Judgment

This matter coming on to be heard upon the temporary restraining order issued by His Honor, J. H. Harwood, Judge Presiding and holding the courts of McDowell County on the 24th day of July, 1929, and said order being by inadvertence dated July 19th, 1929, and being heard at Burnsville, North Carolina, upon the affidavits and argument of Counsel for plaintiff and defendants before the undersigned Judge.

It is now, upon motion of attorneys for plaintiff considered and adjudged by the Court that the said Temporary Restraining Order be and the same is hereby continued to final hearing of this cause, and in the meantime the defendants and each of them, except the defendant Unions as such, and the defendants, Rosa Holland and Zuriah Price, be, and they are hereby restrained and enjoined from:

FIRST: Entering upon the plaintiff's grounds, or in any other manner trespassing upon the plaintiff's property known as Marion Manufacturing Company's mill property, consisting of its cotton mill, offices, warehouses, store and grounds, including wood yards EXCEPTING ingress to and from the branch Post Office of the store and office building;

SECOND: That each and all of the said defendants be restrained from interfering with, intimidating, or in any manner molesting or assaulting any of the plaintiff's employees in their homes or on the grounds of the plaintiff;

THIRD: That the said defendants and each of them be, and they are hereby enjoined, and restrained from holding or participating in any unlawful assembly or assemblies on or in the property belonging to the plaintiff, including the mill village, the ways and streets passing through the same, and particularly from obstructing the plaintiff's gates or modes of ingress or egress, to, upon, around or about the mill;

FOURTH: That the said Alfred Hoffmann and Tom Pettit [sic], their associates and agents and employees, be, and they are hereby enjoined and restrained from in any manner inciting the plaintiff's employees or former employees, or persuading them to maintain an espionage or picketing in, or on any portion of said plaintiff's property, and that they be especially enjoined and restrained from holding unlawful assemblies in, on or about this plaintiff's property, including its mill village; all until the final hearing of this cause.

Providing that this injunction shall not be construed to prevent, and it does not prevent, the said defendants from lawful picketing and espionage at places other than upon the plaintiff's property nor lawful assemblies, nor lawful passage to and from the premises and places of abode now occupied by them, nor from lawful meetings on property other than plaintiff's, nor from holding meetings, speakings and discussions of their rights and grievances upon premises and property other than that of the plaintiff, nor to give the plaintiff any control over the personal liberty or property of any of the defendants restrained hereby, nor shall it have the effect of ejecting any of the defendants from the premises or the property they now occupy.

(Signed) CAMERON T. MACRAE,
Special Judge Holding Court at Burnsville,
Yancey County, North Carolina.

Done at Burnsville, North Carolina,
this August 16th, 1929.

APPENDIX XX
MARION MANUFACTURING COMPANY V. UNITED TEXTILE WORKERS LETTER FROM N. A. TOWNSEND, FEBRUARY 3rd, 1930.

Mr. Duane McCracken,
Guilford College, North Carolina.

My dear Mr. McCracken:

I have your letter of January 22nd, and will be glad to answer the questions contained therein as best I can.

I do not think the injunction furnished the relief sought in the case of Marion Manufacturing Company against United States Textile Workers, and others. About the only effect the injunction had, so far as I could see, was to increase the hostile feelings existing between the manufacturers and strikers. The strikers did not pay any attention to the terms of the injunction. In fact, I do not believe they really understood what the injunction forbade them to do. There was a clause which permitted "peaceful picketing," and the strikers contended that they had never done any kind of picketing except peaceful picketing. Personally, I have never seen any peaceful picketing. All that I have ever seen was decidedly belligerent and hostile. In the Marion case, the condition of the strikers after the injunction was, if anything, more unpeaceful than it was before. In fact, I think that if the injunction had any effect whatever upon the controversy it was to make the tension and feeling between capital and labor more strained and hostile and deferred the day of settlement.

Trusting that this may be of some use to you in your work, I beg to remain

     Sincerely yours,
     (Signed) N. A. TOWNSEND,
NAT:MAJ.   (Executive Counsellor to the
     Governor of North Carolina.)

APPENDIX XXI

Summary of Interviews with Defendants Marion Manufacturing Company v. United Textile Workers.

1. Were you on strike when the injunction came out last summer?
    Yes—27.
    No—3.
2. Was a copy of the injunction served on you?
    Yes—23.
    No—7.
3. What did you think about it when it was served on you?
    I thought it was a bluff.
    I didn't pay any attention to it.
    I didn't know what to think.
    I didn't think it was law.
    I didn't think they would put me in jail.
    I didn't think they had any right to do it.
    I didn't think there was anything to it.
    I didn't think it amounted to much.
    I didn't think much about it.
    I didn't know anything about it.
    I knew in reason it wasn't worth nothin'.
    The people hadn't violated no laws.
    I didn't think they could throw us out of picket lines.
    I thought it was unnecessary.
    I thought it might cause some trouble.
    I just laughed about it.
    It didn't scare me.
    I thought it best to go right ahead.

It wasn't wuth the paper it was wrote on.
I thought I had a right to picket peacefully, as I did.
I thought I had just rights.
I didn't think they could do anything to us.
Some thought it was law.
Thought they might get a man in trouble.
Put me to studyin' in a way.
Went ahead the same as before.
Hadn't done anything to be put in jail for.

4. Do you think the injunction broke the strike?
   Yes—0.
   No—26.
5. Do you think the strike would have been more successful without the injunction?
   Yes—5.
   No—15.
   I believe so—1.
   I don't know—2.
6. Do you think any of the workers were frightened by the injunction?
   Yes—19.
   No—11.
7. Did the workers pay much attention to the injunction?
   Yes—4.
   No—18.
8. Did they stop picketing?
   Yes, a few, for a short time—19.
   No—8.
9. Do you think the injunction had any effect?
   Yes—2.
   No—6.

It made a few of them nervous about picketing.
We stayed off of company property as much as we could.
It made them a little more quiet.
Some didn't know what to do.
It scared a few.
It didn't have any effect on the outcome of the strike.

10. Do you think it is unfair to use the injunction in labor disputes?

Yes—18.
No—1.
Why?
Every man should have his rights.
We didn't have any show.
There is no way to get to 'em and get 'em to come out.
It's wrong unless people are acting more outlaw than we did.
No injunction should be served when a man is not violating the law.

11. Which do you think pay more attention to the injunction: the men or the women?

Men—13.
Women—1.
No difference—6.

Remarks:

"I didn't pay no attention to it."

"I was at summer school at Burnsville at that time. I had never been on picket."

"All those who quit picketing, as far as I know, were men. My wife laughed about it."

"I had an injunction served on me twenty-five years ago at Thomas Creek, Virginia. They didn't do anything to us. They just served 'em on us. I told the boys it wasn't worth the paper it was wrote on."

"Some got mad about it and talked about it, but they went back on the picket line."

"I stayed away from the Post Office one week. I was driven away by two of the men watching gates. They told me I couldn't park my car there. The injunction caused a few to crawfish out."

"I told Mr. Hoffmann if they hung me, I didn't care. I was going to stay on picket."

"It scared outsiders. My wife said pay no attention to it."

"Several talked to me and seemed to be worried."

"Lawyer Giles told me I had a right to do peaceful picketing. Judge MacRae said we had that right too."

"In some ways it stirred them up worse."

"The soldiers and the sheriff and his deputies broke the strike."

"Some tore their injunction papers up and some kept them. I don't think the people understood."

"The injunction wouldn't have amounted to much without soldiers."

"Hoffmann asked us what we were going to do about it. We told him we weren't going to pay any attention. They fired me before the strike for joining the union. They asked me if I belonged to the union. I told them 'yes' and they fired me."

"I didn't think I was doing anything to violate the law. All picketing in my presence was quiet."

APPENDIX XXII

CERTIFIED COPIES OF WRITS OF INJUNCTION AND ORDER TO SHERIFF ISSUED IN THE CASE OF:
AMERICAN GLANZSTOFF CORPORATION AND AMERICAN BEMBERG CORPORATION,

—AGAINST—

GEORGE MILLER, [and twenty-one other named individuals] in their own right and representing each and all employees of the American Bemberg Corporation and American Glanzstoff Corporation, AND ALSO AGAINST:

ELIZABETHTON LOCAL, No. 1630, of the UNITED TEXTILE WORKERS AFFILIATED WITH THE UNITED TEXTILE WORKERS OF AMERICA, an association of the employees of said Bemberg Corporation and Glanzstoff Corporation, its leaders, officers and members; and against G. H. Markland, President; C. S. White, Vice-President; Miss Margaret Bowen, Secretary and Treasurer; Miss Christine Galligher, Recording Secretary; Guy Gibbs, Warden; M. P. Wilson, Conductor, and J. B. Penix, Organizer.

The original bill enjoined the defendants above named from "Entering into or upon the premises of complainants; from congregating or collecting, assembling in groups or mobs around the gates leading into the property upon which complainants plants are located, or around their fences and property lines for the purpose of interfering with complainants, the operation of their plants and business, their employees who are not connected with said strike desiring to enter said premises and work for complainants, or those desiring to engage employment and work for complainants; from interfering with, molesting or damaging complainants plants or property; from interfering with, molesting or intimidating complainants employees in any way whatsoever; from guarding, picketing, or threatening complainants plants, officers, employees, or those seeking employment; from unlawfully procuring complainants employees to breach their contracts of employment or from unlawfully in any way interfering with complainants, their employees or those seeking employment in a proper operation of their business, or the use and enjoyment of its plants, property and business, and all rights, benefits and privileges arising therefrom or incident thereto, and that on final hearing said injunction be made perpetual."

The amended and supplemental bill enjoined the defendants from:

Unlawfully congregating, picketing, confederating, assembling and patroling, complainants' plants, property lines and the highways in front and alongside of complainants' plants for the unlawful purpose of boycotting and interfering with complainants, their property, plants, officers, agents, employees, those seeking employment, their contract, rights, privileges, etc., and that defendants be enjoined from obstructing said highways in front and alongside of complainants' premises and unlawfully congregating on said highways where they have no right or business other than to unlawfully interfere with complainants, their property, etc.;: that they be further enjoined from lining up along said highway and across the roads and entrances to complainants' premises and obstructing same or interfering with same or those desiring to enter or leave said premises in any manner and that they be enjoined from in any way committing trespass or waste against complainants, their plants, premises, property, employees, etc.

At the time the last above injunction was granted, the Court by fiat, issued the following order to the Sheriff of Carter County, Tennessee, to wit:

"The Sheriff of Carter County is hereby ordered and directed forthwith by himself and deputies and such additional deputies as may be required to carry out and execute the terms of the injunction heretofore granted in the original bill and in this amended and supplemental bill so as to protect the property of complainants and so as to prevent unlawful interference by the defendants and their associates with the employees of complainants who are voluntarily at work or who may desire to work.

Protection should be afforded employees whether on the premises or adjacent thereto against unlawful interference by the defendants, their agents or associates.

The Sheriff will report to the Court forthwith as to how he has executed this order.

This March 18, 1929.

S. E. MILLER, Chancellor.

STATE OF TENNESSEE
CARTER COUNTY

I, R. R. Cass, Clerk and Master of the Chancery Court of Carter County, Tennessee, do hereby certify that the foregoing is a true, correct and perfect copy of the two writs of injunction and the order to the Sheriff issued in the above case of American Glanzstoff Corporation, et al., vs. George Miller, and Elizabethton Local No. 1630 of the United Textile Workers of America, et al., as the same appears of record in my office.

Given under my hand and official Seal at office in Elizabethton, Tennessee, on this the 18th day of March, 1929.

Clerk & Master.

Came to hand same day issued and executed as commanded by reading this bill to the officers named and the members of Local 1630 Textile Workers affiliated with the United Textile Workers of America.

This March 18th, 1929.

A. B. WILLIAMS,
Deputy Sheriff.

APPENDIX XXIII
SUMMARY OF INTERVIEWS WITH DEFENDANTS
AMERICAN GLANZSTOFF CORPORATION V. GEORGE MILLER, ET AL.

1. When did you first hear about the injunction?
   "Soon after the first strike [March]."—31
   "Several days after the first strike."—6
   "After the second strike [April]."—7
   How?
   "I heard it read by a deputy sheriff at the tabernacle."—9
   "I was told by union officers."—6
   "I saw a newspaper or posted notice."—4
   "By hearsay."—8
   "I was told by enforcement officers; Sheriff Moreland and others."—15
   "I was told by my father."
   "Notice was served on me by Deputy Sheriff."

2. How did you feel when you first read it or heard about it?
   "I thought I had better stay away from the company's property and vicinity."—7
   "I didn't know anything about it; but I didn't want to break the law."—4
   "I didn't feel like obeying."
   "I didn't care much about it."—6
   "I wanted to fight that much harder."—2
   "I thought I had better obey."—3

"I didn't like it much but there was danger of trouble, right or wrong."—2

"I thought it was rotten. Better stay away from premises."

"It didn't apply to me."

"It was a dirty deal but I thought there would be trouble if we went against it."—2

"I didn't think it was right but I thought I had better obey it."—3

"I thought it was a bluff but I better obey it."

"I thought it was 'damned bull' and I wasn't afraid of it."

"I felt that everybody was against us. We had to quit or go to jail."—2

"I felt it very unjust. Didn't feel like obeying. I told them they could put us in jail."

"It made me mad. I thought there was nothing to it."

"It didn't amount to anything."

3. What did your wife or family say about it?

"She wanted me to stay at home and keep out of jail."—4

"I had better be careful."

"They [my parents] tried to keep me off picket lines."—10

"Nothing."—9

"Nothing, but she was scared about it."

"She said it was an unjust deal."—2

"They didn't know about it."

4. Do you think the injunction broke the strike?

"It had a lot to do with it."—4

"No."—23
"Yes."—5
"It helped break it."—2
"To a certain extent."—2
"Not alone; State Troops on outlying roads did it."
"It and the guards together did."
"It might have."

5. Do you think the strike would have been more successful without the injunction?

"Yes."—41
"I believe so."—2
"It might have."

Comments:

"We could have secured a better agreement without it."—21

"We could have secured a quicker agreement without it."—18

"I know it would."—2

"We could have picketed more."—4

"We could have kept them (scabs) out."—3

"We could have secured a just settlement."

"We could have gone in where the trains stopped."

"The parties could have gotten together easier."

"It sure would."

"We could have talked to people and kept them out."

"Fewer would have tried to work."

"To be sure."

6. Do you think any of the workers were frightened by the injunction?

"Yes."—20
"No."—11

"In a way."
"Not much."—2
"It might have."
Comments:
    "It scared most of them."—2
    "It kept people 'cowed' down."
    "It kept some off picket."—6
    "Several were and several were not."
    "It kept most of them off picket."—3
    "It kept many off picket."—9
    "They laughed at it."
    "It made people more cautious."
    "It scared most of the boys; I don't think it scared the girls." (Girls speaking)—3

7. Were you brought up for contempt?
    "No."—27
    "Yes."—5
    What specific charge?
    "Rioting and breaking injunction."
    "Picketing highway."—2
    "Picketing."
    "Stopping people on highways and threatening them."
    What punishment?
    "Ten dollars' fine."—3
    "Jail one day."
    "None."

8. Do you think the company gained by using the injunction?
    "Yes."—11
    "No."—29

Comments:

"They got men they could not have gotten otherwise."—6

"It caused workers to have less respect for them."—4

"They lost."—3

"It helped them get strike breakers."—10

"It lost people's sentiment; made enemies."—6

"They lost money for guards to enforce it."—7

"No. We went on duty every day, we would get arrested, get bond and go out again."

"They lost the heavy expense from being shut down."

"They got a lot of inefficient workers."

9. Do you think it is fair to use injunctions in such cases?

"No."—39

"Yes, in proper place; not proper when used all over the county like they did in this case."—2

Why or why not?

"Because you can't get a chance to see all the people that go into work and show them right."

"Otherwise, you could talk to people and urge them not to go in."—2

"We should have a right to talk to them."

"The Union didn't intend to destroy property, etc."

"It kept us off of public road where we had a right to be."—3

"The law should give all the same chance."

"Peaceful picketing should have been allowed."

"It was used on some and not on others."

"It gives the company the upper hand of labor."—4

"It takes away a working man's rights; right to picket."
"We should have the right to advise them not to go in."—4
"It's a dirty law."
"If employer had been fair it would have been unnecessary."
"It's against the working class people; it tries to make slaves of people."
"We had a right to strike for better conditions."
"It's all right to protect destruction of property."
"It's generally issued by a man partial to the other side."
"They only serve the mill-owner."
"You couldn't talk to them about joining the union."
"It's a coward's weapon."

10. Would the workers have obeyed the injunction if the soldiers had not been there?
"No."—6
"Yes."—10
"They would have stayed off company property."
"I believe they would."—2
"They would not have destroyed company property."—2

Comments:
"The injunction wouldn't have amounted to anything without the soldiers."
"They would have obeyed better without militia."
"They wouldn't have killed anybody."
"The sheriff had them better in hand."
"It's hard to control a bunch."

"Not all."
"They would have gone out on picket."
"The soldiers made it ten times worse."
"The deputies couldn't have taken care of them."
"The militia caused all the trouble."

Remarks:

"It kept the people divided and kept up the disturbance."

"Soldiers won't carry yellow dogs in if they have another strike."

"They had 800 soldiers here."

"General Boyd told them to run over a girl."

"The injunction was no good."

"In case of another strike I would picket anyway."

"Little good without soldiers."

"The Courts are so corrupt that a man can't get justice."

"The injunction caused the sentiment of the people to be aroused against the management permanently."

"I didn't think much about trouble. I knew I could get out."

"A good many wouldn't have paid any attention to the injunction if the leaders hadn't advised them to obey it."

"I was brought up for contempt on the charge of going on picket duty. There were hundreds brought up for contempt, tried (by the Justice of the Peace) and all turned loose but about five. . . . They wouldn't live up to the agreement. There wasn't any violence at all—only the National guards would get drunk and fight and be put under arrest by some of the other guards."

"I didn't care anything about it but I took the advice of union leaders and obeyed it."

"We went on picket duty but we didn't go on the company's property."

"They took thirty or forty of us to jail without warrants. They issued warrants for fifteen or twenty of them and tried them for contempt. Squire Ryan dismissed the case. The soldiers broke the strike."

"My father was a deputy sheriff. He said they couldn't do anything to me if I stopped on the road. I was on picket near Hunter, four miles from town. The deputy sheriffs picked us up and took us to jail. The magistrate threw the case out of court. We were in jail about forty minutes."

"I helped picket near the plant during the first strike when Captain Elliott told us to leave. We went to the highway to picket. The police came and ran us off. Then we came back to town. Later I helped picket on the Bristol highway."

"I had started to work one morning. I got off and helped on the picket lines. I was on picket on the highway about four miles from town, near Hunter. I was picked up by soldiers and kept in jail about forty minutes. I would advise a man to obey the injunction."

"Conditions are better now. I was getting $10.00 a week before the strike. Now I am getting $15.80. Hours are shorter, too. The bosses are good to me. They are laying several off."

"One of the sheriffs hit a girl with a billy."

"They are helping us more now. They are not so hard on us. Rules are more decent."

"The soldiers went out sixteen miles or farther. It's an unhealthful place to work. Everybody complains with stomach trouble."

"Injunctions and soldiers are unfair. Conditions are now right smart better. A good many would have paid no attention if the leaders hadn't advised them to obey. I can't understand why they would grant an injunction against a peaceful struggling people."

"Soldiers went out eighteen miles and got strike breakers."

"The injunction did help them to get strike breakers."

"I am getting $3.75 a week more than I was before the strike. Conditions are better. They know the people here won't be run over."

"I belonged to the State Guards. A large number of the guards refused to serve. The use of the National Guard here was the dirtiest deal ever pulled. I turned in my equipment when I was ordered to go out and patrol the road. I was dropped from the payroll two weeks later."

"The soldiers raised the ambition and hatred of the workers. They created a deep hatred of military force that will never get out of them."

"The Bemberg Spinning Department was on the verge of a strike anyway. They were hiring about one-third of the regular number when the settlement was made."

"They had a strike in the spinning room at Bemberg about March, 1928. They made an agreement to give a 5 per cent increase in wages. They violated it. Eighty per cent of those at Bemberg were perfectly willing and ready to walk out."

"There had been talk of a strike at Bemberg long before."

"They couldn't have got any workers in without soldiers."

"I was caught in Gap Creek picketing. The soldiers arrested me. I was tried in Chancery Court. They kept us under guard in the court house."

"Soldiers made the matter worse."

"At Glanzstoff, the girls in the reeling department were locked up. The strikers went to get them out. There is still a bad feeling. Dr. Hoffmann, head of the experimental department, is a fine fellow. Dr. Stofenhaufen is too."

"The soldiers put the injunction on the bum. They made it ten times worse. It had little effect except right around the plant. The troops were not ordered out by the government. They were sworn in as deputy sheriffs. The injunction put the clamps on. The people didn't want to go to jail."

"Workers are afraid of injunctions. Injunctions were threatened in the case of each disturbance. . . . Ordinarily, a man is wet from his waist down. There are continuous fumes of sulphuric acid chlorine and ammonia. . . . To be efficient, a man should work four months. The more experience, the better. An inexperienced man damages silk and does more harm than good."

APPENDIX XXIV

Virginia } In the Corporation Court of Danville

RIVERSIDE AND DAN RIVER COTTON MILLS, INC.

VS.

FRANCIS J. GORMAN, ETC.

Bill for Injunction

To the Honorable Henry C. Leigh, Judge of the Corporation Court of Danville:

Humbly complaining showeth unto Your Honor that your undersigned complainant has the following case which it is advised entitles it to equitable relief.

1. Complainant is a corporation organized under the laws of the State of Virginia with its principal office in Pittsylvania County and has located in said Pittsylvania County and in the City of Danville several large textile mills; that it gives employment, when it is able to operate full time, to approximately five thousand (5000) employees; that for forty (40) years or more, there has been no serious dispute or contention between it and its employees, but that recently one, Francis J. Gorman, has organized or caused to be organized a voluntary association known as Local Number 1685 of the United Textile Workers of America; that a considerable part of your complainant's employees have become members of said Union; that recently, on Monday the 29th day of September, 1930, said Union has caused a strike to be declared and both plants of your complainant are now at

a standstill; that the plants of your complainant are surrounded by a fence and that at various points in said fence there are gates which are commonly used so that the employees may pass to and fro into the plants; that at certain points in the plant in the City of Danville these gates are located wholly on the property belonging to your complainant; that the streets or passageways in front of said gates and leading thereto are wholly private ways and not public thoroughfares but are part and parcel of the real estate owned by your complainant:

That said voluntary association, United Textile Workers of America, Local Number 1685 claims to have elected one, J. C. Blackwell, Secretary and one B. F. Nash, President and that with certain executive committees, the names of whom are unknown to your complainant, are undertaking to direct and control the movements and actions of your complainant's foremen and employees who are not members of said Union for the purpose of making effective the strike which has been called by said Francis J. Gorman, B. F. Nash, J. C. Blackwell and others to interfere with and prevent your complainant from using its property; that they have placed large numbers of men at each gate of your complainant's plants; in some instances there being located at said gates as many as twenty-five (25) men and in other cases larger numbers; that they stand in front of and obstruct said gates and by force and by intimidation prevent persons from passing in and out of said gates;

2. That on the 29th day of September, 1930 at about 4:30 o'clock your complainant finding it absolutely necessary for one, Atwell Farley, employed by it as paymaster

of Riverside Division, to enter one of the gates of its plant for the purpose of doing some work on the payroll, sent the said Farley to one of the gates of its plant being commonly known as gate number 6 located at the corner of North Main and River Streets in City of Danville; that at said gate there was crowded around and in front of said gate a large number of persons, to wit, twenty-five (25) persons who represented themselves to be members of Local Union 1685 of the United Textile Workers of America and said persons, who were apparently engaged in picketing said gate refused the said Atwell Farley permission to enter said property, claiming and insisting that they had a legal right to stand before the gates of your complainant's property and restrain by force entry into same of such persons as they wished; that although the said Atwell Farley attempted to enter the said gate peaceably and quietly, rough hands were laid upon him and he was forcibly restrained from entering on complainant's property; That the said Atwell Farley applied to [a] local police officer to disperse said persons who were unlawfully assembled and permit him to enter said property but said police officer refused to take any action; that he then applied to police headquarters and was unable to obtain any officer or assistance of any officer in effecting an entrance into said property; he therefore had to abandon his efforts as he was overcome by superior force and numbers of the members of the said Union; that again at about 7:30 A.M. on the 30th day of September, 1930 your complainant desiring to have employees to enter its gate commonly known as number eight (8) which is located wholly on the private property of your complainant and does not abut upon a public thoroughfare; that at said gate there were located approximately fifty (50) or more persons who claimed to be picketing said gate and represented themselves as members of the aforesaid Union, although your complainant through its agents explained to said persons the purpose of entry of said employees was to finish the process of work on certain goods which were in the slasher, which would be injured and destroyed if the process were not completed, they were forcibly restrained by said persons and not permitted to enter on complainant's property; that complainant again appealed to the Chief of Police of the City of Danville requesting that said unlawful assembly be dispersed and restrained from interfering with complainant's property and the use of same, said police officers in a misapprehension of your complainant's rights refused to take any action unless criminal warrants were secured against each and all of said persons, many of whom were unknown to your complainant except that they represented and claimed to be members of said Union, and your complainant's employees were forcibly restrained and refused admittance to complainant's property.

Your complainant, therefore, prays that Local Union Number 1685 of the United Textile Workers of America, Francis J. Gorman, B. F. Nash, and J. C. Blackwell be made parties defendant to this bill and required to answer the same, but answer under oath is hereby expressly waived; that Your Honor will enter an order enjoining and restraining the said defendants and other persons from congregating in large numbers in front of the gates of your complainant's property and from in any way impeding by force, intimidation, or coercion or threats or other unlawful means the free passage of the said agents and employees of your complainant through these gates and in and out of its property; that the said defendants and all other persons be restrained from trespassing upon and congregating on the private property, ways and streets belonging wholly to your complainant and the officers of Your Honor's court be instructed to post copies of such order at several convenient public places on and around the plant and property belonging to your complainant: that proper process may issue and copy of said injunction order be served upon the named defendants; that Your Honor do adjudge and declare the right in complainant of free, unimpeded and unobstructed use of its own property lawfully and peaceably; and that such further orders may be entered as will specifically and fully protect your complainant and its lawful rights to use the property which belongs to it and its lawful rights to conduct its business without the unlawful interference of the said defendants and other persons.

Your complainant does not deny the equal right of the defendants and all other persons to form and become members of a Union or voluntary association, nor does it deny their right to work or not to work as they may see fit, but your complainant respectfully insists and appeals to the court that it has an equal right to the free and unimpeded use of its property and that its agents and employees who desire to enter its gates for the purpose of working in its plant have a full and complete right to enter in and at all gates at such times and for such purposes as they may see fit without being intimidated, coerced, threatened or otherwise unlawfully interfered with and that your complainant has the right to the use and enjoyment of its private property to prevent persons who constitute themselves trespassers to congregate in large numbers in and about its doors, offices, and its plant and to in any way interfere with the legal and orderly conduct of your complainant's business and your complainant shows that the aforesaid acts of said named defendants and members of said Union are illegally, unlawfully constituting an unlawful conspiracy to do an unlawful act and that the damage to your complainant will be irreparable and that it is without adequate remedy at law.

Therefore your complainant prays that all necessary orders and decrees may be entered and that your complainant be granted such general relief as will protect and preserve its rights as above set out.

Your complainant will ever pray, etc.

  RIVERSIDE AND DAN RIVER COTTON MILLS, INC.
    BY MALCOLM K. HARRIS,
        Counsel.

(Certified by L. J. Rushworth.)

APPENDIX XXV

Virginia

In the Circuit Court of the County of Pittsylvania

RIVERSIDE AND DAN RIVER COTTON MILLS, INCORPORATED

VS.

FRANCIS J. GORMAN AND OTHERS IN CHANCERY

Restraining Order

This cause came on this day to be heard on the prayer of the bill duly filed and affidavits in support thereof, and the court being of the opinion that under the law, while persons have a lawful right to desist from work if they see fit, and have the right by peaceful persuasion to cause others to leave the employment of their former employer, or to persuade others from seeking such employment, it is unlawful to use force or violence, or to terrorize or intimidate new employees; that it is unlawful to congregate in large numbers and by force of numbers, intimidation, threats or violence to prevent employees from entering the property of the Riverside and Dan River Cotton Mills; that it is unlawful to trespass upon, or enter without permission the private property, streets and ways which are the private property of the Riverside and Dan River Cotton Mills; that it is unlawful to interfere with the business of the plaintiff, the Riverside and Dan River Cotton Mills, by patrolling the sidewalk or street in front of same or in the vicinity of the premises occupied by them, for the purpose of preventing persons from entering same by force; that if watching or picketing is carried on to an extent which causes intimidation or which amounts to intimidation, compulsion or coercion in any form of either non-union workmen or their employers, it is unlawful, and the combination making use of such unlawful means is a conspiracy; that no persons individually or by combination have the right, directly or indirectly, to interfere with or disturb another in his lawful business or occupation, or to threaten to do so for the sake of compelling him to do some act which, in his own judgment, his interest does not require, and the court doth therefore grant an injunction to the Riverside and Dan River Cotton Mills, Incorporated, enjoining and restraining the named defendant, Francis J. Gorman, Local No. 1685 United Textile Workers of America, and the members thereof, B. F. Nash as President, J. C. Blackwell, its Secretary, and all other persons, from congregating in large numbers in front of the gates leading to said plants and interfering with the free passage of persons lawfully desiring to pass therethrough, from entering upon and trespassing upon the private property of the Riverside and Dan River Cotton Mills, Incorporated; from congregating on the private steps of said property; from in any way, by force, threats, intimidation, coercion or otherwise, preventing free passage of the agents and employees of the Riverside and Dan River Cotton Mills and of all other persons in and out its gates over and along its property.

This injunction shall become effective and begin to operate as soon as, but not until the complainants or someone for them shall enter into bond before the clerk of this court in the sum of $1000.00 conditioned according to law, and when such bond is given the clerk of this court shall endorse that fact upon this injunction order, showing the time said bond was given. And it is further ordered that copies of this injunction order be promptly served upon the named defendants, and that copies of same be posted in three public places in the County of Pittsylvania, in the vicinity of the village of Schoolfield. This injunction order shall be in force from the time above set out to noon on the 1st day of December, 1930, at which time it shall stand dissolved unless prior thereto it has been enlarged and further injunction ordered.

The clerk of the Circuit Court of Pittsylvania County shall enter this order in vacation.

J. T. CLEMENT, Judge.

Teste: S. S. HURT, Clerk.

Bond with security executed this 30th day of September, 1930.

A Copy—Teste:

S. S. Hurt, Clerk.

APPENDIX XXVI

In the Circuit Court of Pittsylvania County, Virginia

RIVERSIDE & DAN RIVER COTTON MILLS, INCORPORATED
v.
FRANCIS J. GORMAN ET AL.

Answer

The answer of Local Union No. 1685 United Textile Workers of America, Francis J. Gorman, B. F. Nash and J. C. Blackwell, to a bill in equity exhibited against them in the Circuit Court of Pittsylvania County, Virginia, by Riverside & Dan River Cotton Mills, Incorporated.

These respondents, for answer to said bill, answer and say:

Each and all of the defendants admit that the complainant is a corporation under the laws of the State of Virginia and that its principal office is in Pittsylvania County and that it operates several large textile mills in the City of Danville and in Pittsylvania County, Virginia, and that, when operating full time, said mills employ approximately five thousand (5000) persons, as set out in the first paragraph of said bill for injunction;

Each and all of the defendants deny all equities of said bill;

Each and all of the defendants deny that for forty (40) years or more there has been no serious dispute or contention between the employees of the complainant and the management therof but allege that on the contrary in 1919 the management of the aforesaid mills inaugurated a vague, theoretical system called Industrial Democracy and deluded the workers into the belief that they would have some sort of voice in the management of said mills; that this so-called Industrial Democracy operated to keep down labor costs for the mills at a time when wages in every other industry were high and did not permit the workers in the mills to earn wages to which they were entitled during the War time days of inflated values and large pay and that although the theory of this so-called Industrial Democracy embraced the idea that the workers should vote their convictions with reference to representation, that they were continually coerced by second-hands, foremen and overseers of complainant to vote for those representatives which the management knew it could control to the detriment of the workers and for the benefit of the management; that if any worker was bold enough to suggest improvements which did not meet with the approval of the management of the aforesaid mills, that worker was subsequently, on some slight pretext, discharged and placed on the "black list"; that is to say, he was never again permitted to secure employment in said mill; that such a system was calculated to cause distrust and unrest among the workers and that they finally came to the conclusion that the so-called Industrial Democracy had been promulgated exclusively to coerce the workers and to prevent them from organizing for their mutual betterment; that finally, exercising what they conceived to be their right to join together for mutual betterment, a large number of the workers journeyed to Richmond and requested President Green, of the American Federation of Labor, to send them an experienced organizer, purely for the purpose of superintending the mechanics of organization, which the workers of the Riverside & Dan River Cotton Mills, Incorporated, joined voluntarily, and moulded into an association known as Local No. 1685 of the United Textile Workers of America; that, notwithstanding Letter Poster No. 192, issued February 12, 1930, by the Riverside & Dan River Cotton Mills, Incorporated, and signed by its President and Treasurer, H. R. Fitzgerald, in which he said, "However, if or when we become convinced that a majority do not care for or appreciate these principles" (meaning the so-called Industrial Democracy principles) "and they cannot be trusted to adhere to them, of course the system will be withdrawn," when the management found that the entire working force did not care for or appreciate such a system, they refused to withdraw it, and after the workers had repudiated said system by forming a voluntary organization, the management insisted upon forcing them to continue the system of so-called Industrial Democracy by calling a certain election, strapping the ballot boxes around the necks of the overseers, who, flanked by two second-hands, carried the ballots and the ballot boxes to the workers, together with checkers, who checked the ballots as they were voted by the workers, and those who did not vote were discharged from the employ of the said mills and many of those, who were coerced into voting, scratched all of the names on the ballots, only to be told that their services were no longer needed by the mills; that for the proper functioning of the said voluntary organized group, it became necessary to elect officers and committeemen, all of whom were immediately discharged by the said mills for no other reason than that they had exercised their God given right to join a voluntary association for their mutual betterment;

Your respondents deny that recently Francis J. Gorman has organized or caused to be organized a voluntary association known as Local No. 1685 of the United Textile Workers of America, but that such organization was caused by the inability of the employees of said mills to lay before the management of said mills their grievances with reference to their employment and because of the refusal of said management to listen to any of said grievances;

Your respondents admit that a considerable part of complainant's employees have become members of said Union; that, as a matter of fact, nearly all of the employees, except those foremen, superintendents, second-hands and paymasters and clerks who were not affected by the so-called Industrial Democracy system, are members of the said Union; that some time before the formation of the said Union, the stretch-out system was inaugurated in the mills; its members were insulted by foremen and second-hands, were threatened by second-hands with pistols, which situation became so bad that a warrant was about to be issued to Jones, a second-hand of complainant at Schoolfield, and the clamor became so great by the workers that the management was forced to discharge said Jones; that the management permitted certain of its overseers to operate a loan shark business in said mills, charging usurious rates of interest, one employee having borrowed from his overseer five ($5.00) dollars, paying him in return fifty (50c) cents per week for thirty (30) weeks, and then, upon said employee's being discharged, his pay was docked the original five ($5.00) dollars borrowed; that after making repeated efforts to lay their grievances before the management of the said mills through their duly organized representatives and being repeatedly refused and denied a hearing, the workers banded together on Monday, September 29, 1930, and did not return to work, in protest against the inhuman, unjust and unfair treatment that they had been receiving at the hands of the management of the said mills; naturally, a great many members of the Union were not advised of the situation and they arrived at the mill gates on the aforesaid Monday morning to find said gates locked, and your respondents admit that among some of the members there was some confusion;

Your respondents deny that they, or any of them, or that any Executive Committee of said Union, are undertaking to direct or control the movements and actions of the complainant's foremen and employees who are not members of said Union;

Your respondents deny that they have called a strike against complainant but allege that the workers, the former employees of complainant, voted, by an overwhelming majority, not to return to the mill under the inhuman, unfair, unjust and oppressive conditions existing;

Your respondents deny that they have placed large numbers of men at each of the gates of the complainant's plant who, by force and intimidation, prevent persons from passing in and out of said gates;

Your respondents deny that on the 29th day of September, 1930, at about twelve-thirty o'clock, they, or any of them, or any members of said Union, prevented fifteen (15) or twenty (20) workmen to enter a certain gate of complainant's plant;

Your respondents deny that any members of said Union, inspired and directed by other members of said Union and Francis J. Gorman, J. C. Blackwell and B. F. Nash, forcibly prevented the entrance of said employees into said mill for the purpose of saving certain goods then in process in said mills;

Your respondents deny that they, or any members of said Union, on said 29th day of September, 1930, defied officers of the law and they further deny that they continued to unlawfully congregate on the mill's property and deny that they attempted by force to prevent complainant from using and enjoying its property;

Your respondents deny that the acts of them or the acts of the members of said Union in picketing peaceably are illegal, unlawful and constitute an unlawful conspiracy to do an unlawful act;

That contrary to the false charges made in the petition drawn by Malcolm K. Harris, Attorney for the Riverside & Dan River Cotton Mills, Incorporated, and a Director in said corporation, who has repeatedly, both publicly and privately, expressed the wish that the workers would strike, the said Malcolm K. Harris was told by the Police Officers of the City of Danville, and the Commonwealth's Attorney for the County of Pittsylvania, who had discussed the situation with all of the officials of the said Union, that said officials had instructed all of the members of said Union that no force, intimidation or coercion could be used but that only peaceable picketing could be indulged in; that said Union issued orders that any law violators would be disciplined by said Union, and that offers were made by the said Union to co-operate with the law enforcement officers of the City of Danville and County of Pittsylvania to the fullest extent; that the said mill management knew and had been advised at the time said petition for injunction was filed of these facts and, therefore, that the charges that Francis J. Gorman, B. F. Nash and J. C. Blackwell had conspired to do an unlawful act was a deliberate misrepresentation of facts which they had in their possession; and your respondents deny that they have at any time formed any such conspiracy;

Your respondents point with pride to the statement of Honorable Posie J. Hundley, Attorney for the Commonwealth for the County of Pittsylvania, Virginia, that there have been no law violations in the entire County of Pittsylvania since the lock-out by the mills was put into effect, with the exception of one lone drunk, an old man, not in any way connected with said Union, who staggered up to an automobile driven by officers and asked for a ride, which was given him, and he was arrested and brought to the jail;

Your respondents allege that Local No. 1685 of the United Textile Workers of America is composed of former employees of the Riverside & Dan River Cotton Mills, Incorporated, who have given the best years of their lives in loyal service to said corporation;

Your respondents deny that there is any disposition on the part of its officers or members to cause any injury either reparable or irreparable, to the property of the Riverside and Dan River Cotton Mills, Incorporated;

Your respondents further deny that there is any equity in said bill for injunction for the reason that said bill alleges that certain members of the Union, aforesaid, have committed a trespass upon the property of complainant and that said bill, among other prayers, prays that the defendants in said bill and all other persons be restrained from trespassing upon and congregating on the private property, ways and streets belonging wholly to complainant; and respondents here allege that if any such trespass has been committed, complainant has his adequate remedy at law to recover for such trespass, and for the further reason that an injunction will not lie to prevent a trespass unless such trespass does irreparable damage to the property in question, and respondents deny that irreparable damage has been done to any property of complainant.

Your respondents pray that this answer may be treated as a cross-bill and that for affirmative relief, the injunction awarded complainants in this cause may be dissolved and this suit be dismissed forthwith on this answer. And now having fully answered, respondents pray hence to be dismissed.

LOCAL UNION NO. 1685 UNITED TEXTILE WORKERS OF AMERICA

By B. F. NASH, President

FRANCIS J. GORMAN
B. F. NASH
J. C. BLACKWELL

By Counsel

Hugh T. Williams
Ida Mandle
Counsel

APPENDIX XXVII
LETTER POSTER NUMBER 192
TO ALL OF OUR PEOPLE

"We are informed that paid organizers have appeared in our midst and that as usual they are appealing to such prejudices as they can arouse and do not hesitate to distort existing facts to carry their point.

"We think that we can confidently claim to be the friends of our people and that the many years of pleasant relationships that have existed in the organization will speak for themselves as to the truth of this statement.

"Our system of Employee Representation contains every element of collective bargaining that has any real merit. It is true that it does not give either employer or employee a club with which to intimidate or threaten anybody, but is based upon the principles of Justice, Co-operation, Economy, Energy and Service. It has never failed to obtain for the employees the best possible rates of pay and the best working conditions. If any one entertains any doubt as to the correctness of this statement, it can easily be verified with actual facts and authentic figures.

"We do not desire the employees of the Company to be misled by these outsiders for the simple reason that they cause discord and their whole method of operation depends upon agitation and strife. This has been so obvious and so unsatisfactory to those who have tried it that their membership among textile workers has dwindled to almost the vanishing point. You have only to examine the history of the Textile Industry in the New England states and to observe its present condition to see how tragic has been the result; the bitterness engendered; the severe financial losses incurred; and the rapid decline in the number of people employed, being now only a fraction of what it was before prosperity was driven away from them.

"What can such a movement do for you that you do not already have EXCEPT TO TAKE YOUR MONEY IN DUES TO PAY A LOT OF FOREIGN AGITATORS AND SOME FEW DISGRUNTLED UNAPPRECIATIVE PERSONS WHO ARE CONTINUALLY SOWING SEEDS OF DISCORD AND UNHAPPINESS?

"If there were any merit in their claims it seems to us that they would go into those sections where labor is being exploited at low wage rates, with night running, etc., and demonstrate to the world whether they can improve those conditions. They will tell you that they 'are going to do this,' but that they want to get started first; which means of course that they want your money to do it with and, incidentally to fill their own depleted coffers.

"We have confidence in the good sense of most of our people and we believe that they sufficiently recognize the principle of Justice to let the facts speak for themselves.

"For eleven years we have fought hard against the downward trend of post-war deflation, refusing to reduce wages when others were doing it and persistently holding the living standards of our people as high as we could. We carried this burden without one whimper of complaint, trying to gradually increase the efficiency of the organization to meet the many changes in distributive demands and to put out fabrics of superior merit that would win success both for the operatives and the Company.

"The past two years have been extremely difficult, as evidenced by the fact that your Company was compelled to curtail an average of more than 25% of its normal capacity. Furthermore with a wage differential of more than 20% above the average of the entire South it created an unsound economic condition which neither the Company nor its operatives could afford. Not until we became firmly convinced that the situation was serious in that respect and that it would mean more money in your envelopes, instead of less, did we consent to the adjustment of wage and salary rates.

"Now that this has been done, we feel that your prospects have been decidedly improved, and while the goods markets are still very weak, with no real margin of profit for anyone, we are doing our level best to run the Mills as near full capacity as we can. We cannot see very far ahead and can make no promises as to what the future may bring forth, but we confidently hope that you can soon be earning an Economy Dividend; more important, however, is the fact that with your economic condition improved there will be less curtailment and in the long run more money in your envelopes than for the past two years.

"We have tried to encourage our people to think for themselves; not to be unduly influenced by superficial impressions either inside the organization or OUTSIDE OF IT, but to base their judgments upon what is right and fair.

"We regret the insidious temptation that is placed before you by these agitators, who appeal to your credulity with promises that neither they nor anyone else can make good. But we confidently expect that the vast majority of the members of our organization will continue to appreciate what they have accomplished by co-operation and that they will refuse in no uncertain terms to be deluded by these false promises.

"It is our purpose to continue to work for the happiness and prosperity of all our people. We realize that the eyes of the world are upon the organization to see whether it is indeed possible for friendly relationships to be maintained in adversity as well as in prosperity. We believe that it is and that this will be fully demonstrated.

"However if or when we become convinced that a majority do not care for or appreciate these principles and that they cannot be trusted to adhere to them, of course the system will be withdrawn.

"We are, therefore, putting before you this friendly message, and in the kindest spirit, with the hope that you will have nothing to do with these trouble makers. They can do no good but they can cause you much harm.

"With every good wish and kindest personal regards.
Yours very truly,"
(Signed) H. R. FITZGERALD,
President and Treasurer.

Letter Poster Number 192
Issued February 12, 1930.

APPENDIX XXVIII

WISCONSIN STATUTE (1931)

An Act to create section 268.18 to 268.30 of the statutes, relating to litigation growing out of labor disputes and limiting the jurisdiction of courts sitting in equity.

The people of the state of Wisconsin, represented in senate and assembly, do enact as follows:

SECTION 1. Thirteen new sections are added to the statutes to read: 268.18 PUBLIC POLICY AS TO COLLECTIVE BARGAINING. In the interpretation and application of sections 268.18 to 268.30 the public policy of this state is declared as follows:

Negotiation of terms and conditions of labor should result from voluntary agreement between employer and employes. Governmental authority has permitted and encouraged employers to organize in the corporate and other forms of capital control. In dealing with such employers, the individual unorganized worker is helpless to exercise actual liberty of contract and to protect his freedom of labor, and thereby to obtain acceptable terms and conditions of employment. Therefore it is necessary that the individual workman have full freedom of association, self-organization, and designation of representatives of his own choosing, to negotiate the terms and conditions of his employment, and that he shall be free from the interference, restraint or coercion of employers of labor, or their agents, in the designation of such representatives or in self-organization or in other concerted activities for the purpose of collective bargaining or other mutual aid or protection.

268.19 "YELLOW-DOG" CONTRACTS. Every undertaking or promise made after the taking effect of this section, whether written or oral, express or implied, between any employe or prospective employe and his employer, prospective employer or any other individual, firm, company, association, or corporation, whereby

(1) Either party thereto undertakes or promises to join or to remain a member of some specific labor organization or organizations or to join or remain a member of some specific employer organization or any employer organization or organizations; or

(2) Either party thereto undertakes or promises not to join or not to remain a member of some specific labor organization or any labor organization or organizations, or of some specific employer organization or any employer organization or organizations; or

(3) Either party thereto undertakes or promises that he will withdraw from an employment relation in the event that he joins or remains a member of some specific labor organization or any labor organization or organizations, or of some specific employer organization or any employer organization or organizations;

Is hereby declared to be contrary to public policy and shall not afford any basis for the granting of legal or equitable relief by any court against a party to such undertaking or promise, or against any other persons who may advise, urge or induce, without fraud, violence, or threat thereof, either party thereto to act in disregard of such undertaking or promise. This section in its entirety is supplemental to and of subsection (1) of section 103.46 of the statutes.

268.20 LAWFUL CONDUCT IN LABOR DISPUTES. (1) The following acts, whether performed singly or in concert, shall be legal:

(a) Ceasing or refusing to perform any work or to remain in any relation of employment regardless of any promise, undertaking, contract or agreement in violation of the public policy declared in section 268.19;

(b) Becoming or remaining a member of any labor organization or of any employer organization, regardless of any such undertaking or promise as is described in section 268.19;

(c) Paying or giving to, any person any strike or unemployment benefit or insurance or other moneys or other things of value;

(d) By all lawful means aiding any person who is being proceeded against in, or is prosecuting any action or suit in any court of the United States or of any state;

(e) Giving publicity to and obtaining or communicating informating regarding the existence of, or the facts involved in, any dispute, whether by advertising, speaking, patrolling any public street or any place where any person or persons may lawfully be, without intimidation or coercion, or by any other method not involving fraud, violence, breach of the peace, or threat thereof;

(f) Ceasing to patronize or to employ any person or persons, but nothing herein shall be construed to legalize a secondary boycott;

(g) Assembling peaceably to do or to organize to do any of the acts heretofore specified or to promote lawful interests;

(h) Advising or notifying any person or persons of an intention to do any of the acts heretofore specified;

(i) Agreeing with other persons to do or not to do any of the acts heretofore specified;

(j) Advising, urging, or inducing without fraud, violence, or threat thereof, others to do the acts heretofore specified, regardless of any such undertaking or promise as is described in section 268.19; and

(k) Doing in concert any or all of the acts heretofore specified shall not constitute an unlawful combination or conspiracy.

(1) Peaceful picketing or patrolling, whether engaged in singly or in numbers, shall be legal.

(2) No court, nor any judge or judges thereof, shall have jurisdiction to issue any restraining order or temporary or permanent injunction which, in specific or general terms, prohibits any person or persons from doing, whether singly or in concert, any of the foregoing acts.

268.21 RESPONSIBILITY FOR UNLAWFUL ACTS. No officer or member of any association or organization, and no association or organization participating or interested in a labor dispute (as these terms are defined in section 268.29) shall be held responsible or liable in any civil action at law or suit in equity, or in any criminal prosecution, for the unlawful acts of individual officers, members, or agents, except upon proof by a preponderance of the evidence and without the aid of any presumptions of law or fact, both of (a) the doing of such acts by persons who are officers, members or agents of any such association or organization, and (b) actual participation in, or actual authorization of, such acts, or ratification of such acts after actual knowledge thereof by such association or organization.

268.22 PUBLIC POLICY AS TO LABOR LITIGATION. In the interpretation and application of sections 268.23 to 268.26, the public policy of this state is declared to be:

Equity procedure that permits a complaining party to obtain sweeping injunctive relief that is not preceded by or conditioned upon notice to and hearing of the responding party or parties, or that issues after hearing based upon written affidavits alone and not wholly or in part upon examination, confrontation and cross-examination of witnesses in open court, is peculiarly subject to abuse in labor litigation for the reasons that

(1) The *status quo* cannot be maintained but is necessarily altered by the injunction;

(2) Determination of issues of veracity and of probability of fact from affidavits of the opposing parties that are contradictory and, under the circumstances, untrustworthy rather than from oral examination in open court is subject to grave error;

(3) Error in issuing the injunctive relief is usually irreparable to the opposing party; and

(4) Delay incident to the normal course of appellate practice frequently makes ultimate correction of error in law or in fact unavailing in the particular case.

268.23 INJUNCTIONS: CONDITIONS OF ISSUANCE; RESTRAINING ORDERS. (1) No court nor any judge or judges thereof shall have jurisdiction to issue a temporary or permanent injunction in any case involving or growing out of a labor dispute, as defined in section 268.29, except after hearing the testimony of witnesses in open court (with opportunity for cross-examination) in support of the allegations of a complaint made under oath, and testimony in opposition thereto, if offered, and except after findings of all the following facts by the court or judge or judges thereof;

(a) That unlawful acts have been threatened or committed and will be executed or continued unless restrained;

(b) That substantial and irreparable injury to complainant's property will follow unless the relief requested is granted;

(c) That as to each item of relief granted greater injury will be inflicted upon complainant by the denial thereof than will be inflicted upon defendants by the granting thereof;

(d) That the relief to be granted does not violate the provisions of section 268.20;

(e) That complainant has no adequate remedy at law; and

(f) That the public officers charged with the duty to. protect complainant's property have failed or are unable to furnish adequate protection.

(2) Such hearing shall be held after due and personal notice thereof has been given, in such manner as the court shall direct, to all known persons against whom relief is sought, and also to those public officers charged with the duty to protect complainant's property. Provided, however, that if a complainant shall also allege that unless a temporary restraining order shall be issued before such hearing may be had, a substantial and irreparable injury to complainant's property will be unavoid-

able, such a temporary restraining order may be granted upon the expiration of such reasonable notice of application therefor as the court may direct by order to show cause, but in no case less than forty-eight hours.

(3) Such order to show cause shall be served upon such party or parties as are sought to be restrained and as shall be specified in said order, and then only upon testimony under oath, or in the discretion of the court, upon affidavits, sufficient, if sustained, to justify the court in issuing a temporary injunction upon a hearing as herein provided for.

(4) Such a temporary restraining order shall be effective for no longer than five days, and at the expiration of said five days shall become void and not subject to renewal or extension, provided, however, that if the hearing for a temporary injunction shall have been begun before the expiration of the said five days the restraining order may in the court's discretion be continued until a decision is reached upon the issuance of the temporary injunction.

(5) No temporary restraining order or temporary injunction shall be issued except on condition that complainant shall first file an undertaking with adequate security sufficient to recompense those enjoined for any loss, expense, or damage caused by the improvident or erroneous issuance of such order or injunction, including all reasonable costs (together with a reasonable attorney's fee) and expense against the order or against the granting of any injunctive relief sought in the same proceeding and subsequently denied by the court.

(6) The undertaking herein mentioned shall be understood to signify an agreement entered into by the com-

plainant and the surety upon which a decree may be rendered in the same suit or proceeding against said complainant and surety, the said complainant and surety submitting themselves to the jurisdiction of the court for that purpose. But nothing herein contained shall deprive any party having a claim or cause of action under or upon such undertaking from electing to pursue his ordinary remedy by suit at law or in equity.

268.24 CLEAN HANDS DOCTRINE. No restraining order or injunctive relief shall be granted to any complainant who has failed to comply with any legal obligation which is involved in the labor dispute in question, or who has failed to make every reasonable effort to settle such dispute either by negotiation or with the aid of any available machinery of governmental mediation or voluntary arbitration, but nothing herein contained shall be deemed to require the court to await the action of any such tribunal if irreparable injury is threatened.

268.25 INJUNCTIONS: CONTENTS. Except as provided in section 268.23, no restraining order or temporary or permanent injunction shall be granted in a case involving or growing out of a labor dispute, except on the basis of findings of fact made and filed by the court in the record of the case prior to the issuance of such restraining order or injunction; and every restraining order or injunction granted in a case involving or growing out of a labor dispute shall include only a prohibition of such specific act or acts as may be expressly complained of in the bill of complaint or petition filed in such case and expressly included in said findings of fact made and filed by the court as provided herein; and shall be binding only upon the parties to the suit, their agents, servants, employes and attorneys, or those in active concert and participation with them, and who shall by personal service or otherwise have received actual notice of the same.

268.26 INJUNCTIONS: APPEALS. Whenever any court or judge or judges thereof shall issue or deny any temporary injunction in a case involving or growing out of a labor dispute, the court shall, upon the request of any party to the proceedings, and on his filing the usual bond for costs, forthwith certify the entire record of the case, including a transcript of the evidence taken, to the appropriate appellate court for its review. Upon the filing of such record in the appropriate appellate court the appeal shall be heard with the greatest possible expedition, giving the proceeding precedence over all other matters except older matters of the same character.

268.27 CONTEMPT CASES. In all cases where a person shall be charged with civil or criminal contempt for violation of a restraining order or injunction issued by a court or judge or judges thereof, the accused shall enjoy:

(1) The rights as to admission to bail that are accorded to persons accused of crime.

(2) The right to be notified of the accusation and a reasonable time to make a defense, provided the alleged contempt is not committed in the immediate view or presence of the court.

(3) Upon demand, the right to a speedy and public trial by an impartial jury of the county wherein the contempt shall have been committed, provided that this requirement shall not be construed to apply to contempts committed in the presence of the court or so near thereto

as to interfere directly with the administration of justice or to apply to the misbehavior, misconduct, or disobedience of any officer of the court in respect to the writs, orders, or process of the court. All contempt proceedings, whether civil or criminal, brought for the alleged violation of any such restraining order or injunction are, and hereby are declared to be independent, original, special proceedings, and shall require a unanimous finding of the jury.

(4) The right to file with the court a demand for the retirement of the judge sitting in the proceeding, upon an affidavit of prejudice being filed as is now provided by law in other cases. Upon the filing of any such affidavit, the judge shall thereupon proceed no further, but another judge shall be designated as is now provided for in other cases. The affidavit shall be filed prior to the hearing in the contempt proceeding.

268.28 PUNISHMENT FOR CONTEMPT. Punishment for a contempt, specified in section 268.27, may be by fine, not exceeding twenty-five dollars, or by imprisonment not exceeding ten days, in the jail of the county where the court is sitting, or both, in the discretion of the court. Where a person is committed to jail, for the nonpayment of such a fine, he must be discharged at the expiration of fifteen days; but where he is also committed for a definite time, the fifteen days must be computed from the expiration of the definite time.

268.29 DEFINITIONS. When used in sections 268.18 to 268.30, and for the purposes of these sections:

(1) A case shall be held to involve or to grow out of a labor dispute when the case involves persons who are

engaged in a single industry, trade, craft, or occupation; or who are employes of one employer; or who are members of the same or an affiliated organization of employers or employes; whether such dispute is (1) between one or more employers or associations of employers and one or more employes or associations of employes; (2) between one or more employers or associations of employers and one or more employers or associations of employers; or (3) between one or more employes or associations of employes and one or more employes or associations of employes, or when the case involves any conflicting or competing interests in a "labor dispute" (as defined in subsection (3) of "persons participating or interested" therein (as defined in subsection (2).

(2) A person or association shall be held to be a person participating or interested in a labor dispute if relief is sought against him or it and if he or it is engaged in the industry, trade, craft, or occupation in which such dispute occurs, or is a member, officer, or agent of any association of employers or employes engaged in such industry, trade, craft, or occupation.

(3) The term "labor dispute" includes any controversy concerning terms or conditions of employment, or concerning the association or representation of persons in negotiating, fixing, maintaining, changing, or seeking to arrange terms or conditions of employment, or concerning employment relations, or any other controversy arising out of the respective interests of employer and employe, regardless of whether or not the disputants stand in the proximate relation of employer and employe.

268.30 SEVERABILITY OF PROVISIONS. If any provision of sections 268.18 to 268.30 or the application thereof to any such person or circumstance is held invalid, the remainder of these sections and the application of such provisions to other persons or circumstances shall not be affected thereby.

SECTION 2. This act shall take effect upon passage and publication.

Senate: Ayes 20; Noes 9; Paired 2.

Assembly: Ayes 81; Noes 3.

PRESIDENT OF THE SENATE.
SPEAKER OF THE ASSEMBLY.

This act originated in the Senate.

CHIEF CLERK.

Approved , 1931.

GOVERNOR.

SELECTED BIBLIOGRAPHY

BIBLIOGRAPHICAL NOTE

For a study of this kind the most obvious sources of material are the court records. Insofar as they are available these are to be found in the Standard Reporters such as *United States Reports, Supreme Court Reporter, Federal Reporter,* and the reports of the courts of record in the various states, e.g. *North Carolina Reports.* Unfortunately, material derived from these sources is woefully inadequate. Only a small per cent of the cases are reported. Information concerning the unreported cases is buried in the files of the lower courts in which the cases were heard. Even in the reported cases, the printed report omits much of the most valuable material, such as restraining orders, affidavits, and pleadings. In the present study, several of these are reproduced in the appendices.

Other available sources are the various bulletins on the subject, issued by the United States Bureau of Labor Statistics, the *Legal Information Bulletins* issued by the American Federation of Labor, and *Law and Labor*—the official organ of the League for Industrial Rights.

The statement of the law is well covered in the monumental work entitled *The Law of Organized Labor and Industrial Conflicts* by Edwin Stacey Oakes. Sayre's collection of *Cases on Labor Law* is excellent. Frankfurter and Greene's recent book entitled *The Labor Injunction* is the first approach to an exhaustive treatise on this special subject. The Hearings before the sub-committee of the Judiciary on the Shipstead Bill, while not as extensive as those on the Clayton Act, are recent and valuable. A veritable mine of information on the general subject of labor and the courts is found in Volume XI of the *Report of the Industrial Commission* (1916). Excellent criticism is found in the legal periodicals.

BOOKS

Benton, J. H., Jr. *What is Government by Injunction?* Concord, N. H., Rumford Press, 1898.

Berman, Edward. *Labor and the Sherman Act.* New York, Harper, 1930.

Blum, Solomon. *Labor Economics.* Chap. V, New York, Holt, 1925.

Bouvier's Law Dictionary, Rawle's Third Revision. (*See* Injunction.) St. Paul, West Publishing Co., 1914.

Clark, L. D. *The Law of the Employment of Labor.* New York, Macmillan, 1911.

Commons, John R. *Trade Unionism and Labor Problems,* Chaps. 37-39. New York, Ginn & Co., 1921.

Commons, John R., and Andrews, John B. *Principles of Labor Legislation.* New York, Harper, 1927.

Commons, John R., and Gilmore, Eugene A. (Eds.) *Documentary History of American Industrial Society,* Vols. 3 and 4. Cleveland, Arthur H. Clark, 1910.

Douglas, Paul H., and others. *The Worker in Modern Economic Society,* pp. 624-629. Chicago, University of Chicago Press, 1923.

Emery, James A. *Freedom in Industrial Progress.* New York, National Association of Manufacturers, 1927.

Fitch, John A. *Causes of Industrial Unrest,* Chap. XV. New York, Harper, 1924.

Frankfurter, Felix, and Greene, Nathan. *The Labor Injunction.* New York, Macmillan, 1930.

Frey, John P. *The Labor Injunction.* Cincinnati, Equity Publishing Co., 1923.

Furniss, E. S. and Guld, L. P. *Labor Problems,* Chap. XII. Boston, Houghton Mifflin, 1925.

Groat, G. G. *The Attitude of American Courts in Labor Cases.* New York, Longmans, 1911.

High, James L. *A Treatise on the Law of Injunctions,* 4th ed. Chicago, Callaghan and Co., 1905.

Hobbs, R. J. M. "The Use of the Injunction in Strikes," University of North Carolina, Extension Bulletin, Vol. X, No. 2 (October, 1930) *Contemporary Industrial Processes,* pp. 52-60.

Hoxie, Robert F. *Trade Unionism in the United States*, Chap. IX. New York, Appleton, 1923.
League for Industrial Rights. *Act for the Better Protection of Public Welfare against Unwarranted Strikes and Lock-outs.* New York, The League.
League for Industrial Rights. *Social Control of Industrial Warfare.* New York, The League.
League for Industrial Rights. *Struggle for Industrial Liberty.* New York, The League.
Martin, W. A. *A Treatise on the Law of Labor Unions.* Washington, Byrne and Co., 1910.
Mason, A. T. *Organized Labor and the Law.* Durham, Duke University Press, 1925.
Merritt, Walter Gordon. *Liberty Laws.* New York, League for Industrial Rights, 1927.
Oakes, Edwin Stacey. *The Law of Organized Labor and Industrial Conflicts.* Rochester, New York, Lawyers Co-operative Publishing Co., 1927.
Olander, Victor A. *The Inequity of Injunctions* (pamphlet). Chicago, Illinois State Federation of Labor, 1928.
Perlman, Selig. *History of Trade Unionism in the United States*, p. 138. New York, Macmillan, 1922.
Sayre, Francis B. *Cases in Labor Law.* Cambridge, Harvard Press, 1923.
Seager, Henry R. *Principles of Economics*, pp. 592-594. New York, Holt, 1923.
Slesser, Sir Henry, and Baker, Charles. *Trade Union Law.* London, Nisbet and Co., Ltd., 1926.
Wall Street Journal. *History of Organized Felony and Folly.* New York, The Journal, 1923.
Watkins, G. S. *Introduction to the Study of Labor Problems.* Chap. XIV. New York, Crowell, 1922.
Webb, Sidney and Beatrice. *History of Trade Unionism*, pp. 594-634. London, Longmans, 1920.

Public Documents

Great Britain. Royal Commission on Trade Disputes and Trade Combinations. *Report of the Commission* with minutes of evidence, appendices, etc. London, Wyman and Sons, 1906.

New York (State) Legislature. Joint Committee on Housing, *Legislative Document* (1923) *No. 48*. Final Report of the Joint Legislative Committee on Housing. Albany, J. B. Lyon Co., 1923.

New York (State) Legislature. Joint Committee on Housing, *Legislative Document* (1922) *No. 60*. Intermediate Report of the Joint Legislative Committee on Housing. Albany, J. B. Lyon Co., 1922.

United States Bureau of Labor Statistics. *Decisions of Courts Affecting Labor* (annual or biennial). Washington, Government Printing Office, 1913.

United States Commission on Industrial Relations. *Final Report and Testimony*, Vol. XI, pp. 10451-10928. Washington, Government Printing Office, 1916.

United States Department of Labor. *Annual Report of the Secretary of Labor*.

United States. *Report of the Attorney General*, 1894.

United States Senate. *Hearings on the Confirmation of Judge John J. Parker*. April 5, 1930.

United States Senate. *Hearings on S. 1482.* December 18, 1928.

United States Senate. Sub-committee of the Judiciary. *Hearings on H. R. No. 1567* (1914).

INDEX

ADDAMS, Jane, on distrust of courts, 45
Affidavits, false, 66; for injunctions, untrustworthy, 34; Marion employers, 84
Agitators at Danville, 116
Alford, L. F., interviewed, 56, 58
Allen, Murray, interviewed, 58
Amidon, Judge, opinion on affidavits, 33
Arbitration requested, Asheville printer's strike, 62
Army equipment, illegal use, 95
Asheville injunction, mentioned, vii; form of, 66; printer's strike, 62-78; violence threatened, 128
Assembly, right of, 149
Attacks on injunctions in labor disputes, 36, 38, 39
Aymon, Paul, personal letter, 45; interviewed, 129

BAKER, Newton D., attack on injunctions, 36; on distrust of courts, 44
Baldwin, R. W., President Marion Manufacturing Company, assaulted, 82; affidavit, 221
Ballantine, H. W., attack on injunction, 36
Benton, J. H., opinion on injunction, 33; on government by injunction, 38
Bickett, T. W., quoted, 56; attorney, Raleigh printer's strike, 161; argument for defense of employers, 169-172
Blacklisting, injunctions against, 11
Blackwell, J. C., complaint against, 249, 251; enjoined, 255; denial of charges, 262
Bond, Judge W. M., Raleigh printer's strike, 168
Bowen, Margaret, defendant, Elizabethton strike, 234; opinion on Elizabethton strike, 97

Boycott, 41; primary and secondary, 13; in Asheville printer's strike, 73, 199; effect of injunctions on, 137; enjoined, 235; unlawful at Elizabethton, 102
Brandeis, Justice, on constitutional safeguards for labor, 35; on injunctions in labor disputes, 45, 46
Brewer, Justice, opinion in Debs case, 23
Briggs, O. P., on oppressive practices of unions, 29
Brissenden, on injunctions, 12
Brown, Mark W., Asheville printer's strike, 191
Bryan, R. H., affidavit, 162

CAPITALISM, attitude toward injunctions, 5
Carroll, M. J., affidavit, 50; Raleigh printer's strike, 156
Carter, John W., interviewed, 119, 122, 125.
Catch-all phrases in injunctions, 15; Asheville injunction, 66; Elizabethton injunction, 101; Danville injunction, 119; Raleigh injunction, 53, 54
Chancery courts, 8
Clark, Chief Justice Walter, opinion on Asheville injunction, 70; in favor of jury trial for contempt, 144; friend of labor, 208
Clarkson, Justice Heriot, opinion on Asheville strike, 203
Clement, Judge J. T., at Danville, 120; injunction, 256
Clinchfield Manufacturing Company, Marion strike, 80
Complaint, bill of, Asheville printer's strike, 64; complete copy, 187-191; Danville textile strike, 117; Marion textile strike, 84; complete copy, 215-222; Raleigh printer's strike, 51, 52; complete copy, 156

[285]

Conspiracies, injunctions helpful in reaching, 25
Conspiracy charges, vague law, 68; at Marion, 84, 217; at Danville, 117, 255; Asheville strike, 190; Raleigh printer's strike, 157, 158, 160; mentioned, 149, 176, 177, 179; charges denied, 263
Conspiracy doctrine avoided in North Carolina, 136
Contempt proceedings, 10; at Elizabethton, 103, 104; without jury, 138
Contracts, "yellow dog," 14; not contracts, 42; 148, 209, 210
Cope, Elmer, interviewed, 82
Courts, condemned by labor, 75, 76; effect of injunctions on, 59; ignored at Marion, 88; loss of prestige in injunction cases, 44, 130; at Danville, 126; at Elizabethton, 110
Cranmer, Judge E. H., Raleigh printer's strike, 164

D AN River Cotton Mills, Schoolfield, strike, 114
Daniels, Josephus, affidavit favoring strikers, 52
Danville injunction, mentioned, vii; unusual form, 117, 118; strike peaceful, 125; strikers' answer to bill of complaint, 257-264
Danville and Schoolfield compared, 121
Davis, John W., advice on use of U. S. deputy marshals, 142
Debs case, argument for injunction, 23; mentioned, 25; "catch-all'" phrases, 15; injunction, 32
Debs, Eugene, opinion on injunctions, 142
Donnelly, J. Clyde, interviewed, 96, 111
Dunbar, W. H., on constitutional safeguards, 35
Dynamite explosions, Danville, 125

E ASON, S. W., interviewed, 55, 57
Effect of Asheville injunction, 71-74; of Elizabethton injunction, 104-113; of Danville injunction, 121-130; of Marion injunction, 85-93; of Raleigh injunction, 56-61
Elizabethton injunction mentioned, vii; violated, 110; complete copy of, 234; strike violence, 128; second strike, 99
Elizabethton mills described, 95
Emery, James A., testimony on injunctions, 24
Employers, attitude toward injunctions, 3, 5
Equity courts, 8
Eviction from company houses, rules governing, 18
Ex parte proceedings condemned, 150

F ARLEY, Atwell, assaulted, 249, 250
Fitzgerald, H. R., on wage reduction, 115, 116; letter poster of employers, 268
Flagg, open shop crew, 63, 72
Frankfurter, Felix, quoted on injunctions, ix
Frey, John P., attack on injunctions, 39

G ALLIGHTER, Christine, defendant, Elizabethton strike, 234
Gibbs, Guy, defendant, Elizabethton strike, 234
Giles, D. F., interviewed, 85; attorney for Marion strikers, 233
Glenn, Chief of Police A. E., affidavit, Raleigh strike, 175
Gompers, Samuel, attack on injunctions, 39; before Lockwood Investigation Committee, 44
Gorman, Francis J., on "Industrial Democracy," 114; address, 115; enjoined, 116, 118, 126, 255; organizer, 248; denial of charges, 262
Grace, President Bethlehem Steel Company, against unions, 41

INDEX

Green, William, testimony on Parker nomination, 43; address, 114; at Richmond, 115
Gregory, Chas. N., opinion on affidavits, 33; on conditional safeguards, 35
Gregory, S. S., on evasion of jury trial in injunctions, 35

HALL, Robert H., affidavit, 162
Harris, Chas. U., defense of striking printers, 178
Harris, Malcolm K., employers' counsel, 117; interviewed, 119, 122; false charges, 262
Harwood, J. H., Marion strike, 224
Haynes, J. W., attorney for strikers, Asheville, 213
Hillquit, Morris, opinion on injunctions, 33
Hoffman, Alfred, at Marion, 81; enjoined, 83; personal letter, 82, 94; at strike, 91; kidnapped, 99
Holland, Rosa, defendant, Marion strike, 225
Holmes, Justice Oliver W., justification of peaceful picketing, 40
Hours of labor, Marion, 81
Hundley, Posie J., denial of charges, 263
Hurt, S. S., Danville clerk of court, 256

"INDUSTRIAL Democracy" at Danville, 114, 115, 258-260; abuses, 116
Injunctions, against employers, 10, 11; against labor, arguments for, 22-31, 131; arguments against, 32-46; bases of relief, 9, 10; copy of Asheville injunction, 212; copy of Elizabethton, 234; copy of Marion, 223, 224; modified order, Marion, 225, 227; Danville restraining order, 254; Raleigh order, 163, 164; correct form, 150; definition, 7; unusual form of Danville injunction, 117, 118; effect on industrial strife, 77; effect on Raleigh printers' strike, 56, 60; effect at Asheville, 71-74; Marion, 86, 92; Elizabethton, 104-113; Danville, 121-126; expensive, 123; form of, Raleigh printers' strike, 53; form of, at Marion, 83; at Elizabethton, 100, 101; general effect on industrial strife, 129; interference with liberty, 5; law of North Carolina, safer for labor, 140, 141; federal law, 147; lawful acts enjoined, 137, 138; at Marion, injunction modified, 85; most comprehensive ever issued, 19-21; not obeyed, 143; notice given defendants, 132; number against employers, 11; number against labor, 11; in politics, 4; procedure, Asheville, 68; purpose, 7; as relief for labor, 4; scope of, 10; types of, 7, 8; undesirable effects, 139, 140; usual effect on outcome, 127; violated at Elizabethton, 110; widening scope, 18; without effect, 121, 122

JONES, Charles H., defendant, Raleigh printers' strike, 116
Jones, Thomas A., interview, 22
Jury trial, favored by labor, 35, 77, 135, 211

KELLY, William F., on effect of injunction, 109
Koonce, C. F., defendant, Raleigh printers' strike, 166

LAWFUL acts enjoined, 137, 138
Leigh, Henry C., Danville judge, 248
Lindsay, Matilda, address, 115, 116; quoted, 118, interviewed, 125
Lockwood Investigation Committee, 44

MacRAE, Judge Cameron, quoted, 85; Marion strike, 227

INDEX

Marion injunction, mentioned, vii; provisions, 83; effect on strike, 86, 92; modified order, 85; vague, 82
Marion, North Carolina, a mill town, 80; described, 79
Marion strike described, 80; second strike, 87
Markland, G. H., defendant, Elizabethton strike, 234
Martyr spirit, at Marion, 91, 233; Elizabethton, 111
McDowell County, North Carolina, 79
McElroy, Judge P. A., Asheville strike, 196
McGinnis, Marguerite, plaintiff, Raleigh strike, 166
McGinnis, Rosa, plaintiff, Raleigh strike, 166
McGrady, Edward, textile organizer, 98; kidnapped, 99
McLemore, Judge J. L., Danville case, 120
. Meroney, R. S., personal letter, 65, 75
Merritt, Walter G., 27; argument for injunction, 22
Militia, need increased by injunctions, 143
Miller, George, defendant, Elizabethton strike, 234
Miller, S. E., Chancellor, 236
Moore, O. R., affidavit, 162
Moore, V. C., affidavit, 50, 162
Moreland, Sheriff, Elizabethton strike, 97
Morgan, W. T., attorney for employing printers, 221
Mothwurf, Dr. A., employer, Elizabethton, 97, 98

N ASH, B. F., complaint against, 249, 251; enjoined at Danville, 118, 255; denial of charges, 262
National guardsmen as deputy-sheriffs, 94
New York Needle Trades, enjoined, 12; industrial dispute, 15

Nichols, L. E., interviewed, 57; complete interview, 181
North Carolina and Tennessee injunction law compared, 102-104
North Carolina injunction law safer for labor, 140, 141

O LANDER, Victor A., attack on injunction, 38
Opie, Colonel, at Schoolfield, 124

P ARKER, Hon. John J., basis for defeat, 14
Penix, J. B., attempt at kidnapping, 99; interviewed, 99; defendant, Elizabethton strike, 234
Pennell, George, attorney for strikers, Asheville, 71, 213
Pepper, Geo. W., attack on injunction, 36; on abuse of equity power, 43; on widening scope of injunctions, 18, 19
Picketing, dispute, Asheville strike, 63; effect of Elizabethton injunction, 108; effect of injunctions on, 129; enjoined, 12, 235; enjoined at Asheville, 67, 75, 195; at Elizabethton, 101; at Danville, 123, 124; declared unlawful, 216, 218; not enforced at Elizabethton, 112; not usually peaceful, 29; at Marion, controlled by militia, 87; right recognized, 78; rules governing, 17; at Schoolfield, 123, 124; two kinds, 13
Plemmons, W. B., interview, 47, 76; quoted on Marion strike, 86
Pollard, Governor, of Virginia, telegram, 116; order modified, 124
Price, Zuriah, defendant, Marion strike, 225
Procedure in injunctions, need for reform, 143

Q UIGG, Murray T., argument for injunction, 24, 25; personal letter, 27

INDEX

RALEIGH, Chief of Police for striking printers, 53; injunction mentioned, vii; printers' strike, 49-61
Ramsey, D. Hiden, interviewed, 64, 71, 74; mentioned, 201
Religious interests of Southern textile workers, 79
Restraining order, definition, 7, 8; example of prohibitions, 16; copy of order, Asheville strike, 194; Danville order, copy, 254-256; Marion order, complete, 223-224; modified order, Marion, 225-227; Raleigh printers' strike, 163; correct procedure, 151
Right to work, 171
Riverside Mills, Danville strike, 114
Roberts, Gallatin, interviewed, 23, 68; attorney for Asheville strikers, 213

SCHOOLFIELD and Danville compared, 121
Simms, R. N., counsel, Raleigh printers' strike, 168
Smith, Charles Lee, 165; affidavit of, 50; interviewed, 51, 58, 59; complete interview, 173, 174
Song about injunctions, 90
"Stretch-out" at Marion, 81
Strikebreaking, 65, 72, 179, 181, 199, 209
Strikes, enjoined, 14; illegal, 21
Supreme Court opinion on Raleigh injunction, 56; on Asheville injunction, 203

TAYLOR, Ben H., interviewed, 99
Taylor, H. L., interviewed, 96
Temporary restraining order, correct form, 151
Tennessee and North Carolina injunction laws compared, 102-104
Tippet, Tom, organizer, 81; enjoined at Marion, 83
Tomlinson, Dorothy, plaintiff, Raleigh strike, 166

Torlay, Frank J., strike adviser, 187, 192, 199, 210
Townsend, N. A., letter from, 84; letter quoted, 88; letter on Marion injunction, complete copy, 228-229; opinion on Marion injunction, 86, 91
Trade unions, *see* Unions
Trespassing enjoined, 12
Types of injunctions, 7, 8

UNIONS, attitude toward injunctions, 3, 5; power for evil, 27; oppressive practices, 28; use of injunctions, 30; fought by employers at Danville, 266
United Mine Workers, importance of organizing, 43
United States Commission on Industrial Relations, findings, 35

VIOLENCE, at Elizabethton, 106, 127, 128; threatened, Asheville strike, 128

WAGE, dispute at Elizabethton, 96; reduction, Danville, 114, 115; at Marion, 81
Washburn, G. F., interviewed, 82, 84; attorney for employing printers, 221
Watson, E. F., attorney for employing printers, Asheville, 221
Weaver, Guy, attorney for strikers, 213
Weaver, J. W., affidavit of, 50
Webb, Charles A., interviewed, 62, 63, 68; complete interview, 197-202; owner, Asheville printers' strike, 193
Webb, Judge J. L., Marion strike, 224
Weinstock, Anna, strike conciliator, 100, 105
West Virginia field, not organized, 43
White, C. S., defendant, Elizabethton strike, 234
Wicker, E. J., affidavit, Raleigh strike, 49

Williams, H. T., interviewed, 117
Wilson, E. T., personnel manager, 100
Wilson, M. P., defendant, Elizabethton strike, 234
Wilson, R. J., interviewed, 57, 165; affidavit, 162
Witte, E. E., on injunctions against employers, 11; "catch-all" phrases, 15

Women, more loyal to union than men, 89, 108
Wood, Chas. G., at Elizabethton strike, 97
Woodberry, O. E., address, 115

YELLOW dog contracts, *see* Contracts

THE UNIVERSITY OF NORTH CAROLINA SOCIAL STUDY SERIES

Under the General Editorship of Howard W. Odum. Books Marked with * Published in Coöperation with the Institute for Research in Social Science.

Beckwith: *Black Roadways: A Study of Folk Life in Jamaica*	$3.00
Branson: *Farm Life Abroad*	2.00
*Brearley: *Homicide in South Carolina*	In Preparation
*Brown: *Public Poor Relief in North Carolina*	2.00
*Brown: *The State Highway System of North Carolina*	2.50
*Brown: *A State Movement in Railroad Development*	5.00
Carter: *The Social Theories of L. T. Hobhouse*	1.50
Crook: *The General Strike*	6.00
Fleming: *The Freedmen's Savings Bank*	2.00
Gee (ed.): *The Country Life of the Nation*	2.00
*Green: *Constitutional Development in the South Atlantic States, 1776-1860*	3.00
Green: *The Negro in Contemporary American Literature*	1.00
*Grissom: *The Negro Sings a New Heaven and a New Earth*	2.50
Har: *Social Laws*	4.00
*Heer: *Income and Wages in the South*	1.00
*Herring: *History of the Textile Industry in the South*	In Preparation
*Herring: *Welfare Work in Mill Villages*	5.00
Hobbs: *North Carolina: Economic and Social*	3.50
*Johnson: *Folk Culture on Saint Helena Island*	3.00
*Johnson: *John Henry: Tracking Down a Negro Legend*	2.00
*Johnson: *A Social History of the Sea Islands*	3.00
Jordan: *Children's Interests in Reading*	1.50
Knight: *Among the Danes*	2.50
Lindquist: *The Family in the Present Social Order*	2.50
Lou: *Juvenile Courts in the United States*	3.00
*Metfessel: *Phonophotography in Folk Music*	3.00
Miller: *Town and Country*	2.00
*Mitchell: *William Gregg: Factory Master of the Old South*	3.00
*Mitchell: *Textile Unionism and the South*	1.00
*Murchison: *King Cotton is Sick*	2.00
North: *Social Differentiation*	2.50
Odum: *An Approach to Public Welfare and Social Work*	1.50
*Odum (ed.): *Southern Pioneers*	2.00
*Odum and Johnson: *The Negro and His Songs*	3.00
*Odum and Johnson: *Negro Workaday Songs*	3.00
*Odum and Willard: *Systems of Public Welfare*	2.00
Pound: *Law and Morals*	2.00
*Puckett: *Folk Beliefs of the Southern Negro*	5.00
*Rhyne: *Some Southern Cotton Mill Workers and Their Villages*	2.50
Robinson: *A Changing Psychology in Social Case Work*	2.50
Ross: *Roads to Social Peace*	1.50
Schwenning (ed.): *Management Problems*	2.00
Sherrill: *Criminal Procedure in North Carolina*	3.00
*Steiner and Brown: *The North Carolina Chain Gang*	2.00
*Vance: *Human Factors in Cotton Culture*	3.00
*Wager: *County Government in North Carolina*	5.00
Walker: *Social Work and the Training of Social Workers*	2.00
Way: *The Clinchfield Railroad*	5.00
White: *Some Cycles of Cathay*	1.50
Willey: *The Country Newspaper*	1.50
Winston: *Illiteracy in the United States*	3.00
*Woofter: *The Plight of Cigarette Tobacco*	1.00

www.ingramcontent.com/pod-product-compliance
Lightning Source LLC
Chambersburg PA
CBHW021119300426
44113CB00006B/215